STALIN'S GULAG AT WAR

Forced Labour, Mass Death, and Soviet Victory in the Second World War

Stalin's Gulag at War places the Gulag within the story of the regional wartime mobilization of Western Siberia during the Second World War. Far from Moscow, Western Siberia was a key area for evacuated factories and for production in support of the war effort. Wilson T. Bell explores a diverse array of issues, including mass death, black markets, and the responses of both prisoners and prison personnel to the war. The region's camps were never prioritized and faced a constant struggle to mobilize for the war. Prisoners in these camps, however, engaged in such activities as sewing Red Army uniforms, manufacturing artillery shells, and constructing and working in major defence factories.

Stalin's Gulag is revealed as a complex system, but one that was closely tied to the local, regional, and national war effort to the point where prisoners and non-prisoners frequently interacted. Western Siberia's low priority forced-labour camps and colonies saw catastrophic death rates, often far exceeding official Gulag averages. Ultimately, their prisoners played a tangible role in Soviet victory, but the cost was incredibly high, both in terms of the health and lives of the prisoners themselves, and in terms of Stalin's commitment to total, often violent, mobilization to achieve the goals of the Soviet state.

WILSON T. BELL is an associate professor the Department of Philosophy, History, and Politics at Thompson Rivers University.

Stalin's Gulag at War

Forced Labour, Mass Death, and Soviet Victory in the Second World War

WILSON T. BELL

UNIVERSITY OF TORONTO PRESS
Toronto Buffalo London

© University of Toronto Press 2019
Toronto Buffalo London
utorontopress.com
Printed and bound by CPI Group (UK) Ltd, Croydon, CR0 4YY

ISBN 978-1-4875-0408-3 (cloth)   ISBN 978-1-4875-2309-1 (paper)

Printed on acid-free, 100% post-consumer recycled paper with vegetable-based inks.

___

Library and Archives Canada Cataloguing in Publication

Bell, Wilson T., 1977–, author
Stalin's Gulag at war : forced labour, mass death, and Soviet victory
in the Second World War / Wilson T. Bell.

Includes bibliographical references and index.
ISBN 978-1-4875-0408-3 (hardcover)   ISBN 978-1-4875-2309-1 (softcover)

1. Stalin, Joseph, 1878–1953.   2. GULag NKVD.   3. World War, 1939–1945 –
Prisoners and prisons, Soviet.   4. World War, 1939–1945 – Conscript labor –
Soviet Union.   5. Concentration camps – Soviet Union – History – 20th century.
6. Forced labor – Soviet Union – History – 20th century.   7. Political
persecution – Soviet Union – History – 20th century.   8. Soviet Union –
History – 1925–1953.   9. World War, 1939–1945 – Soviet Union.   I. Title.

HV8964.S65B45 2019   940.53'1747   C2018-903915-9

___

This book has been published with the help of a grant from the Federation
for the Humanities and Social Sciences, through the Awards to Scholarly
Publications Program, using funds provided by the Social Sciences and
Humanities Research Council of Canada.

University of Toronto Press acknowledges the financial assistance to its
publishing program of the Canada Council for the Arts and the Ontario Arts
Council, an agency of the Government of Ontario.

Canada Council
for the Arts

Conseil des Arts
du Canada

ONTARIO ARTS COUNCIL
CONSEIL DES ARTS DE L'ONTARIO
an Ontario government agency
un organisme du gouvernement de l'Ontario

Funded by the   Financé par le
Government   gouvernement
of Canada   du Canada

For Martha, Maeve, and Amri.

Contents

Figures and Tables

Figures

Tables

Acknowledgments

Despite the stereotype of the historian who conducts research alone, in old dusty archives, all aspects of the pathway from idea to research to writing to the finished book require considerable feedback and help. In light of this, I am indebted to many, many people.

Norman Pereira and Ieva Vitins at Dalhousie University first sparked and nourished my interest in Russia and Russia's history, although I might not have gone down that path at all without the fascinating *Crime and Punishment* lectures that were part of the University of King's College's Foundation Year Program, or my high school history teacher, Mrs. Cameron. My University of Toronto graduate studies, at both the MA and PhD level, could not have succeeded without the guidance of Lynne Viola. Her kindness, support, suggestions, high standards, and connections were all invaluable to developing my work on the Gulag. She was the first to suggest that I research the Gulag as an MA student. Many of the strengths of this book are due to her mentorship, advice, and knowledge, and I am extremely grateful for all of her help along this often challenging path. My doctoral thesis committee members, Robert Johnson and Thomas Lahusen, significantly impacted my ideas on the practice of history and on Russia itself, and I am very grateful for their input. I was also fortunate to have an internal reader (Alison Smith) and external reader (Kate Brown) who both offered thorough and insightful feedback.

My graduate studies and early academic career have resulted in lasting friendships and professional relationships that have influenced my thoughts on history, Russia, and the Gulag. In particular, of those University of Toronto graduate students with whom I overlapped at one point or another, I thank especially Sarah Amato, Ariel Beaujot, Auri

Berg, Max Bergholz, Seth Bernstein (thanks also for some on-the-ground help in Moscow with securing permissions), Heather DeHaan, Heather Dichter, Sveta Frunchak, Julie Gilmour, Alexandra Guerson, Steve Jobbitt, Misha Kogan, Denis Kozlov, Steve Maddox, Tracy McDonald, and Jennifer Polk. My research in Moscow overlapped with that of other researchers who became friends and colleagues, and I thank especially Edward Cohn, Sean Guillory, Maya Haber, Jenny Kaminer, Lauren Kaminsky, Brigid O'Keeffe, Mike Westren, and Ben Zajicek.

Conferences were and continue to be venues for feedback, inspiration, and networking. Everyone from the audiences to co-panelists and discussants have played important roles. While it is difficult to thank everyone, comments and help from the following individuals stand out in my mind: Golfo Alexopoulos, Alan Barenberg (whom I also thank for many Gulag-related discussions and a lasting friendship), Steven Barnes (who was also instrumental in helping my Gulag research, particularly in its early stages), Olga Cooke, Michael David-Fox, Miriam Dobson, Simon Ertz, Anna Fishzon, Jeff Hardy, Dan Healey, Wendy Goldman, Jehanne Gheith, Bruce Grant, Jean Lévesque, Stephen Norris, Judith Pallot, and Cynthia Ruder. At a 2016 conference in Poland, several commentators read through and discussed an early, manuscript version of this book. I thank Spasimir Domaradzki, Daria Nałęcz, Andrej Nowak, and Boris Sokolov for their valuable feedback at this conference.

I have also had the good fortune to present aspects of this work as part of lecture series at several universities, and as part of departmental and faculty colloquia at my host institutions. In particular, I would like to thank Dana Wessell-Lightfoot (UNBC), Brigitte LeNormand (UBCO), and Barbara Martin and Korine Amacher (University of Geneva), for helping to facilitate lectures on my research. I am grateful to my colleagues in the history department at Dickinson College, and at the Faculty of Arts at Thompson Rivers University, for opportunities to present my research. While all of my colleagues in TRU's Department of Philosophy, History, and Politics have done much to help me feel welcome, I would particularly like to thank Bruce Baugh, Tina Block, and Michael Gorman for their support and encouragement. The Office of Research and Graduate Studies at TRU has also been very important for aspects of my research, including funding my trip to the Hoover Institution Archives.

I have been fortunate to research at a number of excellent libraries and archives. In North America, I thank especially the staff, librarians, and archivists at the University of Toronto's Robarts Library, the Hoover Institution Archives, Harvard University's Lamont Library, the Dickinson College Library, and the Thompson Rivers University Library. In Russia, I am grateful to the staff, librarians, and archivists at the State Archive of the Russian Federation (GARF), the Russian State Archive of the Economy (RGAE), the Russian State Archive of Social and Political History (RGASPI), the State History Library, the Moscow Memorial Society, the State Archive of Novosibirsk Oblast (GANO), the State Archive of Tomsk Oblast (GATO), the Centre for the Documentation of the Contemporary History of Tomsk Oblast (TsDNITO), and the Tomsk Memorial Society. Dina Nokhotovich of GARF, Valentina Piskova of GATO, and Liudmila Pril' of TsDNITO particularly stand out for their help and patience in assisting my work and responding to my queries.

Several Russian scholars assisted my research in Russia. I owe a huge debt of gratitude to Sergei Krasil'nikov, who helped me immensely in Novosibirsk and who gave me access to a lot of his own research material. Vasilii Khanevich of the Tomsk Memorial Society was and continues to be very helpful for my research of the region. Other key assistance and suggestions in Russia came from Oleg Khlevniuk, Boris Trenin, Leonid Trus', and Simeon Vilensky.

Research and teaching often reinforce each other in unexpected and unquantifiable ways. I am very grateful for my students, first at Dickinson College and now at Thompson Rivers University, particularly those students at both institutions who took my "concentration camp" course. I directly thank Anna Savchenko, a research assistant on aspects of this project, but also thank all of my students for their indirect help. With their in-class questions and comments, and with their own research papers, they continue to give me the opportunity to think through and discuss important ideas related to history, Europe, and Russia, among many other topics.

Funding for my Gulag research and conference presentations has come from numerous sources. I thank the Social Sciences and Humanities Research Council of Canada for a four-year doctoral fellowship; the University of Toronto and its Centre for European, Russian, and Eurasian Studies (CERES) for fellowships and grants; the Eurasia Program of the Social Sciences Research Council and the International Research and Exchanges Board, with funds provided by the US State Department under the Program for Research and Training on Eastern Europe and the Independent States of the Former Soviet Union (Title VIII); Dickinson College; and Thompson Rivers University.

Parts of "Forced Labor on the Home Front: The Gulag and Total War in Western Siberia, 1940–45" by Wilson T. Bell from *The Soviet*

Gulag: Evidence, Interpretation, Comparison, edited by Michael David-Fox, © 2016, are reprinted by permission of the University of Pittsburgh Press. I am grateful for this permission.

The University of Toronto Press has been a pleasure to work with, and I thank the staff and my editors, first Richard Ratzlaff and then Stephen Shapiro, and the anonymous peer reviewers who offered helpful and thorough suggestions. Mike Bechthold's map makes this a stronger book, and I am thankful for his work.

Extended family support has also been key to this project and to my development as a historian. My parents, Tom and Jacquie Bell, encouraged and fostered my interest in history from a young age. My sister, Victoria Hagens, and brother, Adam Hammond, have been there to ask pertinent questions and offer their support. My uncle, Donald Hicken, and late aunt, Tana Hicken, hold a dear place in my heart, and were particularly supportive during my three years in Pennsylvania, when they lived not far away. My great-aunt and late great-uncle, Yasuko and James Cogan, provided significant financial support along the way, and I am very thankful for their help.

Finally, and most importantly, I thank my immediate family. Researching the Gulag, I am constantly struck by the disruption that the system caused to families and friendships of all shapes and sizes, and I am especially grateful for the time and experiences shared with my family, particularly those times and experiences that take me away from academic life. My children, Maeve and Amri, are a source of inspiration, delight, and countless smiles. My spouse and partner in life, Martha Solomon, is a wonderful companion, friend, and source of emotional support and advice. Martha is one of the smartest people I know, and her suggestions on various aspects of this work have been invaluable, as has her sense of adventure – she accompanied me to Russia on four separate occasions. Her strong sense of social and environmental justice is inspiring. I am forever grateful for the love and laughter, and for our bond as adventurers and explorers in this world together. I dedicate this work to Martha, Maeve, and Amri.

All translations are my own, unless otherwise noted. I have used the Library of Congress transliteration guide, except with common English spellings (e.g., Trotsky not Trotskii).

Ultimately, if this work has value beyond academic debates and general interest, it is my hope that by understanding suffering in this world, we can learn something about what it means to be human, and empathize within that shared humanity; perhaps this will lead to ways to cause less harm and to help those in need.

STALIN'S GULAG AT WAR

Forced Labour, Mass Death, and Soviet Victory
in the Second World War

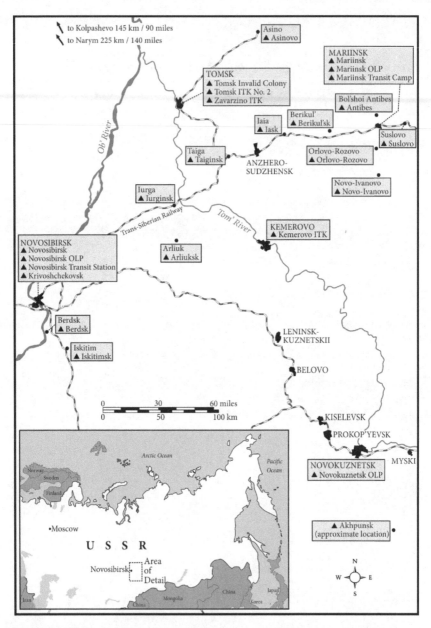

0.1: Map: Siblag Camps and Colonies, May 1941. Each triangle represents a Siblag camp or colony. Map by Mike Bechthold.

Introduction: Stalin's Gulag at War

The German invasion of 22 June 1941 placed the entire Soviet experiment under threat of imminent destruction and collapse. On both the battlefront and the home front, the Soviet Union saw violence and devastation on an unprecedented scale. Stalin and the Soviet leadership had to mobilize all aspects of society in order to have a chance at survival. The Gulag – Stalin's enormous prison-camp system – held a vast number of prisoners who could be deployed quickly to almost any aspect of this mobilization. How was Gulag labour mobilized for the war effort? How did the prisoners and the camp personnel respond? What role did the Gulag play in Soviet perseverance and eventual victory in the Second World War? *Stalin's Gulag at War* describes the Soviet Union's utilization of prisoner labour for the war effort, focusing on Western Siberia, a region crucial to the home front, as it was safe from attack, rich in resources, and easily accessible by rail.

During that fateful June of 1941, the West Siberian Plain was bursting with life, its rich green colours compensating for the long, cold winter. The plain – a swampy, forested lowland, cut dramatically by large, north-flowing rivers – is impressive for its vast scale. The Ob' River and its tributaries constitute the sixth-largest drainage area in the world, and the Ob' itself is one of the world's longest rivers. Even thousands of kilometres south of the frigid Ob' Gulf, the plain rises barely 150 metres above sea level until it finally gives way to the foothills of the Altai Mountains.[1] To the west, the rolling hills of the Ural Mountains divide the plain from European Russia; in the east, the land, as it approaches the Enisei River, gradually transforms from plain into the higher ground of the Central Siberian Plateau. The serene landscape remained largely unchanged during the upheavals of the Second World War. Far removed from the complete devastation and violence of the Eastern Front, the region was peaceful, a place of rest, and relatively safe – on the surface.

Under the surface, however, Western Siberia was fraught with a frenetic energy in support of the war effort, as evacuees, regular civilians, and a large contingent of forced labourers (prisoners, special settlers, and later POWs), were fully mobilized in support of the war. Moreover, the region did not escape the violence of war, as mortality rates soared both in regular society and within the confines of the Gulag. The lives or health of many thousands of prisoners in the region were forcibly sacrificed for the war effort, although their contributions are routinely ignored in accounts and celebrations of the Second World War, the war that Russians still refer to as the Great Patriotic War. Many prisoners were themselves quite patriotic in their response to the war, and the experience of Stalin's Gulag at war highlights both the tragedy and the resiliency of the forced-labour network and, in some ways, the system as a whole. Endemic corruption, a supply chain in chaos, and a sacrifice of almost everything for the war effort meant that during the war, the camps of Western Siberia were a place of mass death. Yet the ability of the Stalinist regime to respond to the war on the home front relied largely on networks of labour – both prisoner and non-prisoner – such as those at the regime's disposal in Western Siberia. The story of the region's camps during the war, then, is a story of both incredible suffering and ultimate victory. Whose victory was it? How did the camp system help achieve that victory? Was the sacrifice worth it?

In answering these questions, this book makes several key arguments about the Gulag during the Second World War. First, despite a modern bureaucratic system on paper, the Gulag's day-to-day operations depended largely on informal networks and personal connections. Second, local officials were focused on economic output even at the expense of ideological concerns and traditional functions of incarceration, such as the isolation of prisoners. These conclusions lead to a third argument, that the Soviet response to the Second World War was not particularly about ideological purity or the isolation of unwanted individuals, but was focused on the total mobilization of all human and material resources for victory, no matter the cost in lives. Comparatively speaking, as we shall see, the wartime Gulag was unusual both as a prison system and as a system of concentration camps, and is thus indicative of the Soviet Union's unusual and uneven modernity. Finally, this book concludes that Soviet victory over Nazi Germany was also the Gulag's victory, but that the Gulag's victory was a Pyrrhic victory, because it was both incredibly costly in terms of lives and resources, and also helped ensure the entrenchment of the forced-labour system, at least until Stalin's death in 1953. Thus, there is a need to recognize the sacrifice that prisoners made for the war effort, and the tragic consequences of the Stalinist version of total mobilization. Instead of the hardships of the war being taken as a turning point for reform, victory meant that Stalin and the Soviet leadership continued with total mobilization policies in the postwar period.

This book focuses on the southern areas of the West Siberian Plain, the area labelled Novosibirsk Province (*Oblast'*) on the eve of the war, and consisting today of three separate provinces: Novosibirsk, Tomsk, and Kemerovo. Novosibirsk Province is today home to Siberia's largest city, Novosibirsk, a thriving metropolis of over 2 million inhabitants that matured as a city during the Second World War. Novosibirsk is a key transit hub as the junction of the Trans-Siberian Railway and the Turksib Railway, connecting Siberia with Central Asia. The mighty Ob' River dissects the city and is a major source of hydropower. One can cross the river via several bridges, even while riding the city's subway system. Although its extremely wide central boulevards and austere architecture owe their existence to Stalinist urban planning, the city now boasts a smattering of gleaming office towers, rising up in tribute to Russia and Siberia's early-twenty-first-century economic transition: banking, oil, and natural gas. Tomsk Province, to the north, was a crucial region for early Russian expansion through Siberia, as its many fur-trading outposts dotted the numerous river routes. The city of Tomsk is today a pleasant university town and wears its past more comfortably than many other former Soviet cities: monuments dedicated to the "memory of those slain" during the "Bolshevik terror" stand in the city's centre, in a small park directly across from city hall.[2] The park overlooks the Tom' River, a meandering tributary of the Ob'. Centuries earlier, both rivers had been key to the Russians' rapid expansion across the Eurasian continent. Kemerovo Province, upriver from Tomsk, is today the most industrial and densely populated region of Siberia. It includes the key Kuznetsk Basin, an area with massive coal deposits and was crucial to the war when the Don River basin – the Soviet Union's primary coal-producing region – was under German occupation. All three of these provinces were home to special settlers and Gulag prisoners during the Second World War.

The region had been an area of fierce resistance to the Bolsheviks during the Russian Civil War, and had long maintained an ambiguous relationship to authorities in Moscow.[3] A colonial outpost during Russia's eastward expansion, Western Siberia was a place where serfs could escape to freedom – there was no serfdom on Siberian agricultural lands – and nevertheless a region of internal exile and even widespread state use of factory serfs in metallurgical industries.[4] Stalin himself was exiled to Narym, in present-day northern Tomsk Province, for a few months in 1912, before the Revolution. That myriad forced-labour and exile institutions were set up in the region under Stalin's watch, and would contribute to the Soviet Union's efforts at defeating Nazi Germany, is an irony that may or may not have been lost on Stalin. Stalin's Soviet Union undeniably needed the human and natural resources of Western Siberia for the war effort, however, and both central and local authorities saw the Gulag as key for extracting and using those resources.

The Western Siberian camps were more or less typical Gulag camps, which highlights their importance as a subject of inquiry. Unlike those of Norilsk, with its crucial nickel deposits, they were never prioritized. They were not a symbol for the entire system, as were the camps of Kolyma. They were neither in the harshest climate nor the most forgiving. More importantly, the camps of Western Siberia included a wide range of economic activity, as prisoners were involved in agriculture, construction, tree felling, mining, and manufacturing – all industries that converted to help the war effort. The regional camp system included special settlements and corrective-labour camps and colonies of all regimen types (from light regimen to one *katorga* camp, the strictest regime during the war, and a term resurrected from the harsh, prison-labour camps of tsarist Russia). Many of the largest camps and colonies were also located within the city limits of major cities, including Novosibirsk and Tomsk.[5] The largest camps in the region were primarily corrective-labour colonies, meant for prisoners serving comparatively light sentences (although, as we shall see, the differences between camps and colonies were, in practice, often unclear). The present book is one of the only studies to cover the corrective-labour colonies, which by war's end housed approximately half of all Gulag prisoners. Unlike town's near the Gulag's more remote camp systems, moreover, the urban areas of Western Siberia did not owe their existence to the Stalinist forced-labour network. This case study thus provides a fascinating look at how Gulag and Soviet society interacted. Western Siberia was crucial for the Soviet home front as one of two main regions for evacuated factories and one of the most important receiving areas for evacuated personnel. Unlike most European areas of the Soviet Union,

Western Siberia actually grew, economically, over the course of the Second World War. While the USSR's industrial output for 1945 was only 91 per cent of what it had been in 1940, Western Siberia's was 279 per cent.[6]

Gulag wartime operations in Western Siberia certainly call into question the idea that the Gulag's central function was to help purify society by removing undesirable individuals and groups. Far from being removed from society, the region's camps and colonies were fully integrated into the local wartime economy, and prisoners regularly interacted with non-prisoners. By and large, moreover, the local focus was more on wartime production than on the isolation of enemies, although we certainly cannot completely separate economic and political motivations. Thus, this case study questions both Amir Weiner's characterization of the Great Patriotic War as the key "purification" event of the Soviet gardening state, and Steven Barnes's related argument concerning the Gulag's role in determining who belonged (and who did not belong) in Soviet society.[7]

The question of the Gulag's central function during wartime also allows for a discussion of the Gulag in comparative perspective. In terms of penal function, the mass mobilization of forced labour and the integrated nature of the Gulag mark it as at least a partial anomaly in modern criminal justice systems, where the stated role of the prison relates, in varying degrees, to deterrence, isolation, retribution, and rehabilitation. Certainly all four were present in the Soviet camp system, but the added emphasis on mass mobilization to aid the economy, a de-emphasis on isolation (in practice), and soaring wartime mortality rates point to important differences in the Gulag. Moreover, if we compare the Gulag to other wartime concentration camps, the Gulag appears to have been *less* important to issues of state power and control than other camp systems *in wartime*, including those of Nazi Germany during the Second World War and the British during the South African War of 1899–1903.[8]

Some of the recent scholarship on the war in the Eastern Front, moreover, has emphasized the similarity between the Nazi and Soviet regimes in terms of the extreme violence on and near the front lines. Timothy Snyder's *Bloodlands* and Norman Naimark's arguments concerning Stalinist repression as genocide are prominent examples of this approach to the Eastern Front, but a close examination of the home-front Gulag certainly highlights the differences, rather than the similarities, between the two regimes.[9] Not only did the Soviet regime arguably decrease the size of the camp system during the war, unlike the Germans, but, as we shall see in this book, there were several other key contrasts between the two camp systems. Forced labour "was not one of [the] founding principles" of the German Nazi camps and was used partially as punishment and only sporadically with significant economic goals in mind, at least until the latter half of the war.[10] In the Soviet case, forced labour was a defining feature of the Stalinist camp system, and one goal of Stalin's Gulag was to conduct significant economic activity in key sectors, including infrastructure, forestry, mining, and agriculture. The Gulag's prisoner population was integrated physically, economically, and ideologically into the Soviet system, rather than removed from it. The camp personnel in the Gulag did not come from those supposedly most committed to the cause; Communist Party membership rates among Gulag camp staff and guards were low. In contrast, most of the staff and even guards for the Nazi camps came from the Nazi SS, at least until partway through the war when they were supplemented by demobilized soldiers and members of local populations, particularly Ukrainians, Latvians, and ethnic Germans in the borderlands. A Gulag job was itself often somewhat of a punishment, rather than a desirable position.[11] Camp operations in the Gulag point to a system that functioned despite its bureaucracy, where the situation on the ground was based more on informal practices than codified rules, whereas the management of Nazi camps has been described (although not without debate) as a "coolly rational bureaucratic process."[12] And, finally, while mass death was prevalent in both camp systems – indeed, the Gulag was at its deadliest during the war – the intentionality of Gulag deaths is debatable.[13] Camp bosses could be punished if the mortality rates were too high, and there were centralized prophylactic directives designed to reduce deaths, although these were not usually implemented or effective. The Gulag's high wartime death rate, moreover, was far exceeded by death rates in the Nazi concentration camps, even excluding the death camps.[14]

Yet, as in the Nazi camps, it is precisely on the level of mass death where we most clearly see the Stalinist Gulag as a system of violence. In *Bloodlands*, Snyder notes that most civilian deaths under Stalin's watch occurred in the Western borderlands, the area of conflict with Germany. In order to show that the Gulag was not the deadliest aspect of the Stalinist system, he points out that 90 per cent of Gulag inmates survived the camps.[15] The 90 per cent figure overestimates the survival rate, but even using official figures, Snyder fails to acknowledge that

932,000 Gulag prisoners perished between 1 January 1941 and 1 January 1946 – over half of all documented Gulag deaths during the entire system's existence.[16] One's chances of surviving Stalin's wartime Gulag were much lower than surviving the peacetime camps. Most of the deaths occurred far from the bloodlands and included prisoners from all across Soviet territory. The camp system was without doubt a key cog in the "violent society" that was Stalin's Soviet Union.[17]

The Gulag in Western Siberia: An Overview

Western Siberia's camp system was well established by the outbreak of the Second World War.[18] Encouraged by the perceived success of the Solovetskii camps in the far north of European Russia, authorities created SibULON (the Siberian Administration of Camps of Special Significance) in 1929, even before GULAG (Main Administration of Camps) came into existence in April 1930. Initially encompassing camps stretching all the way from Omsk to Krasnoiarsk (the rough equivalent of Paris to Budapest by road!), the jurisdiction of "Siblag" (the "Siberian Camp"), as it became known, shrank in size as Western Siberia was divided administratively over the course of the 1930s. By 1937, Siblag was in charge of corrective-labour camps, corrective-labour colonies, and special settlements only in Novosibirsk Province.

By the end of the war, around half of all Gulag prisoners were imprisoned in the corrective-labour colonies, yet most books on the Gulag barely address the history of these colonies.[19] Until 1944, the Gulag also administered the so-called special settlements, which were exile settlements that began with the campaign against the "kulaks" (supposedly well-off peasants) in the early 1930s, and continued with the deportation of suspect ethnic groups in the late 1930s and especially during the Second World War. In 1944, authorities created a separate department within the security police administration for the settlements.[20]

Two separate camp systems – Gornoshorlag and Tomasinlag – also existed in the region in the late 1930s and early 1940s, but both had been decommissioned, with many prisoners reabsorbed into Siblag or other camps, before the German invasion of the Soviet Union in June 1941. Thus, at the time of the German invasion, the Western Siberian camp system appears roughly as pictured in the map in figure 0.1. Many of the camps labelled on this map also had several "stations" (*punkty*) that were often a few kilometres apart from one another, so the actual number of camp-like spaces in the region far exceeds those shown on the map. As we can see from this map, Siblag camps and colonies dotted the region, but most major urban areas had at least one camp or colony, and many of the other camps were located along the Trans-Siberian Railway. Spatially, most of the region's camps were thus not isolated in any noticeable way from the non-prisoner populations. It was the special settlements, many of which were located in the Narym area, that were often far removed from the region's main cities and towns, although even many special settlements existed closer to population centres, particularly in the coal-mining areas of present-day Kemerovo Province.

The region's camps were economically diversified, although agriculture predominated. Indeed, Siblag, along with Karlag in Kazakhstan and Srednebellag in the Far East, was tasked with sending foodstuffs to camps throughout the Soviet Union.[21] Many prisoners, however, also worked under contract from non-Gulag enterprises, particularly construction and defence enterprises, and there were also camp stations devoted to mining, garment production, forestry, and railway and road construction. As will be discussed at length, following the German invasion, all of these prison camps, colonies, and stations shifted to war-related production (if they had not done so already), including the agricultural camps, which now provided food to the Red Army at the expense of sending food to other parts of the Gulag.

Interpreting Stalin's Gulag at War

The war was a test for the Gulag, as it was for the Stalinist system. By June 1941 (or even September 1939), the Gulag, on paper, was a large, modern, bureaucratic institution. The Gulag had accounted for 13 to 14 per cent of the Soviet Union's capital construction projects in 1940–1, and 12 to 13 per cent of the nation's timber over the same period.[22] Yet it had largely grown in the 1930s as an improvised response to the various traumatic upheavals of the decade: collectivization, the five-year plans, and the mass arrests and deportations of 1937–8, also known as the Great Terror. Gulag officials had been so unprepared for some of these events that their responses were inadequate at best and deadly at worst, as Oleg Khlevniuk demonstrates in the case of the forestry camps – including Tomasinlag in Western Siberia – set up to deal with the excess prisoners of 1937–8.[23] Thus, even though Stalin had been planning for war, and had justified many of his campaigns with the need to prepare for war, no one could be sure how the Gulag would respond.

The response, measured in terms of its results, is paradoxical. In many respects, the Gulag at war was the most chaotic period for the Stalinist camp system, with a huge turnover of both personnel and prisoners, mass death, and the frequent disruption of supply chains and basic resources. Despite this chaos, central and local camp authorities successfully mobilized the Gulag into the total war effort, at great expense to the lives of prisoners, but with tangible results in terms of artillery and other military equipment produced. That the system on the ground, as we shall see, functioned haphazardly at best, and largely on the basis of personal, informal networks, was something the authorities partially overlooked. In the end, victory in the Second World War was also the Gulag's victory, because it ensured the survival and growth of a costly, inefficient, and deadly system in the postwar period.

Gulag research to date has only rarely focused on the war. For a more in-depth discussion of recent Gulag historiography, the interested reader should examine the section in chapter 5 on the Gulag in comparative and theoretical perspective. What follows is a brief overview of Gulag scholarship, particularly as it pertains to the Second World War.

Russian-language monographs on the Western Siberian Gulag – such as those by V.N. Uimanov, S.A. Papkov, and S.A. Krasil'nikov – all end their narratives before the war begins.[24] While there are several scholarly articles covering the region's camps during the war, these tend to focus either on particular subjects or provide only very brief overviews, thus missing the chance at in-depth analysis.[25] More useful are several document collections on the region's camps and special settlements that cover the war years, although these studies contain minimal analysis.[26]

The anglophone literature on the Gulag has not focused on the war, despite Edwin Bacon's 1994 book *The Gulag at War*, which was one of the first monographs about the Gulag based on declassified Russian archival documents. Overall, Bacon's account reveals an economic rationale for Gulag operations. Yet Bacon's main purpose was to explain what sort of information one can find on the Gulag in the archives, and he used the wartime framework mostly to limit the chronological scope of his analysis.[27] Much remains to be said on the Gulag's role in wartime mobilization, especially considering the voluminous amount of scholarship on both the Gulag and the wartime Soviet Union that has appeared since Bacon's work. And on the issue of wartime mobilization, most of the more recent book-length studies of the camps either mention the war only in short sections of longer works (as in books by

Anne Applebaum, Steven Barnes, and Alan Barenberg), or do not cover the war at all (e.g., Khlevniuk).[28]

The shorter, article-length or chapter-length studies of the Gulag at war offer a good starting point for discussion. In their study of Norilsk during the war, Leonid Borodkin and Simon Ertz note that unfit prisoners were often turned away from this camp, which had a relatively low mortality rate and remained relatively productive.[29] For Norilsk, at least, it seems that economic concerns trumped penal ones.[30] Barenberg's work on the Gulag in Vorkuta underscores the economic rationale behind Vorkuta's wartime expansion. It was the closest coal supply to the blockaded city of Leningrad, and the largest supply of coal in European Russia following the Nazi invasion and occupation of key coal-producing regions.[31] The Gulag administration, moreover, had divided in 1941 into various *Glavki*, or main administrations, based on *economic* function (e.g., GULDZhS: Main Administration for Camps of Railway Construction) rather than political considerations.[32] Yet economics – that is, a ready supply of forced labour for crucial production activities – does not tell the whole story.[33] Gulag labour was very inefficient and, despite a stated goal of self-sufficiency, generally cost the state more than it gave back.[34]

The politics of release during the war also clearly indicate that penal and political concerns were crucially important. Many thousands of prisoners – often relatively healthy, young men – were released to fight on the front. Without question, these releases hindered the Gulag's economic production. And, while the Gulag remained a "revolving door" for those with lighter sentences, the regime barred from release counter-revolutionaries who had completed their sentences.[35] The so-called counter-revolutionaries, those sentenced under Article 58 of the criminal code, tended to receive harsher treatment than other prisoner populations and were thus more likely to be unfit for work. They were, moreover, by definition politically unreliable, and thus hardly the most likely candidates to help the camp system in the Soviet Union's war effort. As Steven Barnes describes, "At a time when it was mobilized for a total war, the Gulag consisted of a smaller, less healthy, less politically reliable, older, and more feminine detained population with a smaller ... staff."[36] In her earlier work, Golfo Alexopoulos argued that this sort of evidence, along with the frequent releases and arrests, shows that "penal practices fundamentally undermined economic production."[37] Barnes even takes this a step further, pointing to the continued efforts at re-education as evidence of the Gulag's role as a "transformer of man," part of the modern gardening state, where economic concerns were secondary.[38] Alexopoulos's most recent work complicates the question of the rationale behind Gulag operations, as she argues that, by design, a fundamental aspect of the Gulag was the destruction of the health and lives of the prisoners. She shows that labour categories for prisoners, based on physical health and capabilities, were designed to work the prisoners to the point of death or near death. She argues that many releases, particularly in the latter half of the war and in the postwar years, intentionally masked the death rate, as authorities released prisoners on the verge of death rather than counting these deaths in their own mortality statistics. While an economic rationale may be debatable in the release of emaciated prisoners, fundamentally Alexopoulos agrees with Solzhenitsyn's contention that the camps were "destructive-labor" camps.[39]

These emphases in the historiography (economic, penal, and ideological) are, of course, not mutually exclusive. If camp authorities at Norilsk received only the able-bodied prisoners, Siblag's administrators frequently complained about the poor physical condition of the arriving inmates. In a 1943 report on conditions at Camp Station 3 (in Novosibirsk), authorities blamed poor production results on the worsening food supply and the "huge" number of arriving prisoners who were physically able to perform only light tasks; fewer than half of the prisoners at the camp station at the time were even physically able to work.[40] Taken as a whole, then, the motivation for camp operations may have varied between camp administrations, and even between different camps and colonies operating within the same camp system. If some camps emphasized economic output, others emphasized isolation. Many of the light-regimen camps placed more effort on re-education and cultural activities than the harsh-regimen camps. Even the motivations of individual camp commanders likely changed due to external events and pressures. The war carried with it not only the need for home front mobilization at any cost, for example, but also concern about enemies within undermining the war effort, so camp bosses had to be vigilant in terms of both increased production and the punishment and isolation of real and perceived enemies.

Despite the poor condition of incoming prisoners to Western Siberian camps, on the balance, the following pages point to a primarily economic rationale for Gulag operations, at least at the local level. There was an immediate shift to wartime production, in some cases even in support of the Red Army for the 1939–40 Winter War with Finland and

the annexation and occupation of eastern Poland and the Baltics beginning in September 1939; in this sense, the Second World War began for
the Soviet Union in September 1939, although total war began only
after the German invasion posed a clear existential threat to the entire
system. Local authorities granted suspect groups and individuals
positions of responsibility because of their economic contributions.
Prisoners in crucial industries had to remain in the camps even after the
end of their sentences. Finally, camp propaganda was geared mainly
towards increasing economic production. The shift to wartime production itself is not surprising. Similar shifts happened in most non-Gulag
enterprises, and a crucial aspect of Soviet defence planning for most of
the 1930s was an emphasis on the convertibility of industry to military
production.[41] These economic factors, however, intertwined and often
conflicted with political and other factors, as the release of healthy prisoners to the front suggests.

Both the informal practices that pervaded the Gulag and the incredibly harsh conditions helped to undermine economic goals. By
June 1941, the Gulag had evolved, on paper, into a highly bureaucratic
system, with rules and regulations related to almost every aspect of
camp life and death.[42] Understaffing, corruption, and supply problems
meant that those regulations were almost impossible to follow, and informal practices such as black markets, data falsifications, and what has
been called "an economy of favours" flourished.[43] Thus, at the time of
the German invasion, authorities could not be certain how the camp
system would respond: Could it be relied upon to respond to the needs
of the war effort, or would inefficiencies and corruption undermine any
practical contributions?

There is no doubt that prisoners made tangible contributions. From
mid-1941 to the end of 1944, Gulag prisoners as a whole produced over
25 million shells, 35 million hand grenades and fuses, 9 million mines,
and 100,000 bombs, not to mention other military material such as tele-
phone cable, skis, rafts, gas masks, and uniforms.[44] They also helped
build factories that produced airplanes and other military equipment.
Gulag prisoners working in special scientific-research camps, called
sharashki, even helped invent "twenty major weapons systems or pro-
cesses" over the course of the war, although these camps were not in
Western Siberia.[45] Many prisoners, moreover, received early release to
go directly to the front, or were sent to the front at the end of their sentences, often serving in the most dangerous positions. Internal documents estimate that around 1 million former prisoners served in the

Red Army during the war.[46] Camp personnel also left in large numbers for military service. As far as the home front is concerned, however, the Western Siberian case study reveals that other human resources, including the mobilization of underutilized groups such as women and even the elderly, likely had a greater impact on wartime production than the regional Gulag.

The human resources of Soviet society could be moved and allocated as the state desired, regardless of the cost in health and lives. The Gulag as an institution epitomized this type of thinking. Barenberg's impressive work on Vorkuta is instructive on the idea of mobilization. He argues that the terms "prisoner" and "non-prisoner" are more useful than "forced" and "free" in the Soviet context, given the overlap in labour use.[47] Indeed, central and local authorities allocated labour resources, both prisoner and non-prisoner, in remarkably similar ways. I use the term "forced labour" to describe the economic activity of prisoners, special settlers, and POWs because this term underscores the economic rationale behind Gulag operations and the prisoners' place on the home front. My research, however, confirms Barenberg's contention that there was considerable interaction between both prisoners and non-prisoners, and spaces of incarceration and regular Soviet society. I have adopted Barenberg's usage in passages where a distinction needs to be made.[48]

Stalin required full mobilization of the Soviet system in order to defeat Nazi Germany. That system required the use of human resources on a vast scale, a "continuum" of forced and free labour that included non-prisoners sent to various defence enterprises without much choice, and prisoners sent to these same enterprises with no choice at all.[49] The Stalinist system had developed over the course of the 1930s through a series of five-year economic plans, large-scale repressive measures – particularly directed against the peasantry – and modern state-building practices, including increased bureaucratization, standardization of rules and procedures, and increased capacity to gather information and conduct surveillance.

It is within the context of the Stalinist mobilization state that we can speak of the Gulag as "Stalin's Gulag." Stalin himself, at least in the documentation that is currently available to historians, rarely spoke or wrote directly about the Gulag. Gulag projects at times came up for discussion in the Politburo, the key decision-making body of the Communist Party, and the party's Central Committee occasionally discussed the camp system. On the whole, however, wartime Gulag operations were subsumed under the People's Commissariat of Internal Affairs (NKVD) and thus came under the jurisdiction of "Stalin's first lieutenant," NKVD director Lavrentii Beria.[50] Yet there can be no doubt that the camp system was *Stalin's* system. The Gulag as an administration was founded in 1930, in the midst of Stalin's First Five-Year Plan, and owed its dramatic increase in prisoner population and proliferation of camps to Stalinist campaigns, such as collectivization and dekulakization, and the mass arrests of 1937–8.[51] The Gulag that developed over the course of the 1930s was also representative of the Stalinist system's ability to mobilize both prisoner and non-prisoner human resources in whatever ways the state saw as necessary, as well as emblematic of centralized repressive measures that Stalin relied upon for control of various populations. Victory in the Second World War seemed to prove, moreover, that the system had succeeded. Because of the victory, the Soviet leadership could ignore the incredible costs of the system. The Gulag was Stalin's Gulag, even if his name comes up infrequently in the Gulag's myriad operational orders and directives.

Ultimately, the story of the Western Siberian camps at war sheds light on the operation of Soviet power within the camp system, on the effort to mobilize society for the war effort, and on the role of forced labour in Soviet victory. On the operation of Soviet power, we see that top-down orders were routinely ignored or circumvented, and that prisoners and non-prisoners alike formed networks and carried out informal practices that at times reinforced the violence of the camps but could at other times help alleviate some of that violence.

In terms of home front mobilization and the role of forced labour, the Western Siberian camps reveal a pragmatic approach to the war, and a system that had a surprising flexibility to respond to the existential threat posed by Nazi Germany. On one hand, as will be argued, the Soviet system was less reliant on repressive measures than it had been either before the war or would be after the war, and in this respect the Soviet home front represents something of a lost opportunity for the system to have developed into a different, less repressive system. On the other hand, the incredible violence of the system was on full display during the war years, and wartime production was more valuable than everything, including human lives.

This book is organized thematically, focusing on the development of the Gulag in Western Siberia before the Second World War, economic mobilization for the war effort, the prisoners' responses to the war, the personnel's responses to the war, and a final assessment of the wartime

Gulag's role in victory, including a focused discussion of the place of the Soviet camp system in comparative perspective. Chapter 1 assesses the Gulag's readiness for total warfare by providing an overview of the pre-war history of forced labour in Western Siberia, pointing to peculiarities that made the Gulag "Stalin's Gulag," but also showing that the Siberian camps partially addressed age-old questions of Russia's socioeconomic development. Chapter 2, "Total War, Total Mobilization," then provides an overview of the Western Siberian camps on the home front, and reveals that an economic rationale for Gulag operations – at least at the local level – appears the most plausible explanation. While deadly, the camps produced tangible economic results, as they were mobilized for total war in the full sense of the phrase. Chapters 3 and 4 assess the wartime regional camps by examining the prisoners and the personnel, respectively, arguing that while in both cases patriotism was an official motivating factor that could be adopted or largely ignored, the incredibly harsh camp conditions meant that there was an enormous waste of human lives and potential. Both chapters underscore the prevalence of informal practices in day-to-day activities of the camps, and the close connections between the camps and the surrounding communities. Chapter 5, "The Gulag's Victory," places the camps within the context of Soviet victory and explores what the wartime Gulag reveals about the Stalinist camp system in a comparative, theoretical framework. A brief epilogue looks back at the memory, in Russia today, of the Gulag at war.

A Note on Sources

There are two main groups of sources available to Gulag researchers: documentation produced by those in power, and documentation – mostly memoirs, but some correspondence – from former prisoners. Since the opening of the archives in the early 1990s, vast quantities of documents relating to the Gulag have been declassified. If early scholars had to struggle to find enough sources, specialists today have almost the opposite problem: there are too many documents, both central and local, for any one researcher to study, let alone master. In terms of documentation produced by those in power, this book draws on multiple sources in order to examine Gulag operations from various angles. NKVD and Gulag operational orders, statistical reports compiled by camp administrators, and inspection reports by the local procurators (something like a public prosecutor), reveal information about how the authorities wanted the Gulag to exist. However, one can read between the lines of these documents to understand how the system actually existed in practice. If the authorities regularly banned intimate relations between men and women prisoners, or between prisoners and camp personnel, the logical conclusion is not that men and women prisoners, or prisoners and personnel, never interacted but that they interacted in illicit ways on a regular basis.[52] This type of conclusion can be confirmed through another major archival source used extensively in this study: local camp Communist Party organization documents. Camps and colonies formed party organizations for the small percentage of personnel who were party members, and these organizations produced meeting minutes that can now be found in archival repositories. As argued in chapter 4, on personnel, these minutes reveal that the party was most concerned with party business – membership, conference attendance, etc. – but frequent reports by the control commission, in charge of disciplinary infractions within the party, point to significant areas of illicit interaction between personnel and prisoners, particularly fraternization and black market activity. *Stalin's Gulag at War* also relies on a third category of official documentation, the prisoner file, to reveal both the difficulties the authorities had in matching policy to practice, and something of the wartime experiences of non-political prisoners, who rarely left memoirs.

There are now huge numbers of published and unpublished memoirs available to scholars, and even several publications that focus on both censored and smuggled correspondence between prisoners and their families.[53] These sources have the obvious benefit of giving voice to those repressed and marginalized, those who struggled immensely to survive and who suffered in almost unimaginable ways. Gulag memoirs, like any source, must be read critically. Not only do we not have voices of those who suffered the most (those who perished in the camps), the vast majority of memoirists were sentenced under Article 58 of the criminal code, and since Article 58ers represented only a subset of the prisoners, we must be cautious about the representative nature of some of the accounts. This book refers mostly to memoirs of prisoners who spent at least part of the war in Siblag. At times, however, it has been necessary to use memoirs that describe other camps, in order to create as full a picture as possible of the prisoners' wartime experiences. Ultimately, it was the prisoners who sacrificed their health, and frequently their lives, to help achieve victory over Nazi Germany, a victory that Stalin closely associated with himself; the role of prisoners in this victory has been forgotten. It is to this story, the story of Stalin's Gulag during the Second World War – the harshest and most deadly period of a harsh and deadly system – that we now turn.

1 Ready for Total War? Forced Labour and the Development of Western Siberia before the Second World War

That day we covered 25 kilometres. As usual, we were lied to – they told us there were only around 10 kilometres to go. Barely able to drag our feet, we reached the camp in the evening. Its lights shone through the darkness of the forest. We stopped on a hill overlooking a number of dilapidated barracks … Along the walls [in one barrack] stretched three rows of bunks. The room was fully stocked with sweaty, half-naked, emaciated "zeks." Their faces seemed brutalized to us. We recoiled in fear … this is the shack that became our new home.

Iosif Berger, describing his arrival at Siblag's Akhpunsk camp[1]

In 1929, a group of Soviet agronomists, land surveyors, botanists, forestry experts, soil scientists, statisticians, and students set off to assess the viability for settlement of the area north of the Trans-Siberian Railway, between the Siberian cities of Tomsk and Krasnoiarsk. The scientists' report, submitted only in 1931 to the Commissariat of Agriculture, included numerous photographs of the region and an optimistic tone about the prospects of the area for settlement. Relying heavily on the reports of similar expeditions from the early twentieth century, the report noted that the Trans-Siberian Railway had been a boon to colonization throughout Siberia, but that most settlers lived within 100 to 150 kilometres of the railway, making it difficult to extract the rich resources located farther north.[2]

The 1929 expedition was one in a long series of Siberian expeditions dating back to Empress Anna's Great Northern Expedition in the 1730s, which had the purpose of mapping, cataloguing and categorizing Siberia's vast geography, resources and peoples. Occurring almost

200 years later, the 1929 trek is thus also indicative of the difficulties successive regimes had in developing the region, which was still very much a "frontier" area even in 1929 at the time of Stalin's First Five-Year Plan.[3]

While members of the 1929 expedition recognized the need to colonize the area as quickly as possible, they implicitly advocated a gradual approach. In their report, the authors concluded that the region's natural resources could support many factories, which would in turn encourage mass settlement.[4] They noted that previous, tsarist-era initiatives to encourage settlement well north of the Trans-Siberian Railway had failed precisely because of a lack of employment and infrastructure.[5]

The gradual approach advocated by the scientists and students who made the expedition placed them out of touch with the urgency of the times. Nineteen twenty-nine, as the "Year of the Great Turn,"[6] was a watershed year in Soviet history. Trotsky was deported from the Soviet Union; Stalin celebrated his fiftieth birthday, ushering in the "cult of personality"; and Stalin called for faster collectivization of agriculture in the countryside and the "liquidation of the kulaks as a class." This year also saw the creation of the Siberian Administration for Camps of Special Significance (SibULON), later called Siblag.[7]

The Gulag's rapid growth during Stalin's First Five-Year Plan was a result of the "war against the peasantry," which sent many waves of peasants from the Soviet countryside to the Gulag camps and special settlements.[8] Thus, the *primary* causal factor for the Gulag's early expansion was political: to control the countryside. Almost simultaneously, however, authorities realized that these vast numbers of peasants could be used as forced labourers for the fulfilment of the five-year plans and the economic exploitation of developing regions. This economic factor overlapped with the political one by providing further incentive to expand the Gulag system, especially during the "telescoped" development of the 1930s.[9] Tension between political and economic motivating factors continued throughout the Gulag's existence, including the total war effort of the Second World War.

In this way, the Gulag *appeared to be* an attractive solution to two long-standing questions in *Russian* – as opposed to specifically *Soviet* – history: the question concerning the exploitation of resources in underdeveloped regions and the so-called peasant question – the prevention of real and potential unrest in the countryside along with the guarantee of a steady supply of grain.

Long-Standing Questions in Russian History

For centuries, Siberia's resources had supplied governments in Moscow and St. Petersburg with the raw materials for homegrown industries or for the purchase of modern munitions and goods on the international market.[10] In the seventeenth century, Muscovy's military might grew considerably due in large part to huge profits made from the lucrative trade of sable furs, collected by enterprising Russian explorers and trappers who brutally oppressed Siberia's native peoples.[11] Realizing that Russia needed to develop its own arms industry in order to be competitive with the expanding European empires, Peter the Great encouraged the development of the iron industry on the eastern side of the Ural Mountains. By the end of the eighteenth century, Russia was the world's largest producer of pig iron and indisputably a world power. Peter the Great's forceful transfer of Russia into the realms of Western European scientific inquiry also provided the catalyst for the many scientific expeditions to Siberia that would follow his reign.[12]

The nineteenth century saw further economic development as rich polymetallic ores were discovered in the Altai Mountains and geopolitics fuelled increased colonization of the region, especially the construction of the Trans-Siberian Railway, begun late in the century. The railway finally made mass colonization possible, and Siberia saw a huge influx of settlers.[13] From around 1900 until the outbreak of the First World War, over 100,000 settlers came to Siberia *each year*, except during the Russo-Japanese War.[14] The Trans-Siberian snaked its way along the southernmost parts of the Siberian steppe and taiga, which meant that much of the northern Eurasian continent was difficult to access and remained sparsely settled.

Prisoner labour had played at least a small role in Siberia's economic activity from the mid-seventeenth century. Peter the Great's *katorga* system led to an expansion of the use of penal labour, especially in the latter half of the eighteenth century, as the state sent large numbers of convicts to help construct and work in the Nerchinsk Mining District near Lake Baikal.[15] The infamous *katorga* penal system – involving hard labour in remote locations – bore at least some resemblance to later Soviet practices, even if on a smaller scale.[16] The tsarist penal labour system in Siberia received a boost under the governorship of Mikhail Speranskii, the liberal reformer, whose 1822 Exile and Convict Regulations "astronomically expanded the number of convicts and vagrants banished to Siberia."[17] Between 1823 and 1872, authorities forcibly exiled around half a million persons to Siberia.[18]

If the forced labour of *prisoners* played a small but important role in tsarist-era Siberia, forced labour, more broadly defined, had been a huge component of resource extraction for a large portion of the imperial period. It is a misconception to think of Siberia as a land free from serfdom. While peasants in the Siberian countryside were free from bondage, and this contributed to a flourishing agricultural sector, particularly in Western Siberia,[19] the state used huge numbers of factory serfs in the region, most prominently in mining. In 1861, on the eve of the emancipation of the serfs, for example, some 310,752 factory serfs were working in mines and smelting ores in the Altai Mountains. This compares with only 43,522 free workers in the industry at the time. These factory serfs frequently faced violence and lived and worked in harsh conditions.[20] The Soviets were thus hardly the first to make use of a vast pool of forced labourers, largely peasants, for the extraction of Siberia's resources. Nor were they the first to use exiles and convicts as colonizers. The Soviet state's decision to use forced labour in the Siberian periphery, in order provide raw materials to feed the needs of the centre, was a long-standing solution for the economic exploitation of the region and, indeed, the country as a whole.

The extraction of resources for the modernization of the country was a centuries-old issue in Russia's history. The "peasant question," however, in many ways loomed even larger in the country's development. In the seventeenth century, the final codification of serfdom came about in part because of the modernizing needs of the Muscovite state.[21] Actual and potential peasant rebellions also caused persistent fear in the empire's capital. Beginning under Catherine the Great, the growing sympathy among some educated nobles for the plight of the peasantry, not to mention the influence of Enlightenment ideas of rights and equality, meant that serfdom was increasingly seen as untenable, at least in the long term. The abolition of serfdom in 1861 – an attempt at a resolution of the question – in some ways exacerbated the problem, as the onerous settlement terms did nothing to quench the peasantry's desire for land and more independence.[22] Prime Minister Piotr Stolypin's early-twentieth-century agrarian reforms, designed to create prosperous individual farmsteads to supersede the traditional peasant commune, were yet another attempt at ensuring the loyalty of the countryside to the regime while at the same time providing for the needs of the empire in terms of agricultural production.[23]

The First World War, however, seemed to prove that successive tsarist regimes had failed to pacify the countryside. The length and harsh conditions of the war meant that many of the army's troops, the vast majority of whom were conscripted peasants, wanted nothing more than to return to the countryside. In the countryside itself, the clamouring for land grew louder, especially when the collapse of the tsarist regime in early 1917 provided a clear opportunity for reform.

Seeking to seize this opportunity, the Bolsheviks initially promised the land to the peasants in an effort to gain support for the Revolution and, later, their side in the Civil War. Despite this promise, the Bolsheviks met fierce resistance in some parts of the countryside, particularly in Ukraine and Western Siberia. In Siberia, the resistance was strong in part because of the long-standing tradition there of private agricultural enterprise, which made collectivism less appealing.[24] On the whole, the peasantry wanted to be left alone, and the forced grain requisitions by both sides during the Civil War threatened this aspiration. It was not until Lenin's implementation of the New Economic Policy, which provided for limited private enterprise in the countryside, that opposition to Bolshevik rule finally appeared to wane. As punishment for Siberia's fierce resistance to the Bolsheviks during the Civil War, the Bolsheviks delayed implementing the New Economic Policy in the region.[25]

The New Economic Policy led to growing prosperity in the countryside, including Siberia.[26] Successful peasants were hardly successful socialists, however, at least as far as many Bolsheviks were concerned. Central attempts to control grain prices and prices for consumer goods meant that the peasantry, at times, had little incentive to produce for the needs of the state, a regular cause of concern for central planners. Private enterprise, however limited, also seemed anathema to Bolshevik ideology. From a strict Marxist perspective, of course, peasants were capitalists or, at best, representatives of a backward, feudal relationship. Lenin famously adapted Marxism to Russia's peasant question (he had no choice, given that the vast majority of Russia's population was rural).[27] He argued that social stratification existed in the countryside, which was divided into poor, middle, and wealthy (*kulak*) peasants. In this scenario, the kulaks exploited the poor peasants, who were thus obvious allies to the exploited workers and could be considered akin to the proletariat, while the middle peasant wavered between bourgeois aspirations and revolutionary goals. Although revolution, civil war, and famine had done much to level any social stratification that had actually existed among the peasantry,[28] many Bolsheviks held fast to the view of a stratified countryside and, moreover, felt that the New Economic Policy had promoted kulak behaviour. The grain crisis of 1927 contributed to this perception, as peasants appeared to be withholding grain at the expense of the workers. Something had to be done, and Stalin had a solution: collectivization and dekulakization.

Collectivization and dekulakization took place in the context of Stalin's First Five-Year Plan. The plan, which invested primarily in heavy industry, called for nothing less than the transformation of the Soviet Union from a rural, primarily agrarian society into an industrial state. Western Siberia was crucial for Stalin's goals of industrialization and war preparedness. Of exceptional importance was the Kuznetsk Coal Basin (Kuzbass), covering large parts of present-day Kemerovo Province. If industrial cities like Magnitogorsk were to be successful, they would owe that success to coal mining in Kuznetsk. Together, authorities called this project the Ural-Kuznetsk Combine, a project that economic historian Franklyn Holzman referred to in 1957 as "probably the most ambitious single project, apart from the national economic plans themselves, ever attempted by the Soviets."[29] The new steel city of Magnitogorsk, on its own an incredibly ambitious project, was thousands of kilometres from the Kuzbass, but by aligning this Urals city with Western Siberia, planners, as Stephen Kotkin argues, sought to turn a weakness (the vast distance) into a strength.[30] The Ural-Kuznetsk Combine created a second major Soviet metallurgical centre (after the Donbass), and one much more secure from foreign attack or intervention. Although planners allocated resources to the development of this project in the 1930s, the war itself provided the catalyst to focus on the project, as many factories and experts were evacuated to both the Urals and Western Siberia.[31]

Regional development in the 1930s was closely tied to collectivization and dekulakization. The forced collectivization and the accompanying dekulakization campaigns of 1928–32 were, moreover, in effect a "war against the peasantry."[32] This "war" caused a greater upheaval of the peasant way of life than either the abolition of serfdom in 1861 or the Revolution of 1917.[33] It was a "war" that took many prisoners. And many of those prisoners ended up either in the Gulag camps themselves or in the Gulag's extensive network of so-called special settlements.

If peasants comprised most of the first wave of prisoners into the Gulag, they also made up the main contingents of many subsequent waves, emphasizing the key role of the peasantry in the Gulag. Contrary to popular understanding, intellectuals were not the primary targets of Stalinist repression. In fact, it was the peasantry that was crucial for the Gulag's growth throughout the 1930s.[34] Even during the Great Terror of

1937–8, which of course affected intellectuals, officials, and party members, the main target of the so-called mass operations (as opposed to individual investigations of anti-Soviet behaviour) was once again the peasantry. "Mass operations," whereby the NKVD established high arrest and execution quotas for targeted groups, hit former kulaks particularly hard.[35] Other laws during the 1930s, in particular laws concerning "crimes against state property" and the infamous passport laws, in effect targeted peasants, and contributed to making the Gulag an institution populated predominantly by peasants.[36]

While economic factors were initially secondary to the repressive measures aimed primarily at the countryside, they were not unimportant. Some scholars have argued that local authorities encouraged the Gulag's expansion for economic reasons. James Harris notes that local officials in the Urals spurred the Gulag's growth by requesting more forced labourers to fulfil the demands of the First Five-Year Plan.[37] Local authorities certainly treated the Gulag and its prisoner-labourers as an economic resource. Central officials used the language of colonization, too, when discussing the special settlements. In March 1931, the Andreev Commission discussed the resettlement of kulak households in the Western Siberian Territory.[38] From May to July of that year, 40,000 households were to be sent to northern areas of the territory with the explicit purpose of "opening up black earth land tracts" (*chernozem-nykh massivov*) and working in the forestry industry.[39]

Widespread use of forced labour thus helped address both the need to exploit the Soviet Union's natural resources and the need to find an answer to the "peasant question," both long-standing issues for the rulers in Moscow and St. Petersburg. This does not mean, however, that the Gulag – or even forced labour more generally – was a foregone conclusion.

Indeed, while the Gulag addressed long-standing Russian questions, it did so in a particular *Stalinist* way. Stalin's innovation was mass mobilization focused on industrial development, using all coercive state mechanisms at his disposal to achieve this goal. These mechanisms included social mobility, which acted as a form of reward, as Sheila Fitzpatrick has demonstrated.[40] These mechanisms also, however, included tremendous state violence. The rapid speed at which this mass mobilization occurred, moreover, meant that many measures were reactive rather than proactive, and there were simply not enough resources or knowledge to follow regulations and plans to the letter. Thus, Stalinism meant the flourishing of informal networks of exchange and favours. While these networks provided avenues for upward mobility and access to goods, they also reinforced the state's coercive mechanisms of both rewards and violence, by ensuring that almost everyone was in violation of some sort of regulation or law, so that state violence could easily focus on any person (or group of people) at any given time. The Gulag, thus, was an attempt to answer the Russian questions of resource extraction and the pacification of the peasantry, but with a Stalinist twist: mass mobilization and extreme, state-sanctioned violence, held together by the informal practices of those who often found themselves far from Moscow.

The Evolution of Prisoner Labour in the Soviet Union

The Bolsheviks established prison camps not long after the Revolution.[41] They founded these early camps in the context of the Civil War and repressive policies against those who opposed the revolution. While the Bolsheviks were not the first to use the "concentration camp" in a wartime context, they certainly learned from this Civil War experience.[42] The Bolsheviks' militant rhetoric surrounding class enemies, their constant fear of counter-revolution, their hostility towards the viewpoints of other parties and those of non-working-class origin, and even the Bolshevik Party's foundation as a clandestine organization are, taken together, evidence that some sort of large penal system was *likely* to evolve.[43] So, on one hand, one could argue that the Civil War camps led to the Gulag.[44]

A closer examination, however, reveals a constantly evolving system, one that developed in more of an ad hoc manner rather than as the result of any master plan, but that expanded rapidly due to specific Stalinist policies of collectivization and rapid, state-directed industrialization.[45] Whatever the continuities from the early Soviet camps, the Stalin-era Gulag represents an important break. Three factors ultimately reveal that a large penal apparatus was not an inevitable outcome of early Bolshevik rule. The first, and perhaps most important, factor was the very *mild* Bolshevik approach to criminal justice during the early Soviet period. Second, as the 1929 expedition to Siberia indicates, there were alternatives to forced labour that were seriously attempted – and never abandoned – by the authorities. Under a leadership less inclined towards rapid industrialization and collectivization, it is certainly conceivable that such a large penal/exile system never would have developed. And, third, even as the system began to expand rapidly, there were high-level attempts to limit its growth and to find alternative forms of punishment.

Initially, the Bolsheviks approached crime and punishment much more leniently than their tsarist predecessors. Many Bolsheviks understood crime through a Marxist lens as an aspect of the inequalities and class exploitation inherent in capitalist economic systems. Thus, they expected crime – and therefore prisons, too – to wither away under the new, socialist state.[46] The Soviet Union's first criminal code (1922) partially followed tsarist-era law and European tradition, although it added a "socialist" component, particularly in the case of economic crimes such as "speculation," that is, buying and selling to make a profit.[47] Sentencing practices also showed "class favouritism" towards the proletariat, reversing the discrimination of the tsarist-era estate system but effectively "ascribing class" in much the same way.[48] Again, however, leniency of punishment characterized the Bolshevik approach. As Peter H. Solomon Jr. writes, "For most offenses the range of sentencing options revealed a leniency that was new to Russian law. In place of the short prison terms that tsarist law used for lesser crimes, the Bolsheviks used noncustodial sanctions. Even for serious crimes, the terms of imprisonment rarely exceeded a few years."[49]

Early camps were run either by the Cheka[50] or the People's Commissariat of Justice (NKIu), while many of the Justice Commissariat's prison institutions were transferred to the republican-level NKVD in 1922. The republican-level NKVD did not emphasize re-education to the same degree as the Justice Commissariat.[51] The NKVD instead gained favour by promising to make its camps self-sufficient. These ideas – re-education and self-sufficiency – were not necessarily incompatible, and both became stated goals of the Gulag itself, formed under the OGPU[52] (Unified State Political Administration) in April 1930 as the administration responsible for both ordinary and special camps, and transferred to the All-Union NKVD in 1934.[53] Until 1930, however, the criminal justice system had revealed scant evidence that the Soviet system would produce such huge numbers of convicts and exiles.

Official documentation on imprisonment emphasized both isolation and rehabilitation. Declarations on the use of prisoners' labour date back as far as 1919 and 1921, but the first attempt at the codification of "corrective labour" was the Russian Soviet Federative Socialist Republic's (RSFSR) Corrective-Labour Code of 1924.[54] In comparison with later regulations, this early code shows much more concern for the individual welfare and rehabilitation of prisoners. Article 3 makes this explicit, stating that the "Corrective-Labour establishments are set up: a) for the acclimatization [*prisposobleniia*] of the criminal to the conditions of communal life [*obshchezhitiia*] through the path and influence of corrective-labour, connected with deprivation of freedom, and b) for the prevention of the possibility of committing further crimes."[55] Thus the stated goals of punishment in the Soviet Union at this time differed little from the modernizing state elsewhere: to provide for the rehabilitation of the individual prisoner while isolating him or her from society. And it is certainly conceivable that the Gulag could have remained, like the penal systems of other modernizing states, relatively small.

The 1929 expedition to Siberia, for example, had called for investment in infrastructure in order to attract settlers. Certainly massive infrastructure investment in places such as Magnitogorsk, during the First Five-Year Plan, attracted large numbers of non-prisoners, while relying only minimally on prisoner labour.[56] The Soviet government also actively encouraged voluntary settlement to Siberia even in the 1930s. The All-Union Resettlement Committee (*Vsesoiuznyi Pereselencheskii Komitet*) promoted resettlement in Siberia with advertisements in newspapers offering various incentives, and met with some success. In the first half of 1935 – well after the regime was already using forced labour in many remote areas – there were 1,700 requests for resettlement submitted to the committee, representing around 12,000 households, although it is not clear how many households actually resettled in Western Siberia.[57] Twelve thousand households is not insignificant, showing that the gradual approach, like the one advocated by the 1929 expedition, and practised by the All-Union Resettlement Committee, might have worked. During the 1920s and 1930s, the region's population growth was slightly higher than the Soviet average.[58] Even by the late 1920s, however, authorities realized that voluntary schemes had failed to settle many areas. Gradual, voluntary resettlement, moreover, was anathema to the forced, violent transformation of society called for by Stalin's regime.[59]

Investment in mechanization was another possible alternative to forced labour. Forestry – particularly timber – would eventually become one of the Gulag's most significant industries, and Gulag prisoners frequently felled trees with only the most primitive of tools. By the end of the 1930s, the Gulag had mechanized 67 per cent of timber production, but the rate was 90 per cent for non-Gulag timber production, although these official figures mask key problems in both cases, including the frequent breakdown of mechanical equipment.[60] The Soviet Union's vast forests were crucial for the five-year plans, as they supplied much of the fuel needed for industrial development and the timber needed for construction. The Politburo met in February 1931 – when the Gulag was growing rapidly – to discuss the expansion of the forestry industry and focused on mechanization rather than prisoner labour.[61]

By the early 1930s, it was clear that the regime had available huge numbers of convicts and peasant exiles who could be forced to work for the needs of the industrializing, modernizing state. But it is certainly worth noting that the rapid influx of prisoners into the system took both local and central authorities by surprise. As Anne Applebaum writes, "If the arrests [during the First Five-Year Plan] were intended to populate the camps, then they did so with almost ludicrous inefficiency," catching even camp authorities off guard.[62] The OGPU initially had considerable difficulty finding work for all of its inmates.[63] Before the upheavals caused by collectivization and dekulakization, authorities had envisaged a relatively small system. The Gulag was originally intended to hold no more than 50,000 prisoners, and, according to Oleg Khlevniuk, were it not for the "powerful wave of terror" associated with dekulakization, this might have been an achievable goal.[64]

The OGPU had also considered forced *colonization* for prisoners, much like the solution for the dekulakized peasants, as opposed to internment in prison camps. In some areas, prison *camps* ended up playing a colonizing role, especially in remote regions such as Vorkuta, Norilsk, and Kolyma, where whole cities eventually formed as a result of the Gulag's growth.[65] Underscoring early ambivalence about the use of concentration camps, however, Genrikh Iagoda, then deputy head of the OGPU, in 1930 called for a transformation of the camps into "colonization settlements" where prisoners would live more freely and work "more voluntarily" as a stimulus to improve both their character (re-education through labour) and the economy, mostly through forestry work.[66]

These potential settlement colonies, of approximately 1,500 prisoners each, were in some ways similar to what the special settlements turned out to be. The most infamous attempt along these lines was "Cannibal Island" located in Nazino, Western Siberia. In a particularly tragic episode, in 1933 a group of 10,000 prisoner-settlers from Moscow and Leningrad were forcibly resettled to an island where the Nazina River flows into the mighty Ob', some 800 kilometres north of Tomsk, while thousands more languished in an overcrowded transit camp in Tomsk.[67] As Nicholas Werth describes, authorities really did not know what to do with this contingent, and the main Communist Party official in the region, Robert Eikhe,[68] fought against sending this group to the region's remote areas. Bureaucratic negligence and the general hardships of the devastating famine sweeping the country combined to hold up the delivery of foodstuffs. When a huge shipment of flour finally arrived, many on the island ate it raw. Some eventually resorted to cannibalism. After only two months, half of the prisoner-settlers had starved to death.[69] This incident helped convince central authorities that prison camps, as opposed to settlement colonies, were necessary.

To summarize, then, although the Bolsheviks had established concentration camps early in their rule, these camps were initially small, the Soviet criminal justice was initially quite lenient, and the rapid influx of prisoners during the First Five-Year Plan caught most officials by surprise. Even as the Gulag began to expand rapidly, moreover, highly placed officials sought alternatives to prison camps.

The Special Settlements

While the Nazino disaster helped to convince authorities that settlement colonies for prisoners would not work, the Gulag nevertheless continued to rely on exile colonies in the form of "special settlements" for peasants. Often these settlements were little more than designated spots in swampy woodlands, where the peasants were forced to build a new life from scratch. Administratively, the Gulag was directly in charge of the settlements from 1931 until 1944, at which point special settlement administration became its own department within the NKVD.[70] The Siblag administration had its own Department of Special Settlements.[71]

The link between the settlements and the camps remains underexplored in the historiography, but for Western Siberia an awareness of the two together adds to our understanding of the geography of Stalinist repression. Siblag's camps, colonies, and stations themselves were mostly located close to the railway or in Western Siberia's major urban centres (see the map in figure 0.1), and often even within city limits. These areas were growing rapidly at this time, of course, and, as elsewhere, had work-force issues, but the geography of the camps on their own suggests that in Western Siberia, the extraction of resources from difficult-to-reach areas or the extreme isolation of prisoners were not the main motivating factors for camp location. The Western Siberian *camps* were hardly isolated from the surrounding towns and interacted with them regularly.

Even though the region's southern areas also relied partially on special settlements, the majority of these settlements were located in remote areas such as Narym, scattered along the region's northern river routes.[72] Narym was a region consisting of almost 350,000 square kilometres of swampy, forest-covered lowlands.[73] The Stalin-era settlements focused on agricultural work, fishing, and forestry, and it was in places like Narym where attracting a non-prisoner labour force would have required enormous effort and resources. It is quite possible that authorities saw little need to establish a forestry *camp* in the area,[74] as the special settlements were already providing a huge forced labour force to produce timber and transport logs.

Financially, central authorities treated the camps and settlements almost identically, at least in their early years. A 1931 Politburo resolution on the kulaks called for a supply fund for the settlements that would be distributed "analogously" to that of the Gulag camps.[75] In Western Siberia, Siblag was deeply involved in settlement administrative matters, concerning itself with everything from the agricultural expansion of the settlements to the taxation of settlers in Narym.[76]

The special settlements, moreover, share two key characteristics of the "concentration camp" that, interestingly, the Gulag's camps do not share. First, the inhabitants of the settlements were not charged with or convicted of any particular crime. And second, the settlements targeted *groups* of people (first the kulaks, then various national minority groups) rather than *individuals*. Yet the settlements were not concentration camps in the sense of enclosed spaces with well-ordered barracks, barbed wire, and watchtowers. Thus, these settlements are difficult to categorize. The regime restricted the settlers' movement, but the settlers themselves were asked to recreate the collective farm, with the purpose of exploiting the region's economic resources. The settlers were technically not prisoners, nor did they have the rights of regular non-prisoners.[77]

As far as Western Siberia is concerned, special settlers comprised the largest pool of forced labourers in the region. By 1 January 1933, Western Siberia's population of special settlers had reached 227,684, and that number rose to 289,431 the following year. This number would decrease to around 200,000 by the end of the decade, as the regime restored the rights of many settlers.[78] Even given that many of these settlers were children, there would have been more workers in the settlements than in the area's camps.[79] By 1938, Novosibirsk Province contained the largest number of special settlements (517) in the entire Soviet Union, over twice as many as the next highest, Sverdlovsk Province in the Ural Mountains.[80]

Although special settlers supposedly had more freedom than prisoners, conditions in the settlements may have at first actually been worse. The camps at least generally provided some sort of infrastructure, however primitive and inefficient. Special settlers often had to fend entirely for themselves, and it would be years before homes dug out of the earth were no longer the norm. In the early 1930s, proper medical facilities were sorely lacking, and local enterprises often treated the settlers as prisoner labour, falling far behind on wage payments.[81] Many settlers fell victim to starvation or severe illnesses due to hunger and a lack of proper shelter. Suicides were also quite common.[82] The influx of special settlers certainly placed local authorities in an almost impossible situation, even if they had shown much care for the special settlers' living conditions. As I.I. Dolgikh, director of Special Settlements, noted in 1933:

> In [the prior] 25 years of the railway's existence in Siberia 1,000,000 persons were delivered [*bylo zavezeno*] from Cheliabinsk to the nearby Gulf of Saint Olga in Siberia[.] By us in just 3 years, [and] only to one Narym region, were sent more than 200 thousand persons. You see the enormous scope [of the operation] and what enormous work has occurred and all of this has been done without the presence of cadres specially trained for this work.[83]

Special settlers technically had more living space than prisoners. According to official regulations, each settler had at least three square metres of living space (compared to an official regulation of two square metres in the camps, which was in practice usually lower), but in reality often had less.[84] A joint NKVD-Gulag report from 1935 complained that in some areas of Western Siberia, where settlers worked for the People's Commissariat of Forestry, they had an average of around only 0.8 square metres of living space per person, and the Commissariat of Forestry had no plans to build more housing.[85] For Narym as a whole, however, the average at the time was 4.2 square metres per person.[86] Within the Soviet Union more generally, moreover, the rapid urbanization caused by the five-year plans and the upheavals of collectivization/dekulakization meant that living space was an issue almost everywhere, not only in places of forced labour. In 1931 in the new industrial city of Magnitogorsk, for example, there were only 1.9 square metres per non-prisoner (less than the regulated amount for a prisoner), and during the entire decade of the 1930s there was never more than an average of four square metres of living space per non-prisoner in the city, less than the average for special settlers in Narym.[87]

Statistics in 1931 for Narym attest to incredibly harsh conditions. From 1 June to 1 September there were 10,534 deaths among the special settlers, and another 4,961 escaped. The 1 June settler population was 50,687, growing to 215,261 by 1 September. From 1 October 1931 to 1 January 1932, another 7,499 died and 11,473 escaped. Escapes remained at around 3,000 settlers per month until April 1932, with numbers recaptured numbering only in the hundreds.[88] During 1933, the main famine year, official statistics for the Western Siberian special settlements count 26,709 settler deaths and 49,718 escapes; only 12,647 returned from escape attempts.[89]

Conditions improved over the course of the decade. In 1936, the Narym Party Secretary, P.P. Levits, noted that most schools and orphanages were now well supplied with educational materials, and that medical services had reached a satisfactory state. However, he also complained of continued housing problems, with many settlers living in rundown barracks or earthen dugouts (v zemliankakh).[90] Birth rates now exceeded death rates, and the number of settlers with illness was on the decline. By mid-decade there were also many more hospitals and bathhouses, as well as 215 elementary and twenty-one middle schools. At least according to official reports, the average special settler household in Narym now actually worked more land than that of the "native population" (korennogo naseleniia) – 4.2 hectares compared with 2.6 hectares.[91] According to historian Sergei Krasil'nikov, the special settlements at times showed statistically better results than the nearby collective farms in terms of the size of the harvest (although not in all areas). He notes, however, that capital expenditures were much higher in the special settlements.[92]

By mid-decade, too, significant numbers of settlers had already had their rights reinstated, although this usually did not mean that they could legally leave the region. Iagoda himself argued that allowing settlers to leave would "hinder measures to open up uninhabited areas," thus emphasizing the colonizing function of the settlements. Matvei Berman,[93] head of the Gulag at the time, also argued that settlers should not be allowed to leave once rehabilitated.[94] In response, the Central Executive Committee (TsIK) amended its decree (*postanovlenie*) from May of 1934 on the restoration of rights to say, "The restoration of citizenship rights for exiled kulaks does not give them the right to leave [their] place of settlement."[95] In 1935 and 1936 alone, some 53,579 special settlers were rehabilitated in Western Siberia, a much larger number than elsewhere at the time.[96] Children of special settlers could receive certain rights upon reaching the age of majority. This occurred only if they had not run afoul of the law, had cut themselves off from their parents, and were engaged in "socially useful" labour.[97]

Narym was the main area for Western Siberian special settlements, but the Kuzbass also had large numbers of settlements and settlers, mostly engaged in developing the crucially important coalmines of the region. Like Narym, much of the Kuzbass was far removed from the Trans-Siberian Railway, and branch lines had to be completed, such as the Gornoshorskaia Line, built by prisoner labour in the late-1930s. As of August 1931, Kuznetskstroi used 22,077 special settlers as contract labourers, and Vostokugol, a forestry and mining enterprise, contracted out the labour of over 25,000 special settlers in four different Kuzbass towns. In 1933, some 41,512 special settlers were sent to Kuzbassugol', the mining combine, initially to help with mine construction and the construction of workers' barracks.[98] Forced labour, broadly speaking, was thus a major component of Western Siberian development, a development that was key for Stalinist industrialization and particularly important for the Soviet Union's future total war capabilities, as the Kuzbass was deep within Soviet territory.

Siblag, 1929–1941

Siblag proved to be one of the longest-lasting systems in the Soviet Union (1929–1960), but economically Siblag was neither a resounding success nor a dismal failure. Through the 1930s, as central authorities shifted the focus of Gulag labour to important infrastructure and resource-extraction projects, Siblag declined in relative importance to the camps of Kolyma (gold), Vorkuta (coal), Norilsk (nickel), the Far East (railroads), and those involved in infrastructure projects such as the Moscow-Volga Canal. Although Siblag prisoners worked in a variety of sectors of the Western Siberian economy, the very lack of economic focus probably hurt Siblag's chances of becoming a priority camp. Siblag is an important camp for inquiry precisely because there was little extraordinary about it.

Siblag was rarely involved in priority projects, but the camp system nevertheless engaged in a large variety of regional economic activities – most notably agriculture, forestry, construction, and mining – and in this sense replicated the Gulag as a whole. Siblag was one of the larger Gulag camp systems, reaching a peak pre-war prisoner population of 78,838 prisoners, almost 8 per cent of the entire Gulag population at that time (1 January 1938). Like many camp systems, Siblag suffered from high turnover at top administrative levels. From its founding in the fall of 1929 to the German invasion in June 1941, there were at least seven changes in the directorship of Siblag (including at least seven different directors).[99]

Changing political divisions within the region, as Moscow regularly carved the region into smaller political units, affected Siblag. On 30 July 1930, the Central Executive Committee divided the Siberian Territory into the West Siberian Territory and the East Siberian Territory. In late 1934, the West Siberian Territory lost several regions to the newly created Omsk Province and Krasnoiarsk Territory. Then, in September 1937, the Central Executive Committee again divided the remaining territory into two administrative units: Novosibirsk Province, centred in Novosibirsk and consisting mostly of present-day Novosibirsk, Tomsk, and Kemerovo Provinces, and the Altai Territory, with its capital in Barnaul.

In August 1935, the NKVD created the Administration of Camps, Labour Settlements,[100] and Places of Confinement of the NKVD Administration of the West-Siberian Territory, located in Novosibirsk.[101] In 1937, with the creation of Novosibirsk Province, the administration's Corrective-Labour Colonies became part the Department of Corrective-Labour Colonies for Novosibirsk Province (OITK NSO). Two years later, an NKVD operational order signed by Lavrentii Beria – the new NKVD director – created the Administration for Corrective-Labour Camps and Colonies of the NKVD Administration for Novosibirsk Province (with the rather awkward acronym, UITLiK UNKVD po NSO).[102] Often official documents name the camp system "UITLiK UNKVD po NSO (Siblag)."[103] The official name reveals a cumbersome jurisdictional nightmare, whereby Siblag received its operational orders officially from central Gulag authorities, central NKVD officials, and the provincial NKVD administration. In practice, directives came even from provincial and city Communist Party and governmental officials.[104]

Shortly after the 1935 order creating the West-Siberian Camp Administration, the NKVD ordered Siblag's Krasnoiarsk area camps (now located in Krasnoiarsk Territory, in Eastern Siberia) removed from Siblag's jurisdiction.[105] It was now exclusively a West Siberian camp. Siblag also shed subcamps to create an entirely new camp, Gornoshorlag, which lasted from 1938 to 1941. It was founded out of the Akhpunsk subcamp, where prisoners had already been working on the Gornaia-Shorskaia Railway, a task they would continue under Gornoshorlag's administration.[106] Tomasinlag, a camp founded near Tomsk in 1937, also partially merged with Siblag in late 1940, when much of the camp became a receiving centre for "refugees" (*bezhentsy*) from western borderlands, and its largest camp, Asinovo, joined Siblag shortly thereafter. [107]

By June 1941, Siblag administered twenty-seven camps, separate camp stations (OLP), and corrective-labour colonies. Many of these were also divided into several camp stations, so that geographically Siblag was dispersed throughout much of the southern part of Novosibirsk Province (see the map in figure 0.1). Some of these Siblag camps are noteworthy in their own right. For example, prisoners at the Krivoshchekovsk camp helped to develop much of Novosibirsk's left bank. The transit stations in Mariinsk and Novosibirsk at various times held thousands of prisoners headed for camps all over the Soviet Union. The Antibes camp was economically a success and even participated in the 1940 All-Union Agricultural Exhibition, a point that on its own challenges assumptions about the isolation of the Gulag from Soviet society.[108] The Iask camp included one of the Gulag's largest factories, a textile/garment factory. The Siblag economy was incredibly diverse. In all, in May 1941, 23,441 prisoners resided in Siblag contract camps and colonies, in which other enterprises paid Siblag directly for the prisoners' labour; 21,793 prisoners lived and worked in agricultural camps and colonies; 11,182 prisoners were in Siblag-run factories; and 4,412 were in transit camps, invalid camps, or colonies for young offenders. Many of the urban contract-labour camps were, technically, corrective-labour colonies.[109]

As the 1930s progressed, authorities began to emphasize Siblag's role in agriculture. A 1933 report from Iagoda to Stalin on the economic activities of the camps lists three main sectors for Siblag: the supplementation of the workforce of Kuzbass Coal (*Kuzbassugol'*), the major coal-mining enterprise of the Kuznetsk Basin; contracted forestry work; and large-scale, internally run agricultural work.[110] Siblag agricultural activities were meant to help feed the camp system as a whole. In a classic case of Soviet bureaucratic doublespeak, authorities reduced the potato and vegetable supplies to the Gulag in 1933 (the main year of the famine), claiming that the Gulag was reaching a state of self-sufficiency. Official Gulag mortality rates for 1933 were the highest recorded in peacetime (15.3 per cent), illustrating the absurdity of the claims.[111]

Siblag did not become a top-priority camp. In an October 1932 Politburo discussion on the construction of the Far Eastern Baikal-Amur Railroad (BAM), V.M. Molotov[112] and Iagoda listed six core OGPU projects, and none of Siblag's activities made the list: "1) completion work at Belmorstroi, 2) the construction of the Volga-Moscow canal, 3) the construction of the Baikalo-Amur Railroad, 4) Kolyma, 5) work at Ukhta and Pechora, [and] 6) preparation of firewood for Leningrad and Moscow in existing programs."[113]

Priority camps often received healthy contingents, while prisoners in weak physical shape – likely due to long periods of internment elsewhere – were sent to camps such as Siblag.[114] Gulag officials, too, appear to have viewed agricultural camps as prophylactic, which is perhaps another reason why Siblag regularly received contingents in poor health.[115] Siblag was centrally located for the Soviet Union as a whole, and huge numbers of prisoners passed through the Mariinsk or Novosibirsk transit stations. Indeed, memoirs devoted primarily to Siblag are relatively difficult to find, although many former prisoners mention passing through Mariinsk or Novosibirsk on their way to other, more remote camps.[116] Many unfit prisoners and invalids remained in Siblag, rather than continuing along arduous transit routes further east. Notably, the practice of unhealthy prisoners remaining in Western Siberia while healthy contingents moved on to priority areas had also been common during Tsarist exile and *katorga*.[117]

By the middle of the decade, central reports relating to Siblag took on a negative tone. In a September 1935 NKVD operational order, numerous deficiencies were noted: the Mariinsk camp was in an unsatisfactory state, with unsanitary living conditions, poor food, and unclean barracks; many of the camp's Third Department workers drank frequently, a particularly unsettling occurrence given that the Third Department's key role was investigating internal camp security issues. Indeed, by this time, several members of the Third Department had been arrested, censured, or lost their jobs. High-level Militarized Guard (VOKhR) and Cultural-Educational Department (KVO) officials faced similar fates. This was hardly a well-disciplined group.[118] The arrest of Gulag officials and guards, moreover, underscores one of the difficulties in separating the perpetrators from the victims in the Soviet system. In the aftermath of the Great Terror, for example, four of the five highest-ranking Gulag officials were shot.[119]

Some of Siblag's economic problems in the mid-1930s may also have come directly from the outside, via contract work. The use of prisoners as contract workers in non-Gulag enterprises remains an understudied aspect of Gulag historiography.[120] Forestry enterprises made extensive use of special settler labour under contract from the Gulag.[121] But the Gulag also contracted out significant numbers of prisoners from within its camps, which is noteworthy in part because the Soviet Union was hardly alone in using prisoners as contract labourers in key industries.[122] In January 1935, 12,000 Siblag prisoners, or 20.5 per cent of the camp's 58,609 total prisoners, worked as contract labourers, particularly in forestry and construction.[123] The number of contract labourers rose to over one-third of Siblag's total by the eve of the war. This meant that prisoners at times worked alongside non-prisoners, even though authorities attempted to limit contact.[124] At the July 1940 Central Committee Plenum, Stalin himself criticized the tendency for non-prisoners and prisoners to work together, stating, "It's acceptable to use the GULAG in some remote corners, but in the machine industry, in the cities, where criminals work side by side with noncriminals, I really don't know. I'd say it's very irrational and not quite appropriate."[125] Despite Stalin's worries, contract labour appeared to solve multiple problems: on the side of the enterprises, it mitigated the effects of high labour turnover, labour shortages, and cost constraints; on the part of the Gulag, it allowed for increased financial stability and shared responsibility for prisoner welfare. However, contract operations did not always run smoothly.

For Siblag itself, contract labour was not always profitable. The NKVD's financial department complained in 1935 that a "noticeable portion of the contractors are insolvent [*malokreditosposobnymi*], [therefore] receiving money from them for the work force will be delayed for a long period, which will bring financial strain to the camp system."[126] Nevertheless, the area's camps continued to contract out their prisoners to a significant extent.

If contract labour posed specific problems for Siblag, perhaps the camp's internally run agricultural subcamps, sometimes even referred to as state farms, were more successful. By the mid-1930s, agriculture at Siblag was growing considerably. Siblag supplied meat products and grain to the whole Gulag system, making it an important distribution centre.[127] Siblag was particularly important for pork production. While ultimately the level of distribution to other camps is difficult to discern, agriculture also fit nicely into a colonization narrative. A sketch in Siblag's newspaper, *Sibirskaia perekovka*, from January 1935, illustrates this colonization narrative, tying in Gulag labour with the development of the country (see figure 1.1). Note the quaint, almost idyllic depiction of this Gulag farm. The caption reads, "The second pig-farm of Arliuk. Six months prior there was only the empty steppe."[128]

Prisoner labour was hardly reliable. A 1938 report estimated that 20 per cent (179,000 prisoners) of the Gulag workforce was idle due to illnesses, invalid status, pending investigations, work refusal, and even lack of work.[129] The report identified Siblag as one of the worst offenders. Due to what the report termed a surplus of prisoners, 50 per cent of idle days (*prostoev*) for the Gulag as a whole came from just three camps: Siblag, Karlag, and Sazlag. All three camps were agricultural camps.[130]

Siblag's key position as a supplier of foodstuffs to the rest of the Gulag logically should have led to greater emphasis on the health of its prisoner contingent. However, Siblag continued to receive prisoners in comparatively poor health. In 1937, for example, the NKVD administration for Sverdlovsk Province in the Urals was ordered to send 2,500 healthy prisoners to BAMLag in the Far East. On their way, in Novosibirsk, authorities transferred 570 of these prisoners to Siblag because they were unfit for work.[131] One Siblag prisoner, Ananii Semenovich Gebel' remembered a similar occurrence. He was sent to Siberia in early summer 1939, and authorities initially placed him with a transfer contingent to Norilsk, a high-priority camp in the north. The medical commission, however, held him back, along with over 300 other prisoners, because he and the others were too ill to work. According to Gebel', those who had spent time in the Mariinsk transit station were in especially poor shape.[132] The Mariinsk transit station may have acted almost literally (and cruelly) as a filtration camp: intense overcrowding exacerbated health issues among prisoners in transit, and generally the healthy ones were sent to the Gulag's furthest reaches, while unhealthy contingents found themselves distributed among Siblag's many camps and colonies.[133] This type of filtration may have been part of a deliberate attempt to conceal the Gulag's harsh conditions, as it meant priority-camp contingents were comparatively better off than those of non-priority camps and colonies.[134] On the other hand, the filtration could instead have been a response to inefficiencies in the system, rather than a proactive measure.

In any case, the problem of overcrowding and poor health became more acute after Beria took over from Ezhov[135] as head of the NKVD in 1938. Beria emphasized forestry, construction, and industrial camps; as a consequence, many unfit prisoners were filtered into those camps designated for agriculture, as these were less of a priority.[136] The lack of emphasis on healthy prisoner contingents for Siblag contributed to the

Вторая свинсферма Арлюка.Здесь шесть месяцев назад была голая степь.

1.1: Siblag Farm. *Sibirskaia perekovka*, 27 January 1945, page 3. Fiche 485 of *The Gulag Press* (The Netherlands: IDC Publishers and GARF, 2000). Used with permission of the State Archive of the Russian Federation (original image located in the Nauchnaia biblioteka, Gosudarstvennyi arkhiv Rossiskoi federatsii).

overall poor living conditions of the camp, where epidemics were common, barracks were generally filthy and overcrowded, and mortality rates very high.

Living conditions in pre-war Siblag, as one might imagine, were generally terrible. However, individual experiences could vary considerably depending on the time, place, and type of incarceration within the Siblag system, not to mention one's own place within elaborate prisoner hierarchies. Dallin and Nicolaevsky's well-known early study of the Gulag even concluded, based on memoirs available at the time, that Siblag was one of the harshest camps in the entire system.[137] Many ex-prisoners certainly support this contention.

O. Feldheim, who spent time in the mid-1930s in Siblag's Osinovsk camp, recalled that when he arrived at the camp, the "old residents [*starozhily*] of the barracks met us optimistically: they told us that no one makes it more than three months and, if [you] don't die, [you'll] be sent on 'rest,'" a euphemism, according to Feldheim, for agricultural work.[138] Indeed, many prisoners were shocked by their first experience of the barracks. Iosif Berger, who also spent time in Siblag in the mid-1930s, described the barracks at a camp station in the majestic foothills of the Altai Mountains as "dilapidated." On the inside, however, it was the condition of the prisoners that shocked him: "The room was fully stocked with sweaty, half-naked, emaciated 'zeks.' Their faces seemed brutalized to us. We recoiled in fear."[139]

Most Siblag camps and colonies were poorly prepared for the influx of prisoners that accompanied the First Five-Year Plan. One non-prisoner wrote directly to Viacheslav Molotov in 1932 after having visited the corrective-labour colony at Iaia, which at that time housed mostly prisoners in poor physical shape who had been sent from other camps.[140] He noted, "There are those who are completely blind, with eyes burnt by mine drilling cartridges, as well as those who are para-lyzed, disfigured, and completely mutilated, without hands or legs, and those dying of consumption." He then argued that the prisoners had "more than once paid for their crimes, [had] lost strength and health, eyesight and sanity," and that "many of them suffer[ed] almost without guilt, slandered by their co-workers and enemy neighbors." Camp conditions could create almost unimaginable suffering.[141]

The influx of prisoners caused problems with overcrowding. In Tomsk, for example, a camp meant to hold not more than 1,000 prison-ers instead counted 3,100 as of September 1931. Tomsk Procurator Smirnov noted that most prisoners were poorly clothed, filthy, and had suffered considerably due to lengthy travel. A typhus epidemic hit the camp in August.[142] Death rates were very high, although difficult to calculate. In 1932, 900 prisoners in the Tomsk corrective-labour estab-lishments had already died by October, and 276 died in June alone. By this point another 453 had escaped.[143] High prisoner turnover makes rates of both escape and mortality almost impossible to calculate, but the average of approximately 100 prisoner deaths per month in this relatively small camp is certainly striking, and certainly well above the Gulag's overall mortality rate for 1932 of 4.81 per cent. By this time, the famine of 1932–3 was already making itself felt. Even in Western Siberia outside of the camps, there was a massive increase in the mortality rate, although precise statistics are unavailable.[144]

Prisoners attempted to supplement their meagre rations with food packages or money (that could be spent at the camp commissary) sent from relatives. An Orthodox archpriest, Sergei Alekseevich Sidorov, who briefly spent time in a Siblag state farm in Mariinsk in 1932, wrote many letters to family members during his incarceration. Although most of his letters are upbeat, frequently describing the beautiful Siberian countryside – no doubt he wished to both allay any concerns his family may have had and also pass the letters by the censor – the lack of proper food in the camp was a major concern. As he wrote in a letter dated 4 March, "I feel well, but the wounds on my legs (swelling of the feet) are bothering me. They say I need fats. Thus I again risk ask-ing you about [sending] a parcel. Forgive my harassment. How are the children? How is Tania? Kisses to you all. Sergei Sidorov." His next letter, from 23 April, also ends by asking for a food parcel: "I am waiting for a parcel with impatience. If possible, send biscuit cakes."[145] Parcels could play an extremely important part in life in the camps, and not only because they carried food and money. The psychological connection to one's family members was just as important.[146] As one Siblag prisoner, sentenced under Article 58, recalled, "Yes, money, sent from relatives, played an enormous role not only because it offered the possibility of improving one's rations, but most of all as moral support: the realization that [one's relatives] had not forgotten you. Loneliness is nowhere else so terrifying, as in a prison or a camp."[147]

The physical space of the camps could vary considerably. In some camps and colonies barracks were earthen dugouts, spaced haphazardly. The harsher camps and stations of Siblag, however, resembled well-ordered concentration camps. Nikolai Nikolaevich Boldyrev, an engineer, describes the ninth penalty station of Siblag's Akhpunsk camp in the mid-1930s as complete with barbed wire, watchtowers, and crowded barracks where prisoners slept in their clothes to prevent theft. Guards led prisoners to work under the threat of death if prisoners broke rank. Insufficient rations led to a slogan common at Akhpunsk: "You die today, and I, tomorrow."[148] Because of its status as a penalty station (i.e., meant for those with particularly harsh sentences and those who had committed crimes while in the camps), Akhpunsk cannot be considered representative of Siblag as a whole. Even in this harshest of camp stations, moreover, the barracks were not permanent buildings, but large tents (*palatki*) with wood-burning stoves for heat, hardly fitting the image of machine-like efficiency.

Another prisoner, A.S. Gebel', who spent time in Siblag's second Suslovsk camp station on the eve of the war, also remembers the horrible living conditions. The bathhouse, for example, was more than one kilometre from his camp station and had room for only seven to ten people, while authorities usually brought twenty-five to thirty at any one time. For him, the worst aspect of camp life was the dehumanization, as camp personnel "valued [prisoners] lower and cheaper than livestock, fed [them] worse than livestock, and related to [them] as if [they were] slaves." The prisoners worked ten-to-twelve-hour days, slept on hard bunks with no blankets, and did not receive proper food. Gebel' was later transferred to the first Suslovsk station, where the work (in both cases, fieldwork) was not as difficult and the conditions generally better, but extremely cold temperatures meant that what little food the prisoners received was often frozen.[149] In theory, prisoners were not supposed to work in extreme cold, although it is not clear how this worked at Siblag's agricultural camps. Elsewhere, many memoirists report working even in temperatures lower than –40 degrees Celsius.[150]

Many Gulag camps were surprisingly active in the cultural sphere, with newspapers, theatre troupes, orchestras, film screenings, and so on, and these activities could help mitigate harsh conditions for some prisoners.[151] Sporting events within the camps were also common, and Siblag's Cultural-Educational Department had its own soccer and volleyball teams, which regularly played against teams representing individual camps or camp stations.[152] Although many re-education campaigns banned Article 58ers and those sentenced for particularly harsh crimes from participation, some prisoners recall an active pre-war cultural sphere in Siblag.

One of Siblag's better-known pre-war prisoners was Nataliia Il'inichna Sats, who before her arrest and sentencing under Article 58 had been a theatre director at the Moscow Children's Theatre and had even travelled abroad to Berlin and Buenos Aires as part of her theatrical work. She spent two years in Siblag from 1937 to 1939. While recovering from typhus, she was assigned light work in the records office at the Mariinsk camp. One day, while passing by the camp's cultural club, she heard the choir practising and asked if she could accompany the choir on piano. The choir director allowed her to do so, since playing the piano was "technical, not ideological" work. She was popular with prisoners because she frequently received parcels, and popular with camp personnel (except, evidently, the camp boss) due to her work with the choir. Eventually, the camp administration allowed Sats to put on a play. The play – Aleksandr Ostrovskii's *The Dowerless Girl* (1879) – was so successful that Sats's "troupe" went on tour, so to speak, performing at several different Siblag camp stations. The camp's Third Section, in charge of internal security, provided set decorations and costumes. For Sats, this was a taste of freedom: "It was a joy to switch into the world of Ostrovskii, to bear his words, to live in his brilliant play, forgetting about the barbed wire ... This was the one piece of heaven in my life."[153]

Western Siberia's Other Pre-war Camps

While Siblag was the main regional camp system in pre-war Western Siberia, a few words on the other camps are in order. The Tomsk Camp for Family Members of Traitors to the Motherland, a Siblag camp in existence from December 1937 to October 1939, is a curious chapter in

Siblag's history.[154] This camp is most famous for briefly housing Anna Larina, the wife of Nikolai Bukharin (Larina also spent time in the penalty isolator at Antibes and at other Siblag camps).[155] Larina was in the Tomsk camp from December 1937 to March 1938, while her husband was on trial.[156] Although the camp was ostensibly for family members of "traitors to the Motherland," while Larina was there it housed only women, except for the two-year-old son of one of the prisoners.

Larina remembers her time at this camp with a trace of fondness, noting that she and the other prisoners were "relatively happy" because they were no longer in transit, and "no physical labor was required." She recalls using this time to chat and connect with other prisoners, all wives of intermediate and high-level party functionaries. Interestingly, another prisoner at the camp at the same time as Larina, Nina Alekseevna Noskovich, recalls, "There was no possibility of speaking with [Larina], as [the bosses] had surrounded her with informants, and anything said to her would be known by the bosses."[157] Larina states that the guards treated the prisoners horribly, placing them in the penalty isolator on the slightest provocation and frequently verbally abusing them, blaming them for the "crimes" of their husbands. She describes the early spring in 1938 in nostalgic terms, worth quoting in full for the juxtaposition of the beautiful natural surroundings with the harsh reality of the camp:

> That year, 1938, spring came unusually early; in all my twenty years[158] to come in Siberia, there would never be another like it. The birch branches not only bristled with little buds but here and there produced a tender lace of barely opened pale green leaves. How good these birches were, with crowds of gloomy women in threadbare clothing milling around them, some tossing off their dirty gray quilted jackets! How good they looked against the background of dilapidated low barracks and trampled-down earth, the compound it seemed you would never leave![159]

Other prisoners at the Tomsk camp also recall greeting each other with excitement. Kseniia Medvedskaia, whose husband had been deputy head of the Logging-Lumber Office of Leningrad Cooperative Supply, remembers her first night in the camp as one of "great joy," in part because she was no longer in transit and in part because she was able to chat and catch up with so many different people. Still, life was gruelling in the camp, and Medvedskaia even spent time in the penalty isolator. She was most appalled at the lack of basic human decency that the camp engendered. As she writes, "The regimen in prison corrupted people, and that was terrible. Denouncing each other was not only demanded but praised. If someone saw somebody else break the rules and did not report it, they would be punished along with the person who committed the infraction."[160] Following the dissolution of this camp, most inmates were transferred to other Gulag camps.

As the Gulag expanded due to the Great Terror, more camp systems came into existence. Beginning in the late 1930s, two more camp systems briefly existed in Western Siberia: Gornoshorlag in present-day Kemerovo Province, and Tomasinlag in present-day Tomsk Province. Both opened during the period now commonly known as the Great Terror, and both closed for different reasons in the months before the German invasion of the USSR. Gornoshorlag completed its assigned task in a timely fashion, while Tomasinlag abruptly ceased operations as a consequence of external factors: the influx of "refugees" (*bezhentsy*) to the area from the USSR's western borderlands, where both territories and loyalties fluctuated due to the Nazi-Soviet Pact; the outbreak of the Second World War; and the occupation of eastern Poland and the Baltics by the Red Army.[161] Although Gornoshorlag could in some respects be labelled a success (due to the completion of its main assigned task) and Tomasinlag a failure (as it was removed altogether from the Administration of Forestry Camps [ULLP, *Upravlenie lagerei lesnoi promyshlennosti*] when there was still much work to be done), both experienced similar problems with inefficiency, corruption, and escapes. Success for a Gulag camp was clearly a measure of result, not process.

Gornoshorlag, founded in 1938, was originally part of Siblag as Siblag's Ninth Akhpunsk camp, located in what is today the southern part of Kemerovo Province. In 1940, Gornoshorlag came under the administration of the newly formed Main Administration of Camps for Railroad Construction (GULZhDS) but was one of the smaller camps in that system and, for reasons that are unclear, had a proportionately much smaller budget than most of the other railroad camps.[162] In the mid-1930s, prisoners at the Akhpunsk camp had worked on the Gornaia-Shorskaia railway, a railway link for the mines of the crucially important Kuznetsk Basin, and this continued as the primary economic activity once Gornoshorlag became a separate camp.[163]

The basin supplied the coking coal for the massive steelworks in Magnitogorsk in the Urals as part of the Urals-Kuznetsk Metallurgical Combine.[164] The railway was a key project for Siblag and later Gornoshorlag. Upon completion of the railway in 1940, Gornoshorlag's director (I.D. Makarov)[165] issued a statement awarding prizes to many camp personnel (eighty-seven in all) and discussing the project's importance:

> The railroad, connecting the Stalin Kuznetsk Metallurgical Combine with the ore field in Tashtagol, is the key investment [*vklad*] for the purpose of strengthening the defence power [*moshchi*] of our Motherland [*rodiny*], moving forward on the path set forth at the historical XVIII congress of the VKP(b) [Bolsheviks]: to reach and surpass the main capitalist countries economically.[166]

In this case, local authorities clearly linked their projects to broader Soviet goals. The completed railway went on to play an important role during the Second World War, as the Donbass came under German control, and the Kuzbass became crucial to Soviet coal supply.

The Gulag founded Tomasinlag in 1937 as part of a group of new forestry camps that became the Administration of Forest Industry Camps (ULLP) in 1939.[167] The seven initial forestry camps – peaking at seventeen – that made up the Administration of Forest Industry Camps were hardly a resounding success. Oleg Khlevniuk argues that the hasty formation of these camps led to unusually high death rates, so much so that they became "provisional" death camps.[168]

Despite the vast forests of Western Siberia, originally only one camp in the region, Tomasinlag, was part of the Administration of Forest Industry Camps.[169] Given the geography of forced labour in Western Siberia, it is likely that authorities felt more forestry camps would be unnecessary, as special settlers continued to work heavily in the industry in the more remote areas. Centred in Asino, northeast of Tomsk, Tomasinlag initially took over operations from the Tomles Forestry Trust in the area of the Chulym River and its tributaries, one of the regions surveyed in the 1929 scientific expedition of the region.[170]

Waste within Tomasinlag was a major issue. A report from 1939 complained that 59,000 rubles had been wasted at Tomasinlag because "79% of the work to determine the wood-cutting area for planning timber-shipping by railroad proved to be unnecessary."[171] Tomasinlag authorities also complained that they had to conduct their work with fewer specialists than Tomles, the local forestry trust, and thus inadvertently acknowledged a fundamental problem of forced labour: a lack of sufficient training, particularly in specialized positions.[172] Authorities were forced to use prisoners in many key positions: as chief statistician, road foreman (*dorozhnyi desiatnik*), foreman for charcoal burning (*master po uglezhzheniiu*), assistant manager (*Zavkhoz*), planner (*Planovik*), and others.[173] Tomasinlag never functioned well and was closed down in 1940 in order to accommodate "refugees" from the western border-lands and most of its prisoners transferred to other camps, a topic dis-cussed in greater detail in chapter 3.

Conclusion: Ready for Total War?

Looking back at the 1929 Siberian expedition from 1941, there was still much to be done in terms of industrializing and "colonizing" the re-gion. Yes, many remote areas had received large numbers of settlers in the form of forcibly exiled kulaks; special settlers and prisoners had helped to develop key industries; and the non-prisoner population had increased at rates greater than those in much of the Soviet Union. It would take the massive upheavals of the Second World War, however, for the region to gain the influx of human resources and state invest-ment that would truly transform Western Siberia economically.

The ad hoc development of Siblag and Western Siberia's camps and special settlements over the course of the 1930s, combined with the pro-pensity for unhealthy prisoners to remain in the region, suggests that both central and local authorities had little idea how the regime's forced-labour system might perform in the case of war. Prisoners, like non-prisoners, could be allocated to key production projects, but poor conditions meant that economic performance could not be guaranteed. Siblag, as a non-priority, roughly ordinary camp, stumbled into the ex-traordinary conditions of total war and barely survived.

2 Total War, Total Mobilization

The Tomsk Munitions Factory of the NKVD (C[orrective] L[abour] C[olony] no. 5), producing fragmenting 82mm caliber shells, is fully capable of fulfilling its daily output as set by the plans of the State Defence Committee. However, the factory is experiencing systematic disruptions in its electricity supply.

From a February 1943 report of the Novosibirsk Province Camp and Colony Administration director to the secretary of the Novosibirsk Province Communist Party Committee[1]

In *The Gulag Archipelago*, Aleksandr Solzhenitsyn writes that prisoners found out about the German invasion of the Soviet Union on 22 June 1941 only through rumour.[2] While this may have been the case for the Gulag's more remote "islands," and rumour was certainly an important form of communication in the camps, much of the Gulag was fully integrated into the local, regional, and national planned economies, and prisoners were well aware of what was going on and of their role. One Tomsk prisoner, Mikhail Grigor'evich Gorbachev, recalled how the outbreak of war affected a small workshop in Tomsk:

Until this time there was a children's labour colony here. They sent them someplace, and surrounded the territory with a high fence with barbed wire on top with towers on the corners for guards, fully in order. The zone itself was divided into two parts: one part with barracks for living, and the second part [for] production with workshops. When the colonists lived here, they had a mus[ical instrument] factory, making guitars, balalaikas and mandolins.

But for us *zeks* came something entirely different … In these very workshops only in the place of the joiners' benches [they] added lathes, and,
well, we prepared all for the front, all for the war![3] What we produced
were called ready-made mortar shells [*gatovye* (sic) *miny*].[4] But really what
appeared were mortar shells prepared with our hands.[5]

Siblag was fully mobilized for the war effort, even at the expense of
remotely adequate supplies for the prisoners themselves. If the Gulag
had not been a place of mass death before the war, it certainly was
during the war. Official mortality rates reached a staggering 24 per cent
in 1942, with rates exceeding this figure in many Siblag camps and colonies. Indeed, the issue of death is where the wartime Gulag stands out
as significantly different from the peacetime Gulag, at least according
to official statistics. While there were always excess deaths in the Gulag,
those deaths reached incredible numbers during the war. If the Gulag
can be considered akin to a system of death camps – and historians
continue to debate this very issue – then the wartime Gulag, especially
at non-priority camps like Siblag, certainly comes closest. The deadliest
camps of the wartime Gulag were not the most remote camps, such as
those of Kolyma or Norilsk, but the camps – like Siblag – that were not
prioritized. Indeed, although Anne Applebaum partially dismisses the
hardships of corrective-labour colonies, which were generally located
in urban areas and held prisoners with comparatively light sentences,
many of these colonies had higher death rates than the camps, a point
confirmed by Golfo Alexopoulos' recent research.[6] Wartime Western
Siberia provides an important venue for exploring death in the Gulag,
as many of Siblag's camps, including those designated colonies, far exceeded the average death rates for the Gulag as a whole. Thus, Stalin's
Gulag during the Second World War shows the need to view the war
as a distinct period within the Gulag's history. In many respects, the
inefficiencies of the Gulag remained the same (although exacerbated
by wartime conditions), but the scale of the death toll and the goals of
mobilization changed.

Death, destruction, and rapidly deteriorating living conditions meant
that the wartime prisoners experienced total war almost in its most
complete form. Roger Chickering argues that total war is an "ideal
type" in the Weberian sense, with full totality impossible in reality. Yet
the Gulag during the Second World War approaches that totality in its
comprehensive support of the armed forces, even to the detriment of
the prisoners' health and lives. While cautioning against overuse of the

term "total war," Chickering defines the phrase, in a practical sense, as including "the increasing size of armies, the broadening scope of operations, the growing comprehensiveness of the effort to support armed forces, and the systematic, calculated incorporation of civilians into the category of participants."[7] The Second World War was arguably the harshest period of the Gulag's existence, and prisoners died in incredibly large numbers, at the same time as they manufactured artillery shells, built airfields, sewed Red Army uniforms, and produced foodstuffs for the front, to name just a few of the myriad war-related economic activities of Soviet forced labour. These activities clearly fall under Chickering's definition.

Administratively, there were several key changes to Siblag during the war. In 1942, the Gulag moved Siblag's central administration from Novosibirsk to Mariinsk and divided the camp system into two separate camps.[8] Siblag now included agricultural camps, while the Novosibirsk Province Camp and Colony Administration – technically under the jurisdiction of provincial authorities, rather than Moscow – remained headquartered in Novosibirsk as a separate camp system, and was comprised mainly of camps and colonies that contracted out prisoner labour, focusing on defence and construction industries. Later, the formation of Kemerovo Province (1943) and Tomsk Province (1944) out of the larger Novosibirsk Province led to the establishment of a Department of Corrective-Labour Colonies (OITK) for each of these provinces through the division of the old Novosibirsk Province Camp and Colony Administration.

The Gulag population statistics (table 2.1) as a whole show the effects of the war on the camp system. The spike in prisoners from 1939 to 1941 relates directly to the Soviet invasion of eastern Poland and later the Baltics under the terms of the Nazi-Soviet Pact's secret protocols. From late 1939 to 1941, as many as 130,000 people were arrested and 327,000 exiled from former Polish territory.[9] Then, following the 22 June 1941 invasion of the Soviet Union, the Gulag saw a steady decline in prisoner population as many prisoners were released to fight on the front, and many others died due to deteriorating wartime conditions. Once the Red Army was on the offensive, and pushing into enemy territory, the prisoner population again began to increase, but did not reach pre-war levels until the late 1940s. An examination of Gulag data thus supports the argument that, unlike Nazi Germany, the Soviet Union did not rely on its camp system more during wartime than in peacetime. In Germany, the pre-war camp population peaked in late 1938 (following

2.1. January prisoner population, 1939–45, Siblag and Gulag

Year	Siblag (1 January population)	Gulag (1 January population)	Siblag population as a % of the total	Revised estimate (Siblag + other W. Siberian camps)	Revised estimate as a % of the total
1939	46,382	1,672,438	2.77%	69,942	4.18%
1940	40,275	1,659,992	2.43%	61,719	3.72%
1941	43,857	1,929,729	2.20%	51,852	2.69%
1942	77,919	1,777,043	4.38%	77,919	4.38%
1943	30,463	1,484,182	2.05%	79,137[10]	5.33%
1944	29,627	1,179,819	2.51%	74,627	6.33%
1945	39,455	1,460,677	2.70%	84,798	5.81%

Source: M.B. Smirnov et al., eds., *Sistema ispravitel'no-trudovykh lagerei v SSSR, 1923–1960: Spravochnik* (Moscow: Zven'ia, 1998), 204, 392, 482, 533–6; A.B. Bezborodov et al., eds., *Istoriia stalinskogo Gulag*, vol. 4, *Naselenie Gulaga: chislennost' i usloviia soderzhaniia* (Moscow: Rosspen, 2004), 129–30; Danila S. Krasil'nikov, "Lageria i kolonii na territorii Novosibirskoi Oblasti v gody Velikoi Otechestvennoi voiny (1941–1945)," (Diplomnaia rabota, Novosibirsk State University, 1999), 44; I.S. Kuznetsov et al., eds., *Novonikolae-vskaia guberniia – Novosibirskaia oblast': 1921–2000: Khronika. Dokumenty* (Novosibirsk: Sibirskoe otd. RAN, 2001), 146.

Kristallnacht) at approximately 50,000 inmates, while the wartime population (excluding death camps) peaked at 714,211, a dramatic increase.[11] In the Gulag, the peak January 1st population before September of 1939 was 1,881,570 in 1938, while the postwar peak was 2,561,351 in 1953. From 1939 to 1945 the high was 1,929,729 in January 1941, only slightly higher than the peak of the 1930s, but the prisoner population then declined significantly following the German invasion and continued to decline until late in the war.

Siblag data tell a slightly different story. The changing administrative landscape of Western Siberia complicates compiled statistics for the area's camps. According to published figures (column 2 in table 2.1), Siblag's January 1 population from 1939 to 1945 spiked by 1942, declined rapidly, then grew again towards pre-war levels by early 1945. Clearly, there are major discrepancies between Siblag and the Gulag in prisoner population changes from 1941 to 1942 and 1942 to 1943. The disproportionate increase in Siblag prisoners during 1941 was mostly due to the outbreak of the war. The NKVD evacuated close to 750,000 prisoners from corrective-labour camps and colonies under threat from the Nazi invasion. The evacuation was a brutal affair, as many prisoners were forced out of Ukraine and Belarus on foot, leading to extreme transit conditions and the clogging up of roadways that could have usefully been devoted to the movement of military equipment and personnel. The evacuation was so chaotic that the NKVD recommended the release of prisoners sentenced for relatively minor crimes.[12] Nevertheless, many evacuated prisoners no doubt ended up in Siblag or in one of Siblag's two transit stations, Novosibirsk and Mariinsk.[13] Following the liquidation of Gornoshorlag in early 1941, moreover, the NKVD transferred many of the camp's 8,000 prisoners to Siblag.

The most striking change in Siblag's wartime population occurs over the course of 1942, however. The 1 January 1943 prisoner population is only 39.1 per cent of the 1 January 1942 population, at first glance an astounding drop. For the Gulag as a whole, the 1 January 1943 population is 83.5 per cent of the previous year's population, making the Siblag data stand out even more.[14]

What compiled Siblag statistics do not make explicit, however, is that the Novosibirsk Province Camp and Colony Administration functioned as a large camp system after the division of Siblag.[15] In the spring of 1942, just after the division, Siblag reported a population of 33,737 prisoners, while the Novosibirsk Province Camp and Colony Administration housed 50,453 prisoners, the majority working in contract camps.[16] The Novosibirsk Province Camp and Colony Administration remained a large system.[17] As shown in the "revised estimate" in table 2.1, the actual population for the camps in the area increased from 1 January 1942 to 1 January 1943, in contrast to the decrease seen across the Gulag, revealing the importance of the Gulag in the region to the wartime Gulag as whole.

The revised population estimate and revised percentages in table 2.1, above, show that the region went from approximately 3 per cent of the Gulag's population before the German invasion to around 6 per cent by war's end, or from approximately 52,000 prisoners in 1941 to 85,000 in 1945. Given the significant number of wartime releases, extremely high regional mortality rates, and the transit camps in Novosibirsk and Mariinsk, huge numbers of prisoners spent at least part of the war in Western Siberia.

As evidenced by Mikhail Grigor'evich Gorbachev, quoted near the outset of this chapter, the shift to military production had a profound effect on the region's camp system. The Tomsk Corrective-Labour Colony, which Gorbachev describes, became an important part of the

NKVD's munitions production. A plan for November 1941, for example, called for the production of 10,000 50mm shells at the Tomsk plant, out of a total of 65,000 for the Gulag as a whole.[18] Pre-June 1941 munitions plans for the NKVD had not even included the Tomsk Corrective-Labour Colony, revealing the rapid shift to military production in the region.[19]

Alongside the Tomsk Corrective-Labour Colony, the Iask camp had been sewing Red Army uniforms since the second half of 1940 in support of the Red Army's actions in the borderlands.[20] Another corrective-labour colony near Tomsk ceased manufacturing furniture and began to produce skis for the Red Army right after the German invasion in June 1941. According to one Novosibirsk Party Committee (Obkom) document, Siblag engineers even devised a way to attach a machine-gun system to skis, an invention that was tested and approved by the administration of the Siberian Military District (SibVO: *Sibirskii voennyi okrug*).[21] This type of activity – the creation of new military technology – was not that unusual for Gulag prisoners, although it often occurred under the purview of the scientific research camps, called *sharashki*, not in the regular camps and colonies, like those of Western Siberia.[22] In Novosibirsk, prisoners at the large Krivoshchekovsk camp worked on the construction of the enormous munitions factory, People's Commissariat of Munitions Combine 179, and also worked under contract in the combine's various workshops, producing artillery shells and other munitions.[23] Prisoners stepped up construction on the Chkalov Aviation Factory 153 – another key defence enterprise – and on a local airfield.[24] Even the agricultural camps played an important role for the front by sending food and horses to the Red Army. In early 1943, as camp mortality rates reached their highest recorded levels, one of Siblag's wartime slogans was "Give the country and the front more vegetables, more foodstuffs."[25] Despite the extreme hardships, moreover, Siblag managed to increase its area under cultivation over the course of the war.[26]

Central authorities clearly recognized the usefulness of prisoner labour for the war effort. On 30 July 1941, the NKVD in Moscow noted that a significant proportion of Gulag prisoners working on airfields and airports were nearing the end of their terms. The NKVD ordered freed prisoners to remain until the completion of the work, even if their sentences had technically ended.[27] Local camp authorities also recognized this economic imperative. At the same Tomsk Corrective-Labour Colony, mentioned above, authorities granted permission to a convicted Trotskyist to live outside of the camp zone, without guard, because he was a trained engineer and held a crucial position as the foundry shop's acting director.[28] The practice of placing so-called counter-revolutionaries in key camp economic positions, and giving them considerable privileges, was common throughout the wartime Gulag and went against regulations.[29] In November 1941, the Novosibirsk Party Committee specifically called on Siblag's director, G.N. Kopaev, to send "qualified engineers and workers, sentenced for daily life *and* counter-revolutionary crimes," to the region's defence enterprises.[30] In these cases the economic rationale for camp operations, as opposed to political imperatives, is readily apparent.

Even camp propaganda, where one might expect a political rationale to be most visible, emphasized economic production. Of course, the economic and political are difficult to separate in the Soviet context, as proving oneself politically often meant performing competently in economic production roles, while the opposite was also true: authorities often viewed poor economic performance as evidence of political unreliability. As will be discussed in greater detail in chapter 3, wartime camp propaganda focused on inspiring or shaming prisoners to work harder. In particular, camp authorities attempted to inspire prisoners by revealing the exploits of ex-prisoners on the front. As in Steven Barnes's description of Karlag at war, ex-Siblag prisoners supposedly sent letters back to Siblag, recounting their experiences in order to inspire home front production in the camps.[31] Also, as discussed in chapter 3, authorities granted tangible rewards – including early release – to prisoners who overfulfilled their work quotas.

If early release and camp propaganda were meant to increase labour output by the prisoner population, the extremely high mortality rates in the region during the Second World War reveal the opposite: a lack of emphasis by authorities on productive labour. From January 1942 through August 1943, the Novosibirsk Province Camp and Colony Administration saw no less than 1.87 per cent of its prisoners perish *per month*, with a high of 3.52 per cent in May 1942.[32] In 1943, the Novosibirsk Province Party Committee formed an inspection brigade to examine the living and working conditions of prisoners in the region's defence industries.[33] The brigade's report notes huge increases in mortality and invalid rates, particularly at the third Krivoshchekovsk camp, in charge of construction at Combine 179. In January 1943, 2.2 per cent of prisoners in the region's defence industries died; in February, the figure was 2.9 per cent; and in March, 2.6 per cent. At the third Krivoshchekovsk camp in March alone, 5.4 per cent of prisoners died. These percentages reflect monthly, rather than annualized death rates, and translate into huge yearly mortality figures, well in excess of the average for the Gulag as a whole.

These extraordinary wartime death rates in the urban camps and colonies deserve attention. They indicate that the Gulag at its most brutal may not have been Kolyma, Norilsk, or Vorkuta, all areas that were below the Gulag averages for wartime mortality rates.[34] Instead, and perhaps surprisingly, urban corrective-labour colonies like those in Novosibirsk may have suffered the highest mortality rates. One might assume that surviving an urban corrective-labour colony was relatively easy, because an urban area could allow for easier access to black markets, the camp regimen was technically lighter, the workload not as demanding, and the climate generally better.[35] So why did a higher percentage of prisoners perish in some of these camps? As demonstrated in chapter 1, the camps of Western Siberia were not prioritized, and so able-bodied prisoners would be sent to priority camps, while invalids or others who had difficulty with hard, physical labour would be held over in Western Siberia. The incoming contingents in these camps were already in poor physical shape. One can also imagine that the access to black markets was a double-edged sword, as camp officials also would have had an easier time dealing goods meant for prisoners to those on the outside.[36]

Certainly memoirists of the region paint a terrible picture of wartime conditions in the corrective-labour colonies. Wartime shortages and overwork meant that the struggle for survival entered a harsher stage, and prisoners often fought against one another for what little food was available. One prisoner, D.E. Alin, who worked at the Chkalov Aviation Factory 153, remembered that although rations were drastically reduced after the beginning of the war, at first it was possible to live on the minuscule 260 to 460 grams of bread per day, plus a small amount of kasha, and that many prisoners supplemented this ration with food sent in packages from relatives.[37] As the war dragged on, however, the situation became dire. By the beginning of 1942, the prisoners in Alin's camp split a regular ration five ways. The prisoners began to smuggle and hide crowbars, axes, and other items that could be used as weapons, not to try to escape, but to defend their own rations and intimidate other prisoners into giving their rations away. Alin recalls an incident when he found a new arrival at the camp, who happened to be a distant cousin, with his head bashed in, murdered for his small bowl of kasha.

While some memoirists have written of an unspoken moral code that allowed theft of most items except rations, the harsh realities of wartime meant even that code went by the wayside.[38] Alin himself became so ill and malnourished by the fall of 1942 that he lost consciousness one day at work, and considered himself lucky to survive the camp hospital, where patients were "dying like flies."[39]

As Alin's recollections indicate, authorities did not supply sufficient rations, especially during the war. Wartime ration problems related mostly to the general disruptions of supply caused by the war, and the prioritization of soldiers and non-prisoner workers in defence industries. The NKVD had attempted to standardize camp rations with a 1939 operational order, Top Secret Operational Order 00943. Appended to this order were several tables containing various food norms, as well as lists of allowable goods for prisoners.[40] Order 00943 and other orders from this time reveal hyper-bureaucratization, whereby official regulations were detailed and cumbersome to the point of encouraging non-compliance, thereby entrenching and possibly even creating informal practices.[41] Even if there had been a proper supply of food to the camps, it would have been nearly impossible to follow the overly cumbersome regulations.

These food-norm regulations show no concern for variety. Instead, authorities broke down food allotments into grams/day of various types of foodstuffs, from rye bread to fish to potatoes to tea. The charts also contained no mention of quality. The base ration consisted of 1,100 g of rye bread per prisoner per day; 650 g of potatoes and vegetables; and 155 g of fish, as well as small amounts of other items. Alin, with his small amount of bread and kasha, thus received perhaps only one-quarter of the intended amount. The official diet was very low in fruits and vegetables.[42] Of course, according to most Gulag memoirists, fish and even potatoes were extremely rare, with bread and a barely edible broth soup forming the staple diet.[43] During the war, rations were even worse. Thus, to say that actual rations did not conform to Order 00943 would be an understatement. Some prisoners found ways of supplementing rations via packages from relatives, through personal connections with well-placed prisoners or staff, or as reward for performing small tasks. One Siblag prisoner even recalls with a certain amount of satisfaction the ability to "earn" extra food: "In the camp I felt like I was on the outside, as here I was able to 'earn' an extra bowl of gruel [balandy] or a piece of bread, not like in the prison."[44]

On one hand, had local camp authorities been able to follow these ration regimes, prisoners likely would have had enough food. On the other hand, we must consider the possibility that the norms themselves were merely a cynical attempt by the NKVD to pass the blame should problems arise. Due to inefficiencies in supply, the black market, and the skimming of foodstuffs for personal use, central authorities must have known that the regulations would have been impossible to follow. The regulations allowed the centre to blame the periphery for any problems. On the rare occasions when an official received punishment for high levels of starvation and disease in the camps, the punished official was invariably a local camp commander, rather than someone from the central Gulag or NKVD.[45]

On paper, however, ration regulations expose a key difference between the Gulag and the Nazi camps. Food norms in Nazi camps – even the concentration camps as opposed to the death camps – were based on a perceived racial hierarchy of inmates, with those at the bottom, such as Jews, given starvation rations on purpose.[46] While the bureaucratic system and orders from the top were certainly responsible for much of the violence in the Gulag, many Gulag deaths were the result of orders that were ignored or, like these ration norms, subverted down the line.

Margarete Buber-Neumann's fascinating account of her time in both the Soviet and the Nazi camps nicely illustrates this point about the differences in efficiency in the two systems. Buber-Neumann spent time as a Karlag prisoner and then, following the Nazi-Soviet Pact, was transferred as a German communist to Germany, where authorities interned her at the Ravensbrück concentration camp. She recalls finding an official document for food norms while incarcerated in Karlag. She discovered that the prisoners received less food than they were supposed to receive, and assumed that kitchen workers regularly stole the remainder. Camp inefficiencies litter her account of Karlag, where she managed to be unwatched much of the time and where socializing in the barracks – which were hardly well ordered – was a common occurrence. The contrast to Ravensbrück could hardly be more striking. Initially, Buber-Neumann was happy to receive better rations in Ravensbrück than in Karlag (she was not Jewish, and was not on starvation rations), and she was also struck by the orderliness of the camp: "I was astonished at what I saw: neat plots of grass with beds in which flowers were blooming ... large timber barracks painted white ... a big, well-kept lawn with silver firs." Even the barracks had a functioning lavatory and washbasins. However, everything was so regimented, and social ties so tenuous, that Buber-Neumann "almost began to think that the lousy mud huts of Birma [in Karlag] were preferable to this pedantic nightmare."[47]

While Buber-Neumann blamed the kitchen staff at Karlag for the poor state of camp rations, the very regulations themselves were so onerous as to ensure that they were largely ignored. The NKVD called for twelve different food norms, some also containing various modifiers, each very specific in the amount per prisoner per day. The logistical hurdles for distributing food in such a manner surely would have been overwhelming even for the most competent of personnel and managers.[48]

The twelve food norms were as follows: (1) a lower-than-standard ration for those not fulfilling their norms, those under investigation, invalids, and prisoners confined to work within the camp zone (this norm could be modified, too: those fulfilling work norms by less than 60 per cent had different rations than those who fulfilled their work norms by between 60 and 99 per cent); (2) a higher-than-standard ration for those fulfilling their work norms in key production areas; (3) supplementary food rations for Stakhanovite workers, that is, those who significantly exceeded their work norms; (4) supplementary food rations for engineering-technical workers (note that these rations were generally greater than Stakhanovite rations); (5) the standard ration for prisoners in corrective-labour colonies and camps (see table 2.2);[49] (6) rations for underage prisoners, divided into two parts: general and work-norm fulfillers; (7) rations for the sickly and those suffering from pellagra; (8) rations for pregnant and breastfeeding women (mostly higher than Stakhanovite rations); (9) rations for non-working unfit prisoners; (10) rations for working unfit prisoners; (11) rations for those on transfer; and (12) penalty rations. In all cases, rations for those prisoners above the Arctic Circle or in underground work were 25 per cent higher, while rations for several camps – Noril'lag, Vorkutlag, and a Sevzheldorlag subcamp – were set separately, probably because these were priority camps. Thus in the case of rations, the regime categorized prisoners not by type of sentence, as one might expect, but usually by work-norm fulfilment and health status. Authorities were more likely to punish Article 58ers with penalty rations, but there was no explicit targeting of the so-called counter-revolutionaries with these food norms.

While ration differentiation clearly existed in the camps, it is almost impossible to conceive of it working according to the script of NKVD Operational Order 00943. Corrupt camp officials sold foodstuffs on the

2.2. The standard ration (grams per prisoner per day)

Type of food	Amount	Type of food	Amount	Type of food	Amount
Rye bread	1,100.0	Animal fat*	4.0	Potato flour*	0.3
Wheat flour	61.0	Macaroni	10.0	Cayenne	0.13
Cereals	127.0	Tea surrogate	2.0	Bay leaves	0.2
Meat	39.0	Natural tea*	0.3	Salt	20.0
Fish	155.0	Potatoes & vegetables	650.0	Sugar	17.0
Herring*	5.0	Puréed tomato	10.0		
Vegetable oil	14.0	Dried fruits*	0.5		

* Herring was available only for sale in the commissary; animal fat was available only for those who were ill and for Stakhanovites; natural tea, dried fruits, and potato flour were available only for those who were ill.
Source: A.I. Kokurin and N.V. Petrov., eds., GULAG (Gavnoe upravlenie lagerei) 1918–1960 (Moscow: Materik, 2000), 479.

side;[50] supply issues plagued most camps, especially during the war; and prisoners who worked in the kitchen were often able to pocket extra food for themselves and their friends. Even once the food reached the mess hall, however, it is unlikely that those who dished out food portions did so by the criteria set out under the twelve ration regimes. Most likely, prisoners receiving the best rations were the friends of the mess-hall workers or those in the camps – usually from among the hardened criminals – with the most influence among other prisoners. No doubt those who curried favour with camp personnel also received better rations. Women memoirists commonly report that Gulag guards would offer better food or other privileges in exchange for sex.[51] For all of these reasons, then, personal connections, corruption, coercion, ingenuity, luck, and the general inefficiency of the system played a greater role in a prisoner's food supply than did central regulations.

The lack of proper rations meant that prisoners who did not have personal connections or were simply unlucky quickly became invalids. Many prisoners became invalids and could not work, and some prisoners in this category received early release. The Novosibirsk Province Camp and Colony Administration's 1943 inspection brigade, when discussing invalids, noted:

This contingent, on the basis of the instruction of the NKVD of the USSR, the NKIu [People's Commissariat of Justice] of the USSR and the

Procurator of the Union from 23 October 1942, no. 467/18-71/117s, is released from camp ahead of schedule, as it is a large burden for the camp.

By 1 April of t[his] y[ear] the medical commissions under the ITL, as a result of physical examination, had recognized as invalids 7,491 persons. Of these 2,917 were released ahead of schedule and 875 have died.[52]

In a 1944 report based on 1943 inspections of the areas camps and colonies, the procurator overseeing camp operations, A. Kondrashev, actually *encouraged early release for invalids as a way to help improve the camp's mortality statistics.* His statement provides a local example that supports Alexopoulos's contention that large numbers of invalid prisoners were released early, with death beyond the camp zone a real possibility, and underscores the utter disregard for the human misery of the camps, which, while not surprising, is especially galling considering Kondrashev's role as an inspector.[53] As he wrote,

It is worth noting that the Camp Administration and also the procurator in the first half of 1943 paid insufficient attention to fulfilling the directives of the NKVD and Procurator of the USSR, [and] as a consequence in August there was a high mortality rate in the camp, whereas people could have been released in a timely way [*svoevremenno*], thereby considerably reducing the death rate.

Kondrashev went on, however, to suggest that the political reliability of those released must be considered, and cited with disapproval two cases of release – one an Article 58er and one sentenced under Article 162.d (theft of state property) – where "state security has not been observed."[54]

We see here that wartime release was not only about rewards for productive labour or about providing more soldiers for the front, but was often related to relieving local camps of the need to care for dying and severely ill prisoners.[55] That authorities frequently released dying prisoners at first glance supports the argument for an economic explanation for Gulag operations – these prisoners, after all, were a burden economically and could not help production quotas. However, if Gulag economic production had been a top priority, one might expect authorities to place more emphasis on maintaining the prisoners' health in the first place. And although the central NKVD early in 1942 ordered the creation of "preventative health" camp stations for every camp, designed to be well lit, spacious, and with access to increased rations, ostensibly to nurse unhealthy prisoners back to the position of productive labourers, it is clear that local authorities lacked the resources to create such stations.[56]

The upkeep of prisoners required expenses including medical infrastructure and living quarters, as well as the upkeep of personnel and guards, who were often demobilized soldiers. Camp commander Kopaev complained in 1941, for example, that Siblag spent 11 million rubles a year maintaining the 9,000 invalid-prisoners in the camp.[57] Siblag's budget for that same year allotted 25 million rubles for the upkeep of the camp's approximately 4,000 guards, which, as Kopaev pointed out, was enough "to build a decent-sized factory [*nemalen'kii zavod*]."[58] The discrepancy in funding between guards and invalid-prisoners is telling. On a per-person basis, if Kopaev's figures are correct, Siblag authorities spent 1,222 rubles per year on the upkeep of each invalid, and 6,250 rubles on the upkeep of each guard. Given that invalids required, at least theoretically, extra costs in medical care, these figures reveal that care for invalids was minimal at best. As a further comparison, wartime industrial wages peaked in 1944 at an average per worker of 575 rubles per month (6,900 rubles per year), although one must be careful with Stalin-era wage data, as enterprises often made irregular payments.[59]

Kopaev, furthermore, complained not only about the cost of maintaining invalids but also about the fact that they were not involved in productive labour. Indeed, he sought "to break some of our workers of the rotten theory [*gniluiu teoriiu*] of the impossibility of using invalids in light work in the manufacture of consumer goods."[60] As Dan Healey demonstrates, Gulag sanitary departments, in charge of medical facilities, devoted considerable resources to helping those deemed invalids. The authorities, however, expected invalids to work, and only sought to help those who could be nursed back to health, so that they could be productive labourers once again.[61] Kopaev's remarks on using invalids in productive labour had their desired effect, at least partially. During the war, Siblag invalid-prisoners produced felt boots, skis, shoes, and even brooms, which were specifically for use in defence factories.[62] The push to use invalids and severely weakened prisoners in some type of work came straight from the top. The director of the Gulag's medical department, D.M. Loidin, even insisted on it.[63]

The issue of the ill health of prisoners is central to the discussion, but once again complex. From late 1941 through at least the first half of 1943, the Soviet Union was fighting for its very existence, and resources were scarce for everyone. The peak year for mortality in Western Siberia's non-Gulag population was 1942, the same year that the Gulag also reached its highest recorded mortality rates (2.69 and 24.9 per cent, respectively).[64] Even outside of the camps, evacuees to Novosibirsk Province received less bread than what the Gulag prisoner technically should have received before the war began.[65] Oleg Khlevniuk has recently demonstrated that, in certain times and places, rations *in* the Gulag were better than in surrounding towns and villages for certain types of food.[66] So, the lack of emphasis on prisoner health is not surprising given the general circumstances in the country. Nevertheless, it appears that priority camps, such as Norilsk, Vorkuta, and even those in the Kolyma region, may have fared better than the more typical camps, like Siblag and others in Western Siberia, precisely due to perceived economic necessity. Norilsk received only able-bodied prisoners, for example, and its mortality rate peaked at 7.2 per cent in 1943, compared with an overall Gulag mortality rate of 22.4 per cent during that year. The mortality rate in the Kolyma region in 1943 was 12.4 per cent, which was similar to that of Vorkuta.[67] As discussed above, many camps in Western Siberia experienced mortality rates that well exceeded the Gulag average.

The Western Siberian camps thus show us that, at least as far as the evidence on mortality is concerned, both economic and political factors motivated camp operations, and that this motivation varied from camp to camp. We also see that camp conditions, even in the urban areas of the region, were likely far worse in the non-priority camps of Western Siberia than they were in better-known, but more remote, camps. On one hand, the rapid shift to military production, as well as the flexibility in labour use of prisoners and the incentives provided to exhort prisoners to work harder, tips the balance in favour of an economic motivation in the region. On the other hand, the inefficiencies point to more political concerns, as inefficiency in labour and upkeep is not a problem if isolation is the key goal. Yet, the close interaction between prisoners and non-prisoners suggests that one of the main political concerns – isolation of those deemed dangerous to society, a common component of most prison systems – was not the most crucial element of Gulag operations. We see this interaction most clearly when considering issues surrounding the Gulag and total war.

Total War

If most modern penal systems are designed with some degree of emphasis on deterrence, isolation, retribution, and rehabilitation, the total war experience of Stalin's Gulag points to peculiarities of the Soviet system.[68] Certainly, the Gulag contained within it all four of these justifications for imprisonment. Yet, although many modern penal systems use some form of forced labour, the Gulag's focus on prisoner labour in key economic sectors is unusual. As the penitentiary developed in Europe during the nineteenth century, labour became an integral part of daily life, but was usually meant as part of the punitive or rehabilitative process.[69] At most, economically speaking, authorities hoped the products of prisoner labour could offset the costs of running the penitentiary or give convicts necessary skills for future reintegration.[70] The Gulag, however, was different in its application of forced labour, and this difference was especially evident in wartime. Its specific products (artillery shells, uniforms, and so on) were intended to be useful to the state – perhaps even more useful than the convicts themselves, who died in large numbers.

The emphasis on production results also marks the Gulag as unusual compared with other concentration camps. Labour was part of early iterations of the concentration camp in turn-of-the-century colonial contexts, but not a key component.[71] The Nazis established concentration camps soon after coming to power in 1933 and experimented with camps designed for economic production, particularly the Emsland camp in Prussia. However, they settled on the Dachau model, where forced labour was meant more as a form of punishment than as a tool for economic production.[72] And although some camps experimented with forced labour in key economic sectors, it was not until the war began to go poorly for the Nazis that they made a concerted effort to achieve economic value from their concentration camps.

On the surface, the Gulag workshops of Western Siberia appeared to do their job in terms of output of artillery shells, uniforms, foodstuffs, and so on in support of the war effort. Novosibirsk Province Camp and Colony Administration documents proudly report the awarding of the Order of Lenin to Combine 179 in November 1943 and give credit to prisoners for helping to make this happen.[73] Combine 179 participated in all-union "socialist competitions" for the production of artillery shells and won several months in a row in 1943, also receiving the Red Banner (*Krasnoe znamia*) award from the Central Committee of the Communist Party.[74] Chkalov Aviation Factory 153, also in Novosibirsk, was responsible for producing 15,797 airplanes of various types during the Second World War, focusing on the crucially important Yak fighter planes; prisoners helped construct the factory and the airfields. Workers at the Chkalov factory produced approximately 11.5 per cent of all Soviet fighter planes built during the war.[75] The Tomsk Munitions Plant was almost entirely run by prisoners. And, as has been already mentioned, every camp and colony was mobilized for the war, regardless of its production activity.

Combine 179 and the Chkalov Aviation Factory 153 were two of the most important defence enterprises located within the city limits of Novosibirsk. Both of them used a combination of prisoner and non-prisoner labour, and both housed Gulag camps that were technically corrective-labour colonies. Combine 179, situated on the left bank of the enormous Ob' River, was a sprawling complex of munitions factories and workers' barracks, and home to Siblag's largest camp, after May 1942 under the jurisdiction of the Novosibirsk Province Camp and Colony Administration. On the eve of the war in May 1941, Krivoshchekovsk, with its various camp stations, held 7,807 prisoners.[76] The construction and operation of the combine, begun in the 1930s, was the primary social and economic engine for the development of Novosibirsk's left bank. The degree to which forced and free labour overlapped in Combine 179 is striking, lending weight to Kate Brown's assertion that we should understand forced and free labour in the Soviet Union not as a binary but as a continuum, with various degrees of coercion and incentives provided in almost all contexts.[77]

This continuum of coerced and incentivized labour makes it difficult to assess the exact contribution of prisoners, particularly in defence industries like those in Novosibirsk that used a combination of prisoners and non-prisoners. As noted above, Chkalov Aviation Factory produced close to 16,000 planes of various types during the Second World War, focusing on the Yak fighter.[78] Yet how much of this production do we attribute to prisoners, who mostly worked on construction of the factory, barracks, and airfields, rather than on the actual airplanes? At its peak, as discussed in greater detail later in this chapter, forced labour (including prisoners, special settlers, and POWs) made up roughly 20 per cent of the workforce in the Novosibirsk Province defence industries. Many of these contingents were in poor health, and at the factories often worked on supplementary tasks, such as the construction of new workshops or worker barracks. Calculating the prisoners' proportionate contribution remains almost impossible, not least because the authorities themselves did not break down the economic output in terms of worker contingents, at least in the available documentation.

2.1: Yak fighter planes on assembly lines, 1942. World History Archive/
Alamy Stock Photo.

2.2: Siblag prisoners construct a building in Mariinsk, 1940s. Photo-Archive of the International Memorial Society. Used with permission.

However, if it were assumed that forced labour contingents made up roughly 15–20 per cent of the defence-industry workforce in the region, their total contributions in terms of output were significant.

What is clear, though, is that provincial authorities did not particularly care where the labourers came from, as long as they had enough workers to staff the factories. All prisoners and non-prisoners were simply a resource. Already before the official outbreak of war, in expanding Combine 179, the Novosibirsk Provincial Party Committee in December 1940 called for the transfer of 5,000 Siblag prisoners as well as 6,000 non-prisoners from the Soviet Union's central provinces in order to complete the project.[79] The significant mobilization of Soviet troops into eastern Poland and the Baltics from September 1939 to June 1940, plus the November 1939 to March 1940 Winter War against Finland, had necessitated the increased production of war materials,

and local authorities sought to step up the production of this key industrial complex. The resolution's listing of these transfer numbers one after another emphasizes the authorities' wide-ranging ability to draw on
human resources for specific projects, and blurs the distinction between
prisoner and non-prisoner labour.[80]

Even party authorities in Moscow drew on a combination of prisoner
and non-prisoner sources to help build Combine 179. In late December
1940, the Politburo discussed the amount of funding to supply for capital investment in Combine 179, and central plans called for production
of 800,000 shell casings (*korpusov snariadov*) of various types, as well
as numerous other munitions, to be produced in 1941. The Politburo
charged NKVD director Beria with increasing the number of Gulag
prisoners working at the Combine to 10,000. The Politburo also ordered
squared beams and saw timber to be removed from the recently decommissioned Tomasinlag and shipped to the Combine to aid in construction. Authorities in Novosibirsk and Kirov Provinces, the Altai
Territory, and Bashkir ASSR had to send non-prisoners, totaling 11,000
between them, for the first half of 1941.[81] The Politburo ended this particular discussion by calling for the inclusion of Combine 179 as one of
the "country's especially important construction projects."[82] Wartime
orders continued to redirect human resources in a similar manner.[83] The
key issue was having enough hands to complete the task, not whether
that labour was prisoner or non-prisoner. And if non-prisoners could
be forced to relocate for specific projects, this was not free labour in the
technical sense of the term, even if it was far preferable to the horrors of
Gulag life.[84]

The Provincial Party Committee also placed a considerable burden
on Siblag to supply labourers as quickly as possible. At a 10 September
1941 meeting, the committee directed Kopaev to send an additional
3,000 prisoners to Combine 179: 1,000 by 13 September, 1,000 by
20 September, and the final 1,000 by 1 October. Not surprisingly, but
again attesting to poor planning, a month later the Party Committee
criticized Kopaev for not having done enough to build proper barracks
for the incoming contingents.[85] Given the extremely short time he had
in which to transfer the prisoners, the party's demands must have
seemed completely unrealistic. The story does not end there, however.
In December, the Party Committee then ordered Kopaev to clear most
of these prisoners from the barracks to make room for demobilized Red
Army soldiers, who would then work at the factory.[86] These types of
orders from the authorities continued throughout the war. In June 1942,

for example, the vice-director of the all-union NKVD ordered the administration of the regional Novosibirsk NKVD to send 3,000 prisoners to the combine: 2,000 in June and 1,000 in July.[87]

Labour supply posed considerable issues for authorities even in the months leading up to the German invasion. In April 1941, Beria sent a letter to P.N. Goremykin, head of the People's Commissariat of Munitions, complaining that the director of Combine 179 had not properly prepared the combine for an influx of prisoners that had started in January.[88] A week before Beria's letter, the vice-director of the NKVD, S.N. Kruglov, had also sent a letter to Goremykin, complaining that the director of Combine 179 was refusing to take sufficient prisoners as part of the workforce, and asking Goremykin to force the combine to provide sufficient living space for incoming contingents.[89] Notwithstanding the chaos of 1941, or perhaps because of it, we can read some of this tension as evidence of disagreements between competing ministries. In the actual workshops, moreover, the chaos meant that prisoners and non-prisoners often worked alongside one another.

Evidently, there was much opportunity for interaction between prisoners and non-prisoners in these contract camps. Central and local authorities dealt with numerous issues involving de-convoyed prisoners (those permitted to move outside of the camp without guard) during the war, including many who took advantage of their unescorted status and smuggled correspondence, engaged in black market activity, or even escaped.[90] On 18 January 1943, the Gulag in Moscow issued an order to all camp and colony directors, asking them to take measures to prevent interaction at contract camps, as many prisoners were stealing items and foodstuffs from the civilian populations, both at the production sites and while on transfer or moving through settlement points.[91] D.E. Alin recalls that, on the way to the work site, the prisoners at the Chkalov Aviation Factory would stop and wave to mobilized soldiers heading to the front by train. The soldiers would sometimes talk to them and even occasionally throw them food.[92] Thus the evidence suggests that while there may have been some attempts at isolation, there was room for considerable interaction and overlap between prisoners and non-prisoners. Isolation was less important than production in the total war effort.

Even in non-contract camps located in towns, prisoners often negotiated the boundaries between the camp and the surrounding population. In his memoir, G.N. Gorchakov recalls arriving at the Mariinsk camp of Siblag late in the war, before being sent to one of Siblag's agricultural camps. Although he described the agricultural camps as isolated, the camp in Mariinsk certainly was not. There, he ran into an acquaintance from Butyrka, the infamous Moscow prison, who was involved in black market activity along with another prisoner and a civilian worker. Working in the medical unit of the Mariinsk camp, the prisoners used their civilian accomplice to smuggle out camp goods, which were then sold at "the bazaar in the city." According to Gorchakov, "How they shared [the profits] amongst themselves, and who else participated in these operations, was only known to them."[93] Another former prisoner, G.F. Tsivirko, who spent time in Siblag's Mariinsk and Novosibirsk camps during the war, as well as Karlag in Kazakhstan, recalled smuggling correspondence to her family through the civilian workers, by means of bribes. Her main memories, however, are of mass death, including the death of her own son, who was both conceived in, and died in, the camps.[94]

Conditions in these urban camps were extraordinarily harsh, as evidenced by the high mortality rates, discussed earlier, and by Alin's description of wartime rations. One prisoner, P.Kh. Ivanov, who worked in Combine 179 in 1943–5, did not write much about his time there, but his description highlights his precarious position and that of many other prisoners:

> Later [1943] I was sent to work at factory no. 179, which produced munitions. At the first camp station [Krivoshchekovsk] I was placed in the 120th brigade, which included such goners [dokhodiagi] like me, as well as thieves. [My] ration was often stolen. In this same camp were women and children. The latter stole everything. We slept on the floor in the barracks, later bunks were made. As a result [of all of this,] I ended up in the hospital, as I was not able to work. At the end of 1943 I was discharged from the hospital and sent to the factory, but this time with the 117th brigade. The brigade consisted of Article 58ers. Women and men were together. The foreman placed me casting metal, which I did until my third arrest. In March 1945 they arrested me in the camp. I was sentenced in July 1945 for anti-Soviet propaganda and sabotage during the time of my work at the foundry. By the logic of the Chekists, I, as the son of White Guards, could not help, working in a war factory, but cause harm, especially in the production of mortar shells and bombs. And we, all those who had worked in the factory, thought that they'd free us early after winning the war against Germany. They sentenced me to be shot for the second time. On August 28 the death sentence was changed to 20 years in katorga.[95]

While conditions were clearly much worse for prisoners, non-prisoners also experienced horrendous living conditions in the region. In Siberia's urban areas, the mortality rate for regular citizens increased by over 25 per cent in the first year of the war, and Novosibirsk Province saw huge increases in diseases such as typhoid fever, dysentery, typhus, and whooping cough.[96] Non-prisoners in many home front cities also died from starvation and tuberculosis in alarmingly high numbers, and infant deaths due to starvation peaked in 1942, while adult deaths for same reason peaked in 1943. Given German occupation of key food-producing regions in Ukraine, there simply were not enough supplies available to support the population.[97] Due to these and similar conditions, Combine 179 suffered from shockingly high turnover of its non-prisoners, despite extremely harsh wartime labour laws, especially in defence industries.[98] In 1942, 11,497 persons arrived to work at the factory, while 9,324 left. In 1943, 7,703 arrived while 7,600 left, approximately 5,000 of whom deserted.[99] By deserting, these workers chose to live outside the law of the time, and risked a harsh Gulag sentence, which could perhaps send them directly back to Combine 179 or other such factories.

The harsh labour laws of June 1940, whereby one could be punished for showing up late to work or for illegally changing jobs, were made even harsher under wartime conditions. With a December 1941 decree, workers in war industries (more broadly defined as the war progressed) could be sentenced to the camps for five to eight years for leaving their jobs without authorization, although many were sentenced *in absentia*, since they could not be found, and never sent to the Gulag.[100] Transport workers also could receive severe sentences for labour infractions. By 1942–3, "war industries" included the coal, textile, chemical, and gasoline industries. This decree, moreover, stayed in effect until 1948. From 1942 to 1945, over 900,000 persons were sentenced under this decree, and another 200,000 between the end of the war and 1948.[101]

Many non-prisoner workers in the region also left key industries legitimately to join the ranks of the Red Army. Indeed, some 500,000 persons left Novosibirsk Province for the front during the war. Kuzbass Coal lost 11,000 miners to the Red Army in the second half of 1941 alone.[102] By January 1943 in Novosibirsk Province, there were only thirty-five men for every 100 women.[103]

While Combine 179 and the Chkalov Aviation Factory receive much of the attention related to wartime production, the Tomsk Munitions Plant is another strong example of the mobilization of forced labour directly into war industries. The prisoner Mikhail Gorbachev, quoted at the outset of this chapter, shows in his memoir that the transition to wartime production was haphazard, yet it is important to note that the local authorities felt the transition was a success. At a 9 May 1942 meeting of the Tomsk City Communist Party Committee, members discussed issuing awards to thirteen key engineers, foremen, and directors at the factory, because of the successful transition. They note that the factory itself was part of a munitions plant that had been evacuated from Kharkov and reconstructed in Tomsk. The reconstruction took only ten days, and the factory almost immediately over fulfilled its plans for artillery shells, even achieving 203 per cent of the plan in February 1942. The City Party Committee had already awarded the factory the Red Banner for its strong work.[104] Still, despite this report, the transition was not easy. In early 1943, for example, the Tomsk factory had major issues with its electricity supply, severely curtailing output over the course of several weeks.[105]

The total war effort meant harsh conditions within the camps and in the region more generally. War mobilization also contributed to considerable interaction between prisoners and non-prisoners. The war-related interaction between the Gulag and the non-Gulag was not only regional, however. Internationally, the American "lend-lease" program also affected the Gulag. While a portion of the lend-lease program consisted of military equipment, other US machinery and supplies, such as boots, clothing, tractors, trucks, and steam shovels made their way to the Gulag. Even the supply of some ships directly aided the Gulag, as the NKVD occasionally made use of these ships for prisoner transport between Magadan and Kolyma.[106] Given the distance between Siblag and both the Pacific and Arctic coasts, however, it is not surprising to find that the presence of American supplies does not come up in the available regional documentation for Western Siberia. Considering the integration of the Gulag into the total war economy, however, it is not surprising that some lend-lease supplies ended up in the camps.

Mobilizing the Special Settlements

Due to the high turnover – both legitimate and illegitimate – of non-prisoners, the turn to forced labour as a partial solution is not surprising. Indeed, not only prisoners worked in Combine 179 but also exiles. Starting in the late-1930s, but accelerating during the war, Stalin's NKVD launched a series of repressive campaigns to exile certain ethnic groups in their entirety from their homelands to the Soviet interior. The two main ethnic groups sent to Western Siberia were both sent to the region as part of wartime campaigns. The largest was by far the Volga Germans. There is little evidence that these German-speaking Soviet families, whose ancestors had settled along the Volga River during the reign of Catherine the Great, had any sympathy for Hitler. Yet similar in some respects to their North American counterparts, whose distrust of ethnic Japanese Americans and Japanese Canadians following Pearl Harbor led to the internment of these groups, Soviet authorities saw the Volga Germans as potential enemy collaborators and sent them far into the interior. In all, authorities exiled just under 950,000 ethnic Germans from European regions of the Soviet Union, mostly to various parts of Siberia and Kazakhstan, starting in late summer of 1941.[107] The second main wartime group exiled to Western Siberia was the Kalmyks, accused of having collaborated with the Nazis while under German occupation and exiled by an order of the Presidium of the Supreme Soviet on 27 December 1943. Plans called for authorities to send roughly 20,000 Kalmyks (of the 95,000 total) to Novosibirsk Province, and it appears that those plans were roughly carried through.[108]

The Volga Germans and the Kalmyks were not the only wartime exile groups, of course. Authorities had started mass deportations of certain ethnic groups even before the war. The first group was ethnic Koreans living in the Far East, who were exiled mainly to Central Asia beginning in 1937. Like the wartime exile groups, the Koreans were seen by the authorities as potential collaborators with an external threat, as tensions were mounting at the time in Manchuria and East Asia. In the period of the Nazi-Soviet Pact, from 1939 to 1941, many Poles, people of the Baltic states, and the western borderlands (the regions annexed by the Soviet Union) were deported as well (and many to Western Siberia), although these deportations did not encompass entire ethnic groups, as in the case of the Volga Germans, Kalmyks, and others. During the war, other groups, including Chechens, were exiled in their entirety.

Despite their alleged Nazi sympathies, Volga Germans and Kalmyks – the two main exile groups to Western Siberia – were put to work for the war effort. Special settlers from Narym and even POWs joined these exiles and Gulag prisoners in the region's defence industries. An 8 May 1942 directive from the Novosibirsk Party Secretary to the Narym region party organization called for male special settlers born in 1922 and 1923, and unmarried female special settlers of the same age, to be sent to work in three separate defence enterprises in Novosibirsk, including 1,000 to Combine 179.[109] By the second half of 1942, over 20 per cent of the workforce in munitions in Novosibirsk Province was made up of prisoners.[110] By the end of the war, this percentage had fallen somewhat but was still significant. On 1 May 1945, of Combine 179's 25,117 workers, 3,120 were prisoners (12.4 per cent); 1,100 were exiled Volga Germans (4.4 per cent); 822 were POWs; 106 were former "kulaks" from Narym; and 98 were exiled Kalmyks.[111]

In terms of the settlements as they existed in June 1941, there was initially a fair bit of chaos. Many of the Polish special settlers, if they had survived to that point, were released to fight on front. Once the rapid deterioration of the situation on the front was apparent, moreover, Gulag authorities in November 1941 ordered the immediate release of many special settler youth from the settlements, in order to mobilize them into the Red Army, and similar mobilization orders occurred later in the war, too.[112] A June 1943 report on the status of special settlers in Novosibirsk Province stated that from this region alone, 19,515 special settlers had been mobilized into the Red Army between December 1942 and June 1943, and also noted that of the 46,596 special settler youth who had been released from the Novosibirsk Province settlements since October 1938, many had been mobilized.[113] Thus, the German invasion led to both greater repression against many groups and a relaxation of repressive measures against others.

While forced labour appeared to provide benefits, the use of forced labour also created its own problems, as authorities worried about possible counter-revolutionary activity among prisoners and exile groups. In November 1941, I.V. Ivanov, head of the special settlement department of the NKVD, instructed NKVD officials in Western Siberia and neighbouring regions to use exiled Volga Germans in their areas of expertise. At the same time, however, Ivanov reported instances of roaming groups of Volga Germans who, without permission, were going to various organizations and establishments, looking for work. No doubt these Volga Germans were merely trying to survive, to make the best of a bad situation, but from the authorities' point of view this posed problems: "At times this vagrancy [brodiazhnichestvo] by fascist elements is used to establish connections with counter-revolutionary goals."[114] If the Volga Germans had not been anti-Soviet before exile, certainly the conditions of exile itself may have led to anti-Soviet sentiment. As one exile reportedly commented, "They drove us here to starvation ... it would have been better to drown in the Volga."[115] Although accurate data are difficult to find, demographers have estimated excess deaths among the ethnic German deportees to Siberia and Kazakhstan at 228,000 or higher, at least 19 per cent of their total population.[116]

Perhaps due to the exile of Volga Germans to the region and the general upheavals of the early months of the war, Novosibirsk Province saw an increase in death sentences for counter-revolutionary activity in the first six months of the war, but starting in 1942 there was a sharp decline in the number of sentences for counter-revolutionary activity (especially death sentences) in the region, suggesting a relaxation of repressive measures.[117] The initial spike in death sentences was part of what Oleg Budnitskii has termed a "wave of preemptive repression" that accompanied the outbreak of the war. According to Budnitskii, the brief but deadly wave of repression, in combination with the horrors of Nazi occupation and the successful branding of the war as "patriotic," helped shift the general mood of the population away from defeatism and towards a patriotic response.[118]

The regime also saw the Volga Germans as potentially useful. In January 1942, the State Defence Committee[119] called for the mobilization of 120,000 exiled Volga German males fit for physical labour into "work columns" for the duration of the war. Later in 1942, the State Defence Committee expanded this mobilization order to include a greater age range of Volga German males (now from age fifteen to fifty-five) as well as females age sixteen to forty-five, excluding pregnant women and mothers with children under three years of age. These Volga Germans were placed in so-called special zones in Gulag camps, not technically as prisoners, but as "labour soldiers" (*trudarmeitsy*), although the conditions and treatment of these contingents was similar to that of the prisoners, and, like Gulag prisoners, they were forced labourers. In Western Siberia, the labour soldiers worked mainly in forestry, fishing, and in railroad construction.[120]

While data remain incomplete for these work columns, it is clear that conditions were terrible. As we have already seen, 1942 and 1943 were officially the worst years of the war for Gulag mortality, and the Volga Germans acutely felt the harshness of these years. Between January and August 1942, available data indicate that 11.8 per cent of ethnic Germans in these work columns perished, but this number is likely an underestimation of the total mortality.[121]

Prisoner vs. Non-Prisoner Labour during the War

In these examples, then, we see that forced labour was an important aspect of Soviet total war, although just how much emphasis should be placed on forced labour in the context of the home front deserves further examination. Asif Siddiqi, studying the scientific research camps, argues that prisoners indeed made key contributions to the war effort, but these were highly specialized camps.[122] According to Mark Harrison's data, forced labour accounted for roughly 2 per cent of the Soviet Union's total workforce (including agricultural) before the war, and held steady at 2 per cent during the war, too, despite a decline in absolute numbers.[123] In certain industries, of course, including timber and capital construction, the Gulag played a much larger role before the war (around 12–14 per cent of the total), and continued to do so during the war, too, but the war does not appear to have increased the reliance on prisoner labour from what it was in the pre-war period.[124]

In Western Siberia authorities were able to make use of forced labour in military production, and certainly saw it as an important component of available human resources. Yet simply in terms of sheer numbers, we must view the Gulag as being of only marginal importance to the region's economy and, therefore, the Soviet home front. Evacuees and evacuated factories had a larger economic impact. While the area's camps held approximately 74,000 to 85,000 prisoners at any one time during the period of total war (mid-1941 to mid-1945 – see table 2.1), the almost half-million evacuees, even if they included many children and elderly, helped to compensate for the loss of workers to the front in much greater numbers. Of the evacuees, many worked in agriculture, which was crucially important considering German advances into Ukraine.[125] The city of Novosibirsk itself received 150,000 evacuees in the first year and a half of the war, significantly more than better-known evacuee locations such as Tashkent.[126] The huge state investment required to relocate factories to the region also stimulated the economy, and forced the state to recognize the centrality of the region to the Soviet Union's economy as a whole. In August 1943, by a decree of the Presidium of the Supreme Soviet of the RSFSR, Novosibirsk joined a select group of cities as a "republican" city (even though, as one evacuee noted, "only the very center of Novosibirsk resembled an actual city"), meaning that it took its orders directly from Moscow rather than provincial authorities.[127] The granting of republican status was prestigious, but also a way for Moscow to coordinate the war effort among cities that were particularly crucial for wartime production.

The mass mobilization of the region's women and elderly into the workforce played an enormous role, too. As the region's key demographic historian, V.A. Isupov, writes of the workforce in Western Siberia, "The labour-soldiers of work columns, prisoners, and POWs played an important, but secondary role. The main labour resource of the Soviet Union was its own civilian [*grazhdanskoe*] population." In 1939, in Western Siberia alone, there had been almost 800,000 working-age women who were not in the workforce, as well as 600,000 persons over the age of sixty. Many of these people were put to work during the war.[128] These contingents, plus evacuees, meant that there was a large pool of non-prisoner labour mobilized for the war effort.

Even if one focuses only on prisoners, however, the numbers are misleading. By 1 April 1943, the Novosibirsk Province Camp and Colony Administration was reporting that 51 per cent of its prisoner contingent was unable to work due to poor physical condition.[129] This statistic alone is enough to highlight the extreme inefficiencies of prisoner labour. A 1944 inspection of Corrective Labour Colony no. 8 in Tomsk, to cite another example, found that 437 of the 1028 prisoners in the colony were unfit for physical labour, and this was not even during the harshest period of the war.[130] These figures are significantly higher than Gulag wartime averages, which saw approximately 25–30 per cent of prisoner contingents in this category.[131] Overall Siblag data on labour categories for 1942 underscore the comparatively poor state of the prisoner contingents. Available statistics show that 19.2 per cent of Gulag prisoners were "fit for heavy labour" in 1942, while in Siblag this number was only 4.3 per cent. The middle categories ("medium physical labour" and "light physical labour") were relatively similar, at 17 and 38.3 per cent for the Gulag as a whole, and 13.4 and 37.8 per cent for Siblag. The numbers classified as "weakened or invalids" are particularly striking: 25.5 per cent for the Gulag, and 44.5 per cent for Siblag.[132] Siblag had among the highest proportion of invalids and weakened prisoners of any Gulag camp system.[133] Gulag labour was thus incredibly inefficient. Given Alexopoulos's work showing that even those deemed fit for physical labour often suffered from serious diseases and were in extremely poor physical shape, much of the prisoner contingent in Western Siberia likely was on the verge of death.[134]

Thus, the surface analysis of the smooth transition of forced labour as part of the total war effort in Siberia falters under more intense scrutiny. The authorities were not always comfortable with forced labour contingents; those contingents themselves experienced high turnover and low productivity, mostly due to illness; and non-prisoner labour turned out to be a much more critical part of the story.

That prisoners worked in such close proximity to non-prisoners, with local authorities viewing prisoner labour as just one piece in the human-resource puzzle, however, provides evidence that the wartime Gulag was not particularly about the removal of undesirable elements from Soviet society or about using the pretext of war to gain more control.[135] Local authorities were even willing to use so-called enemies (counter-revolutionaries, exiled populations) to help support the war effort. At least as far as our case study is concerned, the total war effort as it included the Gulag appears to have been quite straightforward: an effort to mobilize all available resources to support the military, with little care for the actual cost in human lives – and that cost was staggering.

Wartime mobilization of the Western Siberian camps during the Second World War ultimately highlights the tragedy of the Gulag. Prisoners, with no choice in the matter, sacrificed their health and, frequently, their lives to the war effort, but in the end human resources such as evacuees and underutilized groups were more important to the regional home front, especially considering the inefficiencies of forced labour. While such labour was marginally useful in terms of numbers of shells, uniforms, and so on that were produced, the human cost was enormous. Even so, the interaction between prisoners and non-prisoners in the region, the quick and total shift to military production, and the pragmatic labour use of those labelled ideological enemies of the regime, all suggest that economic motivations for Gulag operations were more important than political motivations during the Second World War.

It is not possible to assess these motivations completely, or to understand on-the-ground operations of the camps during the war, without further inquiry into the two main groups within the Gulag: prisoners and personnel. The Great Patriotic War saw a concerted effort to use patriotism as a motivating factor for both groups, as opposed to specifically communist/Leninist ideology. To what extent were prisoners patriotic in their response to the war? What about personnel? How did the ordinary men and women of the camps respond to the extraordinary threat of war?

3 Patriotic Prisoners

We always felt our blood ties to the Motherland [*s rodinoi*], we were her children, and we wanted to defend her in the same ranks as everyone. We bombarded the director of the camp with hundreds of petitions to go to the front. But all was in vain. Nobody needed our help, [our offer] was rejected mockingly.

> T.M. Khitarova, recalling how the prisoners
> at Siblag's Iask camp reacted to the outbreak of the war[1]

Prisoners, not surprisingly, responded to the outbreak of war in a variety of ways. T.M. Khitarova's description, above, shows a patriotic impulse thwarted by authorities. Despite the rejection of the petitions of Khitarova and her fellow prisoners, however, many hundreds of thousands of prisoners were released to fight on the front over the course of the war. From those prisoners who have left memoirs, responses range from patriotic efforts to be sent to the front, to concern for family members remaining in European areas of the Soviet Union, to the recognition that conditions could only become more difficult during wartime. The authorities attempted to mobilize prisoners through both the carrot and the stick, with propaganda that focused on a patriotic response and tangible rewards for productive labourers, but little to no concern for the lives of prisoners who were too ill or emaciated to fulfil work norms.

Memoirs remain the best source for understanding the prisoner response to wartime mobilization and conditions in the Gulag. Memoirs are not unproblematic as sources, however. Khitarova's brief recollections, cited above, are part of a collection published to commemorate the fiftieth anniversary of the Stalingrad victory, and so it is not surprising to find patriotic recollections, regardless of whether or not this was how Khitarova felt at the time. Memories can fade or even become part of broader narratives.[2] It was mostly the political prisoners – Article 58ers – who wrote Gulag memoirs, moreover, which means that the memoirs at best represent only a minority of the camp population. There are very few memoirs from those with criminal or petty criminal (*bytovye*) sentences. Nevertheless, memoirs clearly have their use. These accounts are some of the only first-hand accounts from those who suffered in the camps, and it is certainly nearly impossible to paint a picture of life in the camps only through Soviet bureaucratic documents. Many of the camp inefficiencies and cruelties described within the memoir literature – meagre rations, overwork, prisoner-on-prisoner violence, black market activity, and so on – are also echoed in the bureaucratic documents, so there is little reason not to accept at least much of what memoirists write as true, at least from the perspective of prisoners serving similar sentences. In short, while Gulag memoirs have their issues, if treated like any other source and read critically, they can be a valuable tool for insight into the camps. In terms of chronology, moreover, memoirs confirm the harsher stage of the wartime Gulag, but also – and perhaps partially because this date became so etched in the Soviet collective memory – emphasize 22 June 1941 as a key turning point, despite the partial wartime mobilization of the Gulag before this date, as seen in chapter 2.

This chapter also uses many documents from the authorities that focused on the prisoners' wartime experiences, particularly those documents produced by the camps' cultural-educational sections. As partial surveillance, partial propaganda departments, the cultural-educational sections produced materials that are also clearly problematic as a source, but they nevertheless reveal the type of information prisoners would have had available to them, and something about how the regime presented itself, Gulag life, and the war effort to the prisoners. Moreover, as the cultural work was meant to focus on those prisoners with criminal sentences or petty criminal sentences, we can also read between the lines for insight into the experiences of the majority of Gulag prisoners, who are largely missing or caricatured in many of the memoirs written by Article 58ers.

Authorities, of course, could not have been certain how Gulag prisoners would respond to the outbreak of war. Indeed, authorities could not even be certain of the response of the general Soviet population, as they evidently found much evidence of a defeatist mood following the German invasion.[3] Within the camps, there had been a consistent propaganda barrage in the 1930s, showing that prisoners were helping – like those outside of the camps – in socialist construction and could, with "re-forging," become useful Soviet men and women, both within the camps and after release.[4] Had this propaganda been successful, the authorities might have expected an enthusiastic response for the war effort. Now, instead of helping to construct socialism, prisoners were defending the Soviet system against a very real existential threat, just like those on the front lines were expected to do. Prisoners, however, were prisoners because they were, in one way or another, suspect in the eyes of the authorities, particularly Article 58ers, who by definition were anti-Soviet. Authorities could thus logically see these prisoners as a potentially subversive group on the home front. To complicate matters further, of course, the actual conditions of camp life would hardly seem conducive to a patriotic response on the part of the prisoner population. Indeed, many memoirists were shocked that some prisoners retained any loyalty for the regime, given the horrendous conditions of the camps.[5]

We saw several possible prisoner responses in chapter 2, from Mikhail Gorbachev's matter-of-fact description of the shift to wartime production in Tomsk, to D.E. Alin's harrowing accounts of the deterioration of camp conditions, to P.Kh. Ivanov's misplaced assumption that his work in wartime industry would help gain him early release. But these were certainly not the only types of responses, and the variety of reactions attests to the persistent humanity of individuals within the system, as well as the myriad experiences the Gulag itself could produce.

Some prisoners saw the outbreak of war as offering the potential to prove one's loyalty to the regime. Steven Barnes begins his discussion of the wartime Gulag in Kazakhstan by describing the case of the prisoner Vissarion Nikolaevich Pilishchuk, who risked his life to explode some ice that was clogging an irrigation floodgate, later claiming that his "goal was to establish the grain base for the front, and then to request Stalin to review [his] case and, if [he] was not guilty, to send [him] to the front."[6] P.I. Belykh, who served time in Siblag, but was a prisoner in Kolyma at the outbreak of the war, recalls immediately writing two petitions for early release upon hearing about the German invasion. He desperately wanted to be sent to the front. The camp boss refused to pass along the petitions. A later boss tried to assure him that each ounce of gold that he mined while in Kolyma was a blow to the enemy.[7] Vasilii Lazarev, a longtime party member who had been arrested before the war, heard Molotov's radio address announcing the German attack on

22 June 1941 while in quarantine before entering the camp system, and immediately petitioned to be sent to the front, but to no avail.[8] Pilishchuk, Belykh, and Lazarev were just three of thousands of prisoners who, whether for patriotic or pragmatic reasons, requested release in order to fight on the front.[9]

Other prisoners thought less about their own situation, and more about those of their families. Nina Alekseevna Noskovich had only just arrived at Siblag's Mariinsk Transit Camp (after two years in a Tomsk camp) when war broke out in June 1941. She recalls thinking immediately of her family in Leningrad. "In the zone there was a radio on a pole," she writes, "and here we learned that war began, and we heard Molotov's speech." Noskovich then wrote a letter home, asking her daughter to evacuate along with other family to Gor'kii. Her mother responded, however, that they had plenty to eat and there was no reason to worry.[10] Noskovich does not say how long it took to send and receive these letters, and she was also a prisoner with certain privileges in the camps, as will be discussed later, but her reaction to the war and the letters home suggest a surprising ease of communication, given camp censorship and the upheaval of the first months of the war.

Yet if Noskovich was able to find out about the war at the same time as most non-prisoners (i.e., via Molotov's radio speech on 22 June 1941), others were in the dark for several days. Alin recalls hearing about the German attack only on 26 June, when camp personnel told the prisoners directly. This is especially surprising, considering he was at the transit camp station in Novosibirsk at the time, and rumours, at the very least, must have been circulating. His first reaction was a sense of foreboding: "Each of us thought to ourselves, 'What will happen to the country, and what awaits us?'" Two days later, armed guards marched Alin and many prisoners from the transit station directly through the streets of Novosibirsk to what was then the outskirts of the city, in order to work at the Chkalov Aviation Factory.[11]

The prisoners were not the only ones who saw the war as a chance for early release in order to contribute on the front lines. Some within the Gulag administration pushed for prisoner releases as well. In August 1941, central Gulag authorities identified some 18,000 former Red Army soldiers or officers serving relatively light sentences in the camps and sent a report to the Presidium of the Supreme Soviet asking for the release of these prisoners. Many were specialists, including pilots and tank operators, and their value to the front was clear. The language used in such documents is telling, as NKVD vice-director V.V. Chernyshev[12] and Gulag director V.G. Nasedkin asked that former soldiers sentenced for "late appearances in particular, and other unimportant [*malovazhnie*] crimes," who had not blemished their records while in the camps, receive release for immediate active duty. The Gulag's main bosses, thus, acknowledged that many prisoners were in the camps for "unimportant crimes." Only seventy-nine such prisoners were identified in Novosibirsk Province.[13] Clearly, authorities felt that these seventy-nine prisoners, along with the other 18,000, would respond to the war in a patriotic way, and fulfil their duties as soldiers. Through the course of the war, nearly 1 million former prisoners were mobilized into the Red Army, often serving in the most precarious battalions on the front lines.

The Cultural-Educational Department and Wartime Mobilization

Mobilizing prisoners on the home front was not an easy task, given the horrendous living and work conditions for most inmates and the forced nature of their labour. One of the ways in which Siblag attempted to mobilize prisoners was with renewed emphasis on cultural-educational activities.[14] Although there are many parallels between this period and the early 1930s, when "re-forging" individuals was rhetorically the Gulag's purpose, the focus during the war was different. In both periods, authorities measured the success of cultural activities by increases in work-norm fulfilment – in other words, by economic indicators. But the early 1930s rhetoric of "re-forging" was replaced during the war by a patriotic impulse: the more prisoners knew about Soviet successes (including the front-line exploits of ex-prisoners) and the horrors of the Nazis, the more they would do their part on the home front.[15] Thus, once again we see the importance of the war for understanding periodization and the Gulag. As demonstrated in chapter 1, the 1930s were a time of rapid expansion and ad hoc development fuelled by Stalinist policies of collectivization and shock industrialization. The camp system retained a focus, in the propaganda at least, on the re-education of individual prisoners. This focus faded as the 1930s progressed, however, to the point where, at camps like Siblag, cultural activities received little emphasis. The war, however, marked a shift. Economically, the Gulag was now a cog in the total war machine. This shift to wartime mobilization necessitated a re-emphasis on cultural activities, however now not as re-education but part of total war.

In December 1941, the Cultural-Educational Departments for individual camps became their own administrative units, separated from the camp Political Departments (*Politotdely*), which reveals that increased administrative importance was placed on the prisoners' official cultural sphere.[16] The Political Departments now focused their activities on camp personnel. As its own separate entity, the Cultural-Educational Department was required to send regular reports to central authorities, and regular reports meant, at the very least, the appearance of regular results.[17]

The Cultural-Educational Department certainly saw its role as important. A directive from 15 August 1941 discusses the "German fascist" attack and the significance of the Gulag for the war effort, noting that "especially serious attention" should be paid to cultural-educational work, including art circles showing the heroic struggles of the Red Army and newspapers emphasizing positive brigade work.[18]

If authorities sought to use the camps' cultural departments to spur wartime production, however, they had a formidable task in front of them, at least as far as Siblag was concerned. Wartime documents reveal an extensive cultural infrastructure with stationary and mobile libraries, multiple film screenings per day, widespread occurrences of political discussions, and so on. Operations, however, occurred haphazardly at best, especially at the beginning of the war. Prisoners themselves remember Siblag's cultural activities mostly for their absence. Ananii Semenovich Gebel', a prisoner of the Orlovo-Rozovo camp, recalling the period 1940–1, wrote "We didn't receive newspapers from anywhere and did not have a clue what was going on in the world; there were also no books. We only knew the barrack, the field, and work."[19] Aleksandr Klein, a prisoner who later became heavily involved in cultural activities in Vorkutlag, was technically forbidden while in Siblag from participating, due to his counter-revolutionary status. He nevertheless managed, clandestinely, to participate in a camp-wide chess tournament among prisoners and even to attend a few theatrical performances, all with the help of bribes.[20] His experience of Vorkuta, however, made Siblag look like a cultural backwater.

If some former prisoners note the absence of cultural activities, others emphasize them. G.N. Gorchakov, for example, noted with some interest that Siblag's Mariinsk camp had a large theatre, while the city of Mariinsk did not have a theatre at all.[21] If one was privileged enough to work in one of the camp's clubs, moreover, survival was certainly much easier during the harsh years of the war. Nina Noskovich, who had been a fine arts student before her arrest in the mid-1930s, was placed in charge of the cultural club at the Iask camp shortly after the outbreak of the war. Along with two other prisoners, she even lived at the club, where they slept on comfortable cots. The camp boss occasionally visited to chat with her, too, and a civilian employee often brought her extra rations. Noskovich recalls her experience with some guilt, noting that she felt sorry for her friends in the barracks who had to work long hours sewing jackets and uniforms. She even refers to herself by the derogatory term *pridurka*, often translated as "trustee." The "trustees" were those who curried favour with the camp administration and received special privileges. In the club, Noskovich and her fellow prisoner workers directed plays, performed dances, made costumes, painted, and played music.[22] Certainly some prisoners, like Noskovich, took the activities of the Cultural-Educational Department seriously. One of the best-known examples comes from the Soviet Far East, where Vasilii Azhaev was a Gulag prisoner, involved in cultural activities in the camps, and became a Stalin Prize–winning author after his release.[23]

From September 1940 to December 1941, Siblag's Cultural-Educational Department lacked a director. Siblag had been admonished several times during 1941 for the poor state of its cultural work. A February 1941 directive from Gavrilin, the head of the Gulag's Political Department, mentioned that many Cultural-Educational Department administrators ignored central directives, not considering them essential. Siblag was among several camps accused of this, and Gavrilin also accused Siblag of not sending its reports on time.[24] In August 1941, another central directive included Siblag among several camp systems which "in reality had achieved nothing over the last quarter."[25]

The December 1941 appointment of a new director, Comrade Karataev, indicates a renewed emphasis on cultural activities. Karataev's first report, on cultural activities for the second half of 1941 (i.e., for the six months following the German invasion), underscores a litany of failures in the cultural sphere. In one Siblag camp, for example, the "red corner" – the Soviet replacement, usually with portraits of Stalin and local leaders, for the typical icon in the corner of the peasant household – was used as a grain-storage facility.[26] In another, the educator was apparently illiterate.[27] Karataev did his best to turn the situation around. At the very least, he and subsequent directors succeeded in reporting data to indicate some improvements. Reports and statistics on the Cultural-Educational Department's activities were sent twice yearly to central Gulag authorities. The reports generally direct more attention to economic production and work-related issues than to strictly "cultural-educational" activities.[28] The statistics on cultural activities during the war reveal a mixed picture, yet were usually interpreted to show an ever-improving situation (despite admissions of failures in certain areas). In general, then, these reports – marked "secret" or "top secret" – cannot be taken at face value. They read as "socialist realist" documents of their own: prisoners become inspired by knowledge of Stalin's orders concerning the war or the exploits of ex-prisoners at the front, and thus over fulfil their work quotas by huge numbers; thousands of prisoners attend newspaper readings and political discussions and information sessions; and incidences of work refusal go down as prisoners become more politically aware.[29]

There is no doubt that both the Novosibirsk Province Camp and Colony Administration and Siblag maintained considerable cultural infrastructure. In the second half of 1941, Siblag's Cultural-Educational Department reported a total of 1,268 film screenings.[30] This works out to approximately seven screenings per day, although Siblag at the time had around twenty-seven camps and colonies, most with numerous camp stations, so certainly not every prisoner would have been able to access the film screenings physically, even if all prisoners had been allowed to attend.[31] The films were more or less the same films as those screened throughout the Soviet Union, even including some Hollywood productions.[32] The overall trend during the war shows an initial drop in film screenings in 1942, followed by some improvements and some setbacks.[33] Some of the initial decline can be attributed to the division of the Novosibirsk Province Camp and Colony Administration and Siblag in April 1942 (see chapter 2), but the accompanying report for this period blames problems with the distribution of films and a lack of electricity in some camp areas.[34] The Novosibirsk Province Camp and Colony Administration also reported problems with showing films in some camp stations due to a lack of projection lamps and safety parts for the projectors.[35] The picture becomes murky in the latter half of the war, as screenings at the Novosibirsk Province camps and colonies increased, while those at Siblag decreased, and more camp administrations were created with the formation of Kemerovo Province (1943) and Tomsk Province (1944) out of Novosibirsk Province.[36]

Even if the films were propagandistic, the availability of the cinema for some prisoners provided an important diversion from the extreme hardships of camp life. Various theatrical groups, choirs, musical ensembles, sports, and even the camp libraries (both stationary and mobile) also gave certain prisoners a respite.[37] Importantly, moreover, the films, plays, and so on constituted a link with Soviet society. Barbed wire did not prevent the same sort of propaganda and entertainment as was consumed by the general Soviet public from reaching the prisoners. Ironically this included political lessons and discussions about the "fascist katorga" of the Nazi regime in the same year (1943) that the dreaded Tsarist-era name *katorga* (the prison camps started under Peter the Great) was resurrected for special strict-regimen camps within the Gulag system.[38] The irony appears to have been lost on Siblag's educators, unless they were being intentionally subversive. Nevertheless, the cultural links to Soviet society as a whole were more than simply propaganda, as films and equipment often came directly from the local cinefication (*kinofikatsiia*) office, the same office that would have been in charge of bringing the cinema to the Soviet countryside.[39]

As Bacon argues, however, "The occasional political meeting could not hope successfully to re-educate inmates, nor could poorly and selectively stocked camp libraries, although both of these phenomena existed."[40] One of the best indicators of this half-hearted effort at cultural-educational activities is the persistent personnel problem at Siblag's Cultural-Educational Department. In the second half of 1941, the department was staffed at only 63 per cent (127 persons out of 190). Turnover was extremely high, too, as 89 workers had arrived during this period, while 88 left, 40 of whom joined the Red Army.[41] And even though Siblag's Cultural-Educational Department finally had a director by the end of 1941 (Karataev), this evidently did not solve leadership issues. The director who signed the report for the first half of 1942 was named Dubinin. Siblag then divided into the Novosibirsk Province Camp and Colony Administration and Siblag, and the second-half reports for 1942 were prepared by Comrades Sushchev and Bekbulatov, respectively. Bekbulatov remained Siblag's Cultural-Educational Department director for the remainder of the war. At the Novosibirsk Province Camp and Colony Administration, however, the high turnover continued. For the first half of 1943, the director remained Comrade Sushchev, but in the second half Comrade Lebedev took on that role.[42] Staffing was an issue at all levels of the Cultural-Educational Department. For the second half of 1942, Siblag's department was staffed at 68 per cent, while Novosibirsk's was only at 48 per cent (53 of 111). The Novosibirsk Province Camp and Colony Administration improved this to 59 per cent by the first half of 1943 and 72 per cent by the second half, and Siblag managed to increase its staffing levels to 80 per cent by the second half of 1944.[43]

Camp cadres who worked in the cultural-educational sections were mostly poorly educated, although as we will see in chapter 4, this was true of camp personnel more generally, too.[44] In the second half of 1942 at the Novosibirsk Province Camp and Colony Administration, only three out of the fifty-one department cadres had any sort of higher education, although just over 90 per cent had completed at least some middle schooling. Of this same group of fifty-one, only 41 per cent had received training at Cultural-Education Department seminars, and fewer than one in four had been at the job for more than one year.[45] Most department cadres had some sort of party affiliation, whether as full, candidate, or Komsomol members. For most of the war, too, women made up slightly more than half of the department's employees, likely due in part to the many men leaving for the front.[46]

As in the 1930s, prisoners conducted a significant proportion of the "educational" work directed towards other prisoners. By far the most common department activity was the newspaper reading. For instance, in the second half of 1943, a total of 15,265 newspaper readings were reported at the camps and colonies of the Novosibirsk Administration, and 28,936 readings occurred at Siblag.[47] Within the Novosibirsk Administration, 28 party and Komsomol members (presumably department cadres), along with 231 different prisoners, conducted the 15,000-plus newspaper reading sessions.[48] The newspaper readings were likely from the camps' own wall newspapers and production bulletins, although some reports mention including information from *Pravda* in political discussions.[49]

The emphasis of the Cultural-Educational Department had, by this point, shifted from the "re-forging" theme of the 1930s. None of the cultural-educational documents from Western Siberian camps during the war mention re-education. Indeed, as one report states, "The purpose of political discussions, reports and lectures is for the mobilization of prisoners to overfulfil production tasks in the output of defence materials [and] collecting the harvest, mainly by labour competitions."[50] However, clearly some of the re-education "blueprint" of the 1930s remained in the purview of the Cultural-Educational Department, even during the war. Shaming rituals, which had been prominent in the Gulag press of the mid-1930s, continued and, at least according to the department reports, helped turn some of those who refused to work into prisoners who overfulfilled their norms.[51] Just as in the early-to-mid-1930s, moreover, Gulag propaganda emphasized examples to emulate. During the war, these examples came mostly from ex-prisoners who had been released to fight on the front. For camp authorities, these ex-prisoners were the perfect propaganda tools, providing evidence that a camp sentence could turn a prisoner into a productive Soviet citizen. The wartime reports usually include descriptions and excerpts of letters supposedly sent from ex-prisoners to the camps, letters that would inspire prisoners in the camp to do their part "on the home front." One example from Siblag in 1943 reads as follows:

> The former prisoner of Iurginsk camp, K.A. Novak, now a soldier with the Red Army, twice awarded governmental awards, writes to his former camp comrades: "On the approach to Belgorod I destroyed [*unichtozhil*] 10 Fritzes and seized a trophy, for which they awarded me the medal "For Bravery [*Za otvagu*]." On the right bank of the Dnepr they awarded me the Order of the Red Banner and at present they have removed [my] previous conviction and accepted [me] as a candidate of the party [*VKP/b/*] ... But it is necessary to be fearless, for the Fritzes love cowards ... but Russians do not cower before them, overcoming all difficulties and moving fearlessly forward," and so on. He asked [his comrades] to tell all prisoners not to feel sorry for themselves in work, [or to feel sorry for] the idler or saboteur – direct helpers of the enemy. He sends his regards to the advanced brigades and the best workers and asks them to write him a letter.
>
> In response to the letter the prisoners of Iurginsk camp sent him an answer. They wrote, "By the Stalin Constitution Day we had fulfilled our obligations, having executed the repair schedule at the tractor park by 113%. We send our greetings and assure you – glorious defender of the Motherland [*rodiny*] – that we, just like you, are working selflessly on the home front for the rout of the enemy.[52]

While we should no doubt be sceptical about the truth of these reports – after all, conditions were terrible in the region's camps and colonies, especially in 1942 and 1943 – there are, indeed, numerous examples of ex-prisoners who were awarded for their exploits at the front. Several even received status as heroes of the Soviet Union.[53] This particular example is important, too, for the inclusion of prisoners as "comrades" and as a key part of the overall war effort.

Thus re-education, while no longer explicit in the rhetoric, continued to play a role in the Gulag in Western Siberia. And, even though the practice of formally reducing a prisoner's sentence by giving credit for days worked had ended in 1939, prisoners continued to receive early release for good work. In 1939, the Politburo had explicitly stated that prisoners must serve their full terms, with incentives in the form of rewards (higher rations, better barracks, etc.), rather than early release.[54] Local authorities, however, recognized the need for strong positive incentives. The continued use of early release also, of course, under-scores the penal – and perhaps ideological – aspects of the Gulag sys-tem. Prisoners could be rehabilitated, so to speak, if they proved their usefulness through their work on the home front. Barnes argues that, "to some extent, the drive to involve Soviet prisoners emotionally in the battle at the front was successful," and prisoners tried to prove their usefulness.[55] Many of the cultural reports include a section on "early release and reduced sentences."[56] In the second half of 1943, the Novosibirsk Province Camp and Colony Administration allowed the early release of 161 prisoners and reduced the sentences of another 262. Part of the work of the Cultural-Educational Department was to inform prisoners that only through "selfless labour and excellent behaviour in daily life [*v bytu*] can they receive conditional early release."[57] According to the report, prisoners throughout the camp studied the orders per-taining to early release and reduced sentences as an incentive to work harder. The Cultural-Educational Department recognized improved norm fulfilment *and* improved behaviour as the main reasons for granting early release, calling it "one of the best measures" to increase production and teach prisoners good behaviour. In his brief work on Siblag's agricultural camps during the war, Russian scholar R.S. Bikmetov discusses numerous instances of monetary and other awards (including improved rations), along with early release, for especially productive prisoners.[58] The official encouragement for individual pris-oners for self-improvement, with the possibility of tangible awards, clearly echoes the 1930s re-forging campaigns without, importantly, using the same language.

The practice of early release for productive labour, moreover, high-lights the problematic nature – from the historian's point of view – of release from the Gulag. On the one hand, we have seen that the authori-ties released many prisoners precisely because these prisoners were unfit to work and were a burden on the system. At the same time, camp officials held out the promise of early release as a reward for productive labour. Many prisoners with relatively light sentences received early release to fight on the front or, even at the beginning of the war, to make the cumbersome evacuation process a little bit easier for the authorities. Many prisoners left the Gulag simply because their terms had ended. On the other hand, prisoners serving sentences under Article 58 or for especially dangerous crimes were kept in the camps after the end of their sentences, as were some prisoners working at especially impor-tant defence enterprises. Wartime release from the Gulag thus defies

3.1: Siblag prisoners at a Mariinsk work site, 1940s. Photo-Archive of the International Memorial Society. Used with permission.

easy explanation, as a mix of political and economic motivations are apparent in many of these decisions.

Resistance and Survival

If some prisoners exhibited a patriotic response, and the regime certainly emphasized such responses as proper, the reality is much more complex and reveals something of the ad hoc nature of operations on the ground. Resistance was common during the war, whether in the form of day-to-day survival strategies that subverted Gulag regulations, escapes and escape attempts, planned uprisings, or even extended strikes.

In important respects, resistance was everywhere in the Gulag. Lynne Viola argues that Soviet authorities in general tended to see resistance in day-to-day survival strategies: "The greater part of official 'resistance' consisted of acts of resistance that could be described as survival strategies, cultural and religious customs, opportunism, and, at times, sheer common sense, transformed into resistance by the Stalinist lens."[59] Clearly, this holds true of the Gulag. From the cohabitation of men and women prisoners, to black market activity and the smuggling of correspondence, to the procurement of extra rations through favours and connections, many prisoners found ways of subverting Soviet authority in the camps. Falsification of work data, black market activity, and so on, also help constitute the everyday resistance that occurred in the Gulag, resistance that was often necessary for survival.[60]

Evsei Moiseevich L'vov, a prisoner of Siblag's Orlovo-Rozovo camp, recalled that in 1941 the villagers near the camp almost all wore clothing "of the camp type." There was a thriving black market between de-convoyed prisoners and the villagers, involving camp clothing and supplies leaving the camp and cigarettes and alcohol coming in.[61] Official documentation confirms this type of interaction. In 1942, Siblag's Political Department complained of this very activity, although they placed the blame on camp personnel, stating that both civilian employees and guards participated in black market exchanges with prisoners and the nearby population.[62] In one specific case, a party member within the camp administration was accused of smuggling both money and food to a Siblag prisoner from that prisoner's mother, who lived in Novosibirsk.[63] Indeed, as we shall see in chapter 4, illicit interactions and even fraternization between prisoners and personnel was common, violated camp regulations, and could work both to ameliorate and to deteriorate camp living conditions for prisoners.[64]

Subversive activity in the day-to-day lives of prisoners frequently included illicit relationships. According to official regulations, male and female prisoners were to be kept strictly separate, but this was often not the case in practice. Key infrastructure, such as medical and cultural facilities, was usually located in the men's zone of a particular camp or station, and male and female prisoners regularly worked at the same work site, even if their barracks were located separately.[65] Mixed-gender work sites were certainly common at Novosibirsk's Krivoshchekovsk camp.[66] At a December 1940 meeting of the Communist Party organization of Siblag's Corrective Labor Colony no. 6 (Tomsk), a report mentioned, "In our colony there is open cohabitation [sozhitel'stvo, a euphemism for sexual intimacy] of women with men," and later noted, "The struggle against those who violate camp regimen (work refusal, waste, drunkenness, sexual promiscuity) has not yet taken on an inten-sified character."[67] While female prisoners were often exploited and abused sexually by personnel or other prisoners, they could also use their sexuality as a form of barter within the camp economy.[68] Margarete Buber-Neumann viewed this type of barter as relatively ordinary with-in the camps, although she could not refrain from judgment when she wrote, "If you were pretty enough and not overburdened with moral scruples, there was no need to work."[69] Some prisoners even found love in the camps. Anna Larina, widow of Nikolai Bukharin and perhaps Siblag's most famous wartime prisoner, met her second husband while they were both still prisoners, although she says little about this in her memoir.[70] Still, accounts such as Elena Glinka's, which reveal how sex-ual violence contributed to mass death, underscore the extra dangers involved in camp life for women.[71]

Male-on-male sexual violence and sexual intimacy is more difficult to uncover in the documentation, in part because official reports were more concerned with the consequences of heterosexual intimate rela-tions (pregnancies, breastfeeding, nurseries, and so on) than homosex-ual intimate relations, and in part because memoirists rarely discuss these issues or do so "with a shade of disgust."[72] Certainly, homosexual men who found themselves in the camps due to their homosexuality (in late 1933, the Politburo had passed an "anti-sodomy" decree, which was adopted by the various Soviet republics in early 1934) faced dis-crimination and extra hardships.[73] Authorities turned a blind eye, how-ever, to common practices of homosexual relationships between males in the camps that appear to have been based more on informal power networks among prisoners, whereby the "active," usually older, par-ticipant in the relationship gained certain power within prisoner hierar-chy, while the "passive," usually younger, men were at the bottom of the social hierarchy. Certain barracks in certain camps also reportedly functioned informally as male brothels, and men, like some women in the camps, exchanged sex for favours such as better food or other privi-leges.[74] Such activity certainly ran counter to official Stalinist ideology and law, and thus could possibly be categorized as resistance.[75] Like other informal practices in the Gulag, however, some prisoners benefit-ed while others experienced even greater suffering.

The suffering of the Gulag at war is clear, statistically. Although official figures include many problems, not the least of which was the tendency to release prisoners on the verge of death, so that if they sub-sequently died, their deaths were not technically Gulag deaths (see chapter 2), the dramatic increase in mortality during the war is undeniable, and points to a system on the verge of complete collapse (table 3.1). Clearly, too, what these figures underscore is that even though the Soviet Union had partially mobilized in the period from August 1939 to June 1941, the invasion of the Soviet Union by German forces in June 1941 had a profound and immediate effect on the camps, and the situation started improving only after the Red Army began to make significant gains in late 1943, after victories earlier that year in Stalingrad and Kursk. As noted in chapter 2, moreover, living and working conditions were poor for non-prisoners as well, particularly during 1942 and 1943, and much of the mortality in the Gulag was due to the placement of prisoners at the bottom of the supply chain. As Donald Filtzer writes in his study of home front starvation, "Some groups, however, very clearly were deemed expendable, in particular Gulag prisoners and *trudarmeitsy* [the "labour soldiers," mostly Volga Germans, forcibly conscripted into work duty – see chapter 2]. There was no policy to starve them to death, but they were at the bottom of the hierarchy for the receipt of scarce food, and so mass deaths were inevitable."[76]

The mass death of the wartime Gulag meant that survival was always a struggle and a matter, no doubt, of a combination of ingenuity, luck, and one's precise work position within the camps. One of the most common forms of everyday resistance was *tufta*, or the falsification of work norms. The regime's emphasis on production norm fulfilment, both at the individual prisoner level and at the camp level, often meant that documented results were more important than actual results. *Tufta* was widespread. Many former prisoners, for example, report the practice of sawing off the ends of already felled trees in order to make the trees appear freshly cut; these logs then were included in the prisoner's quota.[77] Brigade leaders, it seems, would sometimes turn a blind eye to this practice – they too would benefit from the appearance of (over)fulfilled production norms.

The practice of *tufta* was, of course, economically absurd. One former prisoner, Evgeniia Borisovna Pol'skaia, refers to *tufta* as "the scourge of all creative work, eating into the pores of the entire country."[78] Indeed, according to Siblag prisoner Evsei Moiseevich L'vov, *tufta* was one of the many Gulag-related words that entered the general lexicon of the Soviet population.[79] *Tufta*'s effects were more than just linguistic. Kate Brown, for example, shows how the haphazard, informal practices of the Gulag had a direct impact on the creation and construction of atomic cities in the Soviet Union in the immediate postwar years.[80] But *tufta*

3.1. Official wartime Gulag mortality, 1939–1946, all prisoners

	1939	1940	1941	1942	1943	1944	1945	1946
Deaths	44,730	41,275	115,484	352,560	267,826	114,481	81,917	30,715
Percentage	3.1%	2.72%	6.1%	24.9%	22.4%	9.2%	5.95%	2.2%

Source: Anne Applebaum, *Gulag: A History* (New York: Doubleday, 2003), 582–3.

was necessary, both for the individual prisoner's survival (avoiding as much hard labour as possible) and for the brigade leader's job (reporting positively on the fulfilment of work quotas). As Khlevniuk writes, "Falsifications and exaggerations were a foundation of the forced-labor economy. Both prisoners and their wardens depended on 'trash' [*tufta*] for survival."[81] The *appearance* of a functioning bureaucracy and economic system, in other words, was more important than an actually functioning bureaucracy and economic system. As Viola argues, Stalinist planning resembled socialist realism in the sense that planning reflected "reality" as it was supposed to become, rather than as it actually was on the ground.[82]

The link between *tufta* and survival is clear, as *tufta* allowed a certain respite from the gruelling quotas. As Alin notes, working diligently to fulfil quotas could lead to death by exhaustion, while not fulfilling norms could lead to death by starvation, since rations were tied to norm fulfilment. *Tufta* was thus widespread, as prisoners sought to,

> gain influence with the civilian master who covered duty details. Our brigade leader solved this problem, reaching an agreement with a civilian engineer-master so that he would cover our duty details at inflated rates, and the brigade received more funds in hand, and then those funds were returned to the master. This kind of "action" was then widely practiced throughout the camps of the country. [83]

For some, informal practices were not enough, and luck was the only way to avoid the mass death that accompanied the wartime Gulag. Mikhail Gorbachev writes that he had become a goner (*dokhodiaga*), and the only thing that saved him was that he became de-convoyed, and was therefore able to move outside of the camp zone without guard.[84] His work burden eased, and he now had the chance to forage for berries and other food. Ananii Semenovich Gebel', who was arrested in 1937 and spent almost twenty years in the camps, recalls his wartime experience in a remote camp station of Siblag's Orlovo-Rozovo camp as the most difficult of his entire time in the camps. In 1943 and 1944, he writes, "hundreds" of prisoners died from starvation, and dystrophy was widespread. To make matters worse, de-convoyed prisoners regularly stole from the other prisoners, and informants made life miserable for Article 58ers. Gebel' suffered from a severe case of avitaminosis, had sores and boils all over his body, and survived only because he was finally declared an invalid and admitted to the camp hospital.[85]

It is a curiosity of the Gulag that rations were so inadequate and work so gruelling that prisoners – especially during the war – starved to death or were worked to death quite regularly, but that, if a prisoner could be declared an invalid, camp medical authorities would frequently do everything they could to nurse him/her back to health. The wartime Gulag was a place of mass death, but with considerable medical infrastructure. During the war, the Gulag administered over 1,000 medical institutions, including infirmaries, clinics, and hospitals, with a total of 165,000 beds.[86] Golfo Alexopoulos has demonstrated, however, that as the Gulag evolved, authorities modified lists of ailments, diseases, and disabilities associated with certain labour categories so that it became increasingly difficult to qualify as an invalid and receive anything even remotely approaching adequate care. Alexopoulos sees in these modifications an intentional effort to destroy the lives of Gulag prisoners. Authorities then masked mortality rates by releasing prisoners on the verge of death.[87] Dan Healey shows that the Gulag's Sanitary Department, in charge of the camp hospitals, did what it could within strict parameters to nurse invalids back to health. However, the Sanitary Department followed "the same logic found in civilian industrial and military medicine," where only those deemed "recoverable" were helped, the rest were denied access, and even those declared invalids were still meant to engage in some sort of labour, no matter how symbolic.[88] Siblag's wartime care for invalids certainly came under criticism. One observer described the convalescent area as "typically the most filthy section of the barracks, with overcrowded two-level bunks without any bedding or linens, and no defined regimen or health care for prisoners."[89] Thus, the Gulag frequently reduced prisoners to something approaching bare life, a biological existence without social or political meaning.[90] Camp authorities refused to cure some, removed others (via early release) from the system altogether, while at the same time tried to cure others, so that they could be productive once again within the camp.

Gebel' himself, once he had recovered in the hospital, temporarily gained work there, which helped raise his chances of survival.[91] One of the key survival methods was to manoeuvre one's way into – or even just luck into – a job at the camp hospital or someplace like the Cultural-Educational Department (as in the case of Noskovich), as this usually brought with it a reprieve from heavy labour and the opportunity to secure other privileges. Many well-known Gulag memoirists, such as Eugenia Ginzburg and Janusz Bardach, found work in camp hospitals, and credit this work with easing the burden of camp life.[92] The Sanitary Department conscripted prisoners (along with civilians) with medical training into the camp hospitals, and the Gulag also provided some training courses for prisoners. Many prisoners just learned on the job.[93] These efforts could be life-saving not only for the invalids under care in the camps, but clearly also for those who worked in the medical facilities.

If Gulag authorities frequently turned a blind eye to resistance as a survival strategy – black markets, *tufta*, and so on – there were certain forms of resistance that they punished severely. One major and consistent concern of authorities was escape. In mid-November 1941, the Gulag's deputy director and director of corrective-labour colonies, G.S. Zavgorodnii,[94] issued a report on the Gulag's work from mid-July to mid-November of that year. Clearly, many prisoners saw the outbreak of the war as a chance to exploit the chaos and uncertainty of the times. Zavgorodnii's report shows an increase in escapes from 948 in July to 1355 in September in the camps, and from 512 in July to 1339 in September in the colonies. Roughly 75 per cent of escapees from the camps and 54 per cent of escapees from the colonies had been recaptured by the time of the report.[95] The escape problem persisted into the following year. An April 1942 NKVD operational order (number 0149) directly from Beria noted the unsatisfactory isolation of "state criminals" and the high level of escapes in many camps. In May and June 1942, escapes from the Gulag increased even more, prompting the censure of several Militarized Guard commanders from various camps.[96]

Beria had expressed special concern about escapes even before the German invasion, stating in April 1941, "The escape of prisoners from the camps is considered to be one of the most heinous [*zlostnykh*] forms of sabotage and the disorganization of camp life and production."[97] In an attempt to discourage escapes, he ordered that all recaptured escapees be sentenced under article 58–14 of the RSFSR's criminal code, a counter-revolutionary offence, and that the death penalty be administered to escapees who were "especially dangerous criminals," those who had made repeated escape attempts, counter-revolutionaries, and other serious offenders. Another circular, issued right after the outbreak of the war, actually relaxed these rules somewhat but still made escapes punishable by death under certain circumstances.[98]

Alin, who spent time in several Siblag camps during the war, describes successfully escaping from a camp station near the Chulym River, although he was recaptured. Working by night for two weeks, he and two other prisoners dug a tunnel under a building to an area at the edge of the zone, which was not completely surrounded by fence. They then waited for a thunderstorm to make their escape and were on the run for three days. They became lost, however, and a young boy ("a local Pavlik Morozov," as Alin called him, after the famous thirteen-year-old boy who had supposedly denounced his father to the authorities in 1932, only to be murdered by his own family)[99] turned them in to the authorities in a village where an elderly woman had given them food and tobacco. NKVD officers then took them back to the camp, where members of the Militarized Guard beat them so severely that one of his co-escapees died. Alin and his other friend, Ivanov, got off lightly, however, with six months in a strengthened-regimen barrack before going back to the regular regime. As Alin explains it, he and Ivanov both claimed that they had left spontaneously during the thunderstorm when they saw that the Militarized Guard had left the camp gate open. Thus, not wanting to risk reprisals against themselves for their own negligence, the camp officials covered up the issue.[100]

Escape is one clear form of resistance to camp rules and regulations. While most historical studies of resistance in the Gulag have sensibly focused on the major strikes and uprisings that took place in the camps following Stalin's death, the war also led to an increase in organized resistance, at least if official reports are to be believed.[101] Alan Barenberg highlights the major armed uprising at a remote camp of Vorkutlag in 1942, an uprising that eventually included the occupation of a town and even a battle between the rebel prisoners and 125 guards, with the prisoners emerging victorious. The rebellion was eventually crushed, and the authorities accused the rebels, whose leaders were mainly Article 58ers, of wanting to support the German war effort. Barenberg cautions against taking the authorities' investigation at face value.[102] Such accusations were not uncommon during the war, however, and placed the Article 58ers in an even more precarious position within the camps.

While not nearly as dramatic as events in Vorkuta, armed uprisings – or at least the planning of such uprisings – occurred in wartime Western Siberia, too. A report issued in early December, 1941, listed Siblag as one of a handful of camps where organized rebel groups had planned either an armed uprising, the murder of guards, or a mass escape. In the case of Siblag, former monarchists and others with anti-Soviet sentiment, including Mensheviks, had allegedly planned an armed uprising to coincide with such a time when the Germans reached Siberia.[103] In February 1942 another similar report described a Siblag prisoner who had organized a group of Article 58ers at the Mariinsk Transit Camp. They had planned to seize weapons from the Militarized Guard and then take control of communications, including the telegraph, at the camp.[104] A Third Department special report from 4 July 1942 stated that, due to the work of an informant, the department had uncovered a plot by four prisoners at the Iask factory, all women, who had prepared and hid kerosene at the factory with the intent to burn it down, thus halting the production of uniforms for the Red Army. Two of the four had been sentenced under Article 58, while the other two were serving time as "socially dangerous" individuals.[105]

That authorities uncovered all three of these conspiracies before the planned uprisings took place points to several possible conclusions. Perhaps informant networks in Siblag worked fairly well (especially evident in the third case), enabling camp officials to uncover conspiracies in the planning stages. Or perhaps the authorities simply wanted to show that they were being vigilant, and thus uncovered conspiracies that were not, in reality, anything of the sort, but nevertheless targeted the usual suspects (monarchists, Mensheviks, other Article 58ers). At several other camps, prisoners from the western borderlands, including the Baltics, reportedly organized resistance groups, an explanation that sounds more plausible than a conspiracy of monarchists roughly twenty-five years after the monarchy had ceased to exist. As Steven Barnes points out, "the Westerners carried with them experiences and social memories outside the Soviet system," and during both the war years and afterwards, contributed to fundamental changes in prisoner culture. Prisoners from these borderlands later constituted some of the main participants in the post-Stalin-era Gulag uprisings.[106]

The effect of this borderland contingent was immediately felt in the region's camps. Indeed, the largest recorded act of resistance in the Western Siberian Gulag during the period 1939–45 occurred in the summer of 1940, as Tomasinlag, a forestry camp northeast of Tomsk, was decommissioned in order to make room for incoming contingents of "special-settler refugees" from the western borderlands.[107] Tomasinlag officials seem to have had no idea that their camp was to be closed down. On 3 July 1940, the NKVD ordered the transfer of 5,000 so-called refugees from western Ukraine and Belarus.[108] The NKVD designated Tomasinlag as a receiving area for this contingent, with its conversion to occur in the quickest time possible. Tomasinlag's prisoners were to be transferred elsewhere: the camp administration needed to send the first contingent (3,000 physically fit prisoners) to Unzhlag between 1 July (two days after the order) and 15 July. All prisoners were to be gone by 15 September, distributed to Unzhlag, Usol'lag, Temlag, and Belbaltlag (but not the local Siblag). This "refugee" transfer was part of a larger 1940 campaign directed against various groups from eastern Poland, a campaign that included the forced displacement of many Poles, Ukrainians, Jews, and Belorussians. The campaign related direct-ly to the Soviet annexation of eastern Poland under the terms of the Nazi-Soviet Pact's secret protocols. According to historian Viktor Zemskov, there were three main roundups of Polish "refugees" in 1940, and by April 1941 there were 19,628 "refugees" in Novosibirsk Province, the third-largest contingent after Arkhangel'sk Province and Sverdlovsk Province.[109] The first of these waves occurred in February 1940, the sec-ond in April, and the third from May to July. There was also a fourth wave in May to June 1941. Most of these waves included a combination of ethnic Poles, Ukrainians, Jews, and Belorussians. Given the timing, the transfers to Tomasinlag appear to have been part of the third wave, which included a particularly large number of Jews.

Not surprisingly, Tomasinlag officials were unable to meet the hous-ing and supply needs of the "refugees." Already by 18 July, just two weeks after the original order, there were 18,500 "special settlers" (*spetspereselentsev*) in Tomasinlag, when the camp itself was designed to hold no more than 10,000 prisoners (at this time, too, some prisoners remained in the camp).[110] This meant that the per-person living space in the camp was less than one square metre.

Reeling from the war, the loss of their homes, and the hardships of a haphazard deportation thousands of kilometers to the east, these de-portees from the western borderlands saw the Gulag as the last straw and launched a massive strike. The strike started in the Tomasinlag camps of Asinovo and Taiga, spreading the next day to Kitsa, and the following day to Beregaevo. Although details are lacking in the documentation, it appears that the strikes were not violent but consisted mainly of anti-Soviet slogans, refusals to work, and demands for better living conditions.

A Novosibirsk Provincial Party Committee (*Obkom*) commission arrived on 17 August to investigate the "riot strikes" (*bunta zabastovok*), which allegedly consisted of anti-Soviet agitation, including pro-Hitler slogans. The commission placed the blame squarely on the head of Tomasinlag's Third Department, Saltymakov, and the head of the Political Department, Bekbulatov, who had both left the scene during the strike. Although both had done so ostensibly to obtain help, the Party Committee's commission found them negligent in their duties, as their absences made it easier for the strikers to organize. Clearly, however, despite any anti-Soviet sentiment, overcrowding was the main catalyst for the uprising. The commission noted, "A whole host of families with small children were living entirely under the open sky."[111] The commission itself oversaw the arrest of 49 "organizers" within two to three days and claimed that by 22 August all "refugees" were back at work.

The commission's decisive action was evidently not decisive enough. On 6 September 1940, the Provincial Party Committee met again to discuss the situation at Tomasinlag, noting that strikes were ongoing at several Tomasinlag camps.[112] One participant at the meeting claimed that Tomasinlag's personnel "did not realize that this contingent should be treated differently than prisoners" and again blamed the Third Department and the Political Department for failing to act. Tomasinlag's leadership defended itself by noting that it had not received lists of the incoming contingent in advance, and that the refugee contingent was entirely different from what they were used to, as it included many young children and babies, and many adults who were not accustomed to forestry work. Work at the camp, according to one Comrade Aksenov (position not mentioned), had been going very well in the two years prior to the arrival of the refugees, making the disruption that much more noteworthy. Those present at the meeting recommended relieving Saltymakov, Bekbulatov, and the director of the camp, Borisov, from their duties, with the possibility of party reprimands and criminal investigations. While the fates of Saltymakov and Borisov are unknown, Bekbulatov shows up again in the regional camp administration in 1942 as the director of Siblag's

Cultural-Educational Department, so clearly not all – if any – local punishments were severe.

What is most fascinating, however, is that the Provincial Party Committee blamed both the "clumsiness" of the Tomasinlag leadership *and* the poor planning of central Gulag administrators, who had sent the "special settler-refugees" without sufficient consideration of the amount and quality of living space at the camp.[113] Thus although local scapegoats had been found, local party officials placed blame on central authorities, too. Surely this was a risky strategy. On 6 September, the Party Committee resolved:

> To inform the C[entral] C[ommittee] [of the Communist Party] about the violation of the decision of the C[entral] C[ommittee] and the SNK of the USSR concerning the sending of special-settlers to Tomasinlag and the irresponsible relation of the GULAG leadership to the directing of refugee-special-settlers to Tomasinlag without accounting for the possibility of their settlement and the organization of labour[.] [D]espite the full awareness on the part of Gulag management about the available housing in the camps, and as a result of a superficial and irresponsible relation to the resolution of this problem, intolerable conditions were created in the camps, [including] an unbelievable overcrowding of people ... resulting in diseases and a [high] death rate amongst the settlers.[114]

While it is not clear what happened to this specific contingent, which included ethnic Poles, Jews, Ukrainians, and Belorussians, ultimately many Polish deportees (including some 43,000 Polish prisoners in Gulag camps) were freed by order of the Presidium of the Supreme Soviet on 12 August 1941, in response to the German invasion of the Soviet Union in June.[115] Others were freed later in the war, and a third group freed and resettled in Poland after the war. Many, of course, died in exile in Siberia or Kazakhstan. In any case, after the August 1941 decision, the Asinovo camp of what had been Tomasinlag was then incorporated into Siblag, becoming a prison camp once again.

Experiencing the Special Settlements at War

The fates of the Polish deportees highlight some of myriad issues facing special settlers during the Second World War. As noted in chapter 2, of the minority groups that Soviet authorities targeted in their entirety, the two main groups exiled to Western Siberia during the war, were the

Volga Germans and the Kalmyks. Many other national minority groups experienced exile elsewhere, too, particularly to Kazakhstan. Expanding the definition of wartime to include the 1939–41 period, when the Soviet Union was in a state of partial mobilization due to the Winter War and the annexation of eastern Poland and the Baltics, means that deportees from these regions should also be considered wartime exiles. Unlike groups such as the Volga Germans and Kalmyks, however, Soviet authorities did not exile these other groups in their entirety.

If the experiences of prisoners are difficult to describe due to the small number of available memoirs, this problem is certainly more acute in relation to the special settlements, although there are a few first-hand accounts.[116] The experience overall was one of displacement, almost unimaginable hardships, followed by a sense of perseverance, at least for those who managed to survive. U. Ruta, a Latvian deportee, wrote a detailed memoir of her family's experience of wartime Western Siberian exile. Much of the travel to their place of exile was by barge along the Ob' and its tributaries. These barges were overcrowded but stopped at towns where it was sometimes possible to purchase food and other provisions. Initially, Ruta and her family lived with a "kindhearted" Russian woman, in the corner of a room, and over the first winter ended up trading all of their clothing and supplies for food, sometimes walking long distances to other villages in order to trade. They moved frequently, and life became more difficult as they ran out of supplies to trade. Many of their friends and fellow Latvians did not survive the first winter, and her own grandmother died in early April 1942. Work on the collective farms was difficult due to the harsh climate and improper nourishment of both people and livestock, and Ruta recalls many horses dying, particularly in the spring, when provisions had run out and new crops were not yet available. In all, Ruta's family moved frequently, living in both towns and collective farms.[117]

The oral history project, "European Memories of the Gulag," contains eight interviews of those exiled to Novosibirsk, Tomsk, or Kemerovo Provinces, and of these interviewees only two experienced exile in the region during the war. The first, Rafails Rozentals, was four years old when he and his mother were deported from Riga to a village in the Tomsk region in June 1941, just a week before the German invasion. Rozentals's father had been arrested as a Zionist. As was the case for many other Jews deported to Siberia and other eastern regions, deportation inadvertently saved Rozentals from a more deadly fate under the Nazis. As he states, "The Communists saved our lives." He stresses that there was little chance his parents would have left Riga, had they remained in Latvia, and, indeed, the rest of his relatives were murdered in the months following the German occupation of Latvia. Only a child at the time of deportation, Rozentals expresses few specific memories of wartime exile. Notably, however, he emphasizes the kindness of the Siberian people, stating that, despite knowing that he and his mother were exiles, the Siberians were not hostile and had "good relations with the deportees."[118]

The second, Peep Varju, was, like Rozentals, only four years old when exiled to the Tomsk region in 1941 from the Baltics (in Varju's case, Estonia), and his father, too, had been arrested. Soviet authorities exiled Varju along with his mother and siblings. This is where the similarities end, however. Varju was the only member of his family to survive the experience, and authorities then placed him in a Siberian orphanage during the war. He was transferred back to Estonia in 1946. In his interview, Varju emphasizes the extremely harsh conditions of the settlements and the orphanage. There was such overcrowding in the settlement that he and his family slept on the floor. For food, Varju's mother bartered away what items they had managed to take with them, including, eventually, their clothes, so that they were basically naked, even in the cold. In the orphanage, Varju was forbidden from speaking Estonian, and soon lost his ability to speak the language. His most poignant memory is of a young Estonian girl approaching him, suggesting that they speak together in Estonian. It was at this point he realized that he "remembered not a single word." In the orphanage, Varju became quite ill with typhus, and almost lost his life.[119]

Documents from the settlements confirm Varju's accounts of severe supply issues related to both clothing and food. For example, January 1944 special correspondence from the director of Narym's regional NKVD to the Narym party secretary highlights the extremely poor living conditions that plagued many of the settlements: "All special settlers have completely worn out their clothes, have neither clothing nor shoes, [and] therefore most of them cannot work beyond the premises [of the settlement]. In the majority of cases, this has led to the fact that, at the present time, not one organization will accept them for work. Most special settler families are in a catastrophic situation."[120] Still, an August 1943 report on special settlers in the Kuzbass region had emphasized that many settlers were overfulfilling their work quotas and even volunteering to work harder on the home front. This same report, however, reveals that in the first half of 1943, deaths in the special settlements exceeded births.[121] The high number of deaths attests to a deterioration in conditions, since, by the mid-1930s, births had exceeded deaths in the settlements, as noted in chapter 1.

The Wartime Prisoner File

The experiences of the Article 58ers, the so-called counter-revolutionaries, often called "politicals," form the basis for most of our understanding of day-to-day life inside Stalin's prison camps. They wrote the majority of the camp memoirs, and for many decades their memoirs provided the bulk of the primary evidence concerning the Gulag. Yet they were not a majority of the Gulag population.[122] As we know from memoirs, criminal gangs held considerable power over camp life, and hardened criminals frequently harassed the "politicals," compounding the difficulties of camp life.

This picture, however, is only partial at best, especially when one considers the war years. First, the picture of two main subsets of prisoners (hardened criminals versus the politicals) is inaccurate. Many prisoners in the camp and colony system were the petty criminals (*bytoviki*), those who had relatively short sentences for relatively minor crimes, a point which will be discussed in greater detail below. Second, the strict separation of criminals and politicals into distinct worlds warrants further examination. While most memoirists highlight the huge chasm between these two groups (in terms of education, culture, and behaviour), some, like Janusz Bardach, complicate the picture by showing that prisoner networks at times crossed these boundaries.[123]

The reason historians routinely ignore the petty offenders mostly comes down to geography. Because memoirists were Article 58ers, and therefore tended to be sent to more remote camps, they did not experience the corrective-labour colonies that became increasingly important over the course of the war. By the end of the war, the prisoner population of the corrective-labour colonies exceeded that of the corrective-labour camps. By 1 January 1945, prisoners in colonies accounted for 51 per cent of all Gulag prisoners, and by 1 January 1946 this figure had risen to 61 per cent. They had constituted only around 22 per cent of the prisoners at the outbreak of the war.[124] Article 58ers occasionally ended up in these colonies. The Tomsk engineer (mentioned in the previous chapter), who was granted permission during the war to live outside the zone even though he had been sentenced under Article 58 as a Trotskyist, is one such example. But most of those sent to the corrective-labour colonies were theoretically there under short sentences (fewer than three years) and for relatively minor crimes. Thus, colonies had large numbers of petty criminals. Because scholars have focused on the Gulag's more notorious and more remote camps, this subset of the prisoner population has been mostly ignored not only in the memoirs but also in scholarly accounts.[125] The camps of Western Siberia thus provide a crucial view of the lives of non-political prisoners, as the region's camps included a number of large corrective-labour colonies.

Since few petty offenders or hardened criminals wrote memoirs, the prisoner file becomes an important window into the lives of these prisoners while in the camps. At the same time, these files also highlight the experiences of Article 58ers. Although these sources represent at best only snapshots of the prisoners' lives – snapshots taken by or collected by the administration – we can partially recover the experiences of many prisoners through an examination of these sources.[126] While only a comprehensive study of hundreds or even thousands of prisoner files could point towards a clear picture of the prisoner population, the individual stories that can be ascertained through a more in-depth reading of a smaller number of files still hold value in their ability to rescue individuals who have largely been overlooked, even in the aggregate.

Many prisoner files for those with short sentences are themselves also quite short and contain little information that can shed light on the prisoner experience. A thirteen-page file of a recidivist, sentenced in 1942 to two years (Article 192, section II), who served out his time in Corrective Labour Colony 6 in Tomsk, reveals almost nothing about his time in the camps. From his arrest report, it appears that he had been homeless and unemployed prior to arrest. Of his time in the camps, there is little evidence, except that work refusal got him two days in the penalty isolator in May 1944. He was released at the end of his term in September 1944.[127] In another brief file, a collective-farm worker, forty-eight years old at the time of his arrest in October 1942, spent two years in Corrective Labour Colony 6 for a sentence under Article 79 of the criminal code. He was convicted of allowing the escape of twenty-three of the farm's sheep. Authorities rejected his petition to have his sentence reduced, but he received de-convoyed status in August 1943 and was released from the colony in October 1944, the end of his term. Medical documents had pronounced him healthy throughout his time at the camp.[128]

In some ways, other files reveal more about the hardships of wartime life *outside* of the camps, because they show the type of actions ordinary

Soviet men and women took in order to make do during the war. A prime example of this type of file is that of a mother from Tomsk, sentenced to the Gulag in March 1945, several months after her husband had died.[129] She was released in August 1945 as part of the postwar amnesty, just six days shy of five months after her arrest. Her short time in the camps marked her as fortunate within the context of the Gulag. Her crime, however, was simple speculation in tobacco and matches. She had been convicted of buying and selling tobacco and matches on the black market in order to make a profit. According to the documentation in her file, she started to do so after her husband's death, presumably because his death had led to the deterioration of her family's finances. Authorities accused her of making approximately 5,000 rubles in profits over a period of only several months, a sum approaching the average factory worker's yearly wartime wage.[130] Her initial sentence, moreover, was for five years, meaning she should have been sent to a corrective-labour camp, rather than a local corrective-labour colony, as was the case. Her six[131] children, ranging from a one-year-old toddler to a fifteen-year-old, were to be sent to orphanages, as was common for children of convicted prisoners when relatives could not be easily located.[132] The risks that this prisoner took show the hardships of wartime Tomsk: many people felt forced to risk imprisonment in order to better the welfare of themselves and their families. Yet that one could be sent to the camps simply for trading in tobacco and matches also attests to the harshness of the system as a whole.

Especially lengthy files frequently indicate something unusual about the prisoner's experience. One prisoner, for example, spent the war in the psychiatric hospital in Tomsk. He had originally been sentenced for ten years as a counter-revolutionary (Article 58–8) in February 1929. The exact crime is missing from his file, but the horrors of his situation shine through even in piecemeal documentation. He had been sent in 1936 or 1937 (depending which document one believes) to serve under the jurisdiction of Corrective Labour Colony 6 in Tomsk after being diagnosed with schizophrenia. Instead of housing him at the camp, authorities took him directly to the Tomsk psychiatric hospital. The file reveals an almost Kafkaesque scenario, in which the prisoner's family wrote to authorities, and authorities wrote to each other, trying to figure out whether or not the prisoner could be released. As early as 1939 (the year his sentence technically ended), the deputy director of the hospital wrote to Siblag authorities requesting that the prisoner be transferred to relatives, but to no avail. Several inquiries from relatives (including the prisoner's wife and children) can be found in the file, dating from 1936 and continuing through the war, asking about the prisoner's health and requesting his release. In December 1944, the procurator for Novosibirsk Province refused to grant release, since Novosibirsk Province no longer had jurisdiction over Tomsk (Tomsk Province had been created earlier that year). Finally, the prisoner was released to relatives in July 1945, more than six years after the end of his term.[133]

Many files underscore the declining physical health of wartime prisoners. One such prisoner, the son of exiled kulaks, was only twenty-five years old when sentenced to his second term in the Gulag in 1937.[134] He received his sentence in Western Siberia, and was sent to Tomasinlag, northeast of Tomsk. He initially showed signs of good health. Pre-war reports consistently pronounced him healthy and placed him in the first category of physical labour. He was apparently a hard worker, and even had his sentenced reduced by several months by the time workday credits were cancelled. In early 1940, if not before, he began to send petitions for early release. The first one was rejected in August 1940 and gives no indication that the prisoner is in poor health. Once Tomasinlag was decommissioned, the prisoner remained in the camp, which later became the Asinovo camp of Siblag and then a labour colony within the Novosibirsk Province Camp and Colony Administration. A document signed by a commission from the local procurator's office, dated 5 December 1943 noted that the prisoner was in horrible physical condition and recommended his release. Yet, he was not finally released until after the war, and then only to work as a civilian within the same camp. He was not freed from his civilian work in Asinovo until July 1946 and was sent back to his home in rural Kemerovo Province at the end of September. Another prisoner, also sentenced in 1937 for eight years under Article 58, began the war working in the fields at a camp station near Mariinsk. As his health deteriorated, he switched jobs and worked as a bootmaker in a small workshop within the camp zone. Many of the documents in his file are responses (all rejections) to his various petitions to have his case reconsidered. By the end of the war, he was a physical wreck, declared an invalid, and ordered released in June 1945 "on the basis of the [All-] Union NKVD and USSR Procuracy directive no. 185 of 29 April 1942, freeing from confinement [prisoners] for the inability to use [them] at work in the camp." He was released the following month, however, simply due to his term ending.[135] The documentation does not reveal if these two prisoners died after leaving the camps or if they made a partial or full recovery.

Deteriorating health could, and often did, lead to death. In one prisoner file that contains conflicting information about the prisoner's sentence – a two-year sentence under either article 58 section 10, or 58 section 14 – and conflicting information about the prisoner's birth year, we learn that the prisoner died from TB in September 1944. She had been sentenced in 1940, evacuated to Tomsk during the war, and held past the end of her term under directives limiting the release of Article 58ers during the war. Early in her term, medical reports pronounced her healthy. Documents from the Asinovo camp also reveal that she was well behaved. Although the information is sporadic, we can ascertain that her health deteriorated very quickly, leading to her death in 1944.[136]

The goner (*dokhodiaga*), the prisoner on the verge of death, was a regular, haunting figure of the Gulag. Particularly during the war years, when mass death joined forced labour as a defining feature of camp life, many prisoners suffered from extreme malnutrition and exhaustion, and hundreds of thousands died in the wartime camps as a result. As Alexander Etkind has pointed out, descriptions of the goner reveal him or her to be little more than a purely biological being, whose death lacked meaning.[137] Life in the camp, for the goner, was no longer life in society, a life within recognized legal and social boundaries, but bare life, reduced to its biological functions.[138]

Despite its horrific conditions and appalling mortality rate, a rate that obscures the true number due to the release of emaciated prisoners before they could die in the camps, the concept of bare life does not entirely fit the wartime Gulag. First, as we saw in chapter 2, Gulag prisoners were not exceptions to the regular legal functions of Soviet society, although clearly the criminal justice system became increasingly arbitrary and harsh over the course of Stalin's rule, and the NKVD-run trials of Article 58ers hardly conformed to Enlightenment concepts of justice.[139] Still, Gulag prisoners were tried and convicted under criminal codes.

The responses of prisoners to the war, moreover, suggest that the reduction to bare life was not the main purpose of the camps. Many prisoners had a patriotic response to the war. Others used connections to secure better rations, participate in the black market, or engage in illicit relationships. Still others maintained connections with family outside of the camps. Prisoners and personnel frequently fraternized, suggesting a level of mutual recognition that defies the very idea of bare life. Even the goners, if declared invalids and given medical care, could sometimes recover and serve out their terms.

There is no easy explanation for the paradoxes of the wartime Gulag. Why work many prisoners to the point of near death and then release some, cure others, and allow others to die in the camps? Why reward prisoners who worked hard in the camps with early release, while forbidding others – depending on type of sentence or, at times, type of work – from leaving the camps even after their terms had ended? Why show films and offer other cultural activities to subsets of the prisoner population, integrating them rhetorically into the broader propaganda campaigns of the Stalinist total war effort? Why declare individuals and groups internal enemies, but then allow them to work in key defence industries, at times even with privileges such as de-convoyed status? The paradoxes may be difficult to explain, but they all point to a system that in its combination of formal rules and informal practices, did not reduce prisoners to bare life, or at least, did not seek to reduce *all* prisoners to bare life.

Adding to this complicated picture of Stalin's Gulag at war is the far-from-unified reaction of the camp personnel to the war effort. They, like the prisoners, responded in numerous ways to total war, from reacting patriotically, to using their own informal networks to improve their personal positions. If authorities in Moscow could not be sure how Gulag prisoners would respond to war, they must have been nearly as uncertain about the response of personnel who, like the prisoners themselves, were mostly ordinary Soviet men and women who found themselves in the most extraordinary of situations.

4 Patriotic Personnel

Podrugin, ex-employee of the transit station, is expelled from the [Communist Party]. Podrugin directed a prisoner-support echelon. In May and June Podrugin, along with Komsomol-member Volynkin (dir[ector] of supply), stole food and other tangible assets from the prisoners' fund in the market-value sum of 270,000 rubles. Podrugin was sentenced by the order of 7 August 1932 to ten years deprivation of freedom.

> January 1945 Party Conference for the Novosibirsk
> Province Camp and Colony Administration[1]

"A person?" roared [the Boss]. "There aren't any here! Here are enemies of the people, traitors of the Motherland, bandits, crooks. The dregs of humanity, scum, riff-raff, that's who is here!"

> From the memoir of Sergei Vladimirov, Siblag prisoner[2]

The wartime arrest and sentence of Podrugin for stealing from prisoners and Sergei Vladimirov's description of a camp boss suggest two different views of Gulag personnel. In the first, camp personnel were clearly expected to be competent and honest employees, tasked with ensuring the proper upkeep of the prisoners; they risked significant punishment if they abused their positions. In the second, camp personnel viewed prisoners as expendable, less than human. While these fragments may be based on a difference in voice – with the former representing one perspective of the administration, and the latter a prisoner's viewpoint – they nevertheless point to a curious absence in the literature on the Gulag. We know remarkably little about those who ran the camps and their motivations for doing so.

Ultimately, an in-depth analysis of the personnel in Western Siberia during the Second World War highlights the importance of personal, informal relationships (as opposed to central directives) in the Gulag's day-to-day operations. Camp personnel, for the most part, do not appear to have been highly ideologically motivated. In many respects, they can be considered ordinary Soviet men and women, and nothing stands out in terms of education levels or even membership within the Communist Party. The war gave these ordinary citizens a greater sense of purpose, and, like some prisoners, camp personnel showed patriotism in their efforts to secure victory. Many called for greater vigilance against the enemy on the home front, and thousands more left the Gulag to fight on the battlefront. Yet this greater sense of purpose did not prevent some personnel from abusing their positions for personal gain or from regularly violating camp regulations set in Moscow. Indeed, on the operational level, Stalin's Gulag became the Gulag of local bosses and their subordinates, or even the Gulag that formed through the myriad informal practices of personnel and prisoners alike.

The lack of studies on camp personnel is striking, given the huge amount of scholarly work devoted to the role of the perpetrator in Nazi Germany.[3] Lynne Viola argues that scholars of the Stalin era have ignored the "question of the perpetrator" due in part to lack of archival access during the Soviet period, combined with the different historical trajectories of the Soviet Union and Nazi Germany, where the Soviets were not defeated in wartime nor held to account for human rights violations. She acknowledges, too, that part of the issue relates to the at times unclear boundaries between perpetrator and victim in Stalin's time, with multiple grey zones.[4] Viola notes that Christopher Browning's characterization of perpetrators in Nazi Germany as "ordinary men" may be useful for understanding the perpetrator in the Soviet system.[5] Browning demonstrated that many of those involved in the atrocities of the Holocaust – at least outside of the camps themselves – were not from the Nazi SS or even members of the Nazi Party, but ordinary men with relatively average backgrounds and levels of education. Outward signs of ideological commitment to the cause were not necessary for participation in mass murder. Is this a useful framework for understanding Gulag personnel? To what extent was the Soviet perpetrator "ordinary"?

In Western Siberia, there was nothing extraordinary about those who ran the camps. They were, as we shall see, "ordinary" Soviet men and women. Galina Ivanova's *Labor Camp Socialism* includes a large section on camp personnel, and she demonstrates that despite the Soviet stereotype of the "morally pure, self-sacrificing Chekist,"[6] Gulag guards and staff were generally poorly educated – even in comparison with non-Gulag officials from the NKVD. Indeed, the NKVD often sent its own cadres to work in the camps as a punishment for poor behaviour. Standards of living for staff were quite poor, and there was, at least initially, little concerted effort at training.[7]

While highlighting living standards and educational levels that suggest a certain "ordinariness" of camp personnel, Ivanova and most scholars who have described camp cadres argue that authorities placed considerable importance on "cultivating a sense of hatred in the guards towards the prisoners."[8] Even Anne Applebaum and Steven Barnes, who both uncover many of the grey areas between guards and prisoners (particularly illicit interactions and the acknowledgment that guards could become prisoners and vice versa), argue that guards and personnel were meant to feel hatred towards the prisoners.[9] In one of the most in-depth studies of camp personnel, Oxana Ermolaeva notes the difficulty in recruiting qualified medical staff, the large percentage of prisoners used in key medical positions, and a somewhat ambivalent pragmatism to the NKVD's hiring practices, as the NKVD accepted those with suspect or foreign backgrounds who had difficulties finding employment elsewhere. Despite this ambivalence, Ermolaeva argues that authorities taught the medical staff to see the prisoners as "enemies of the people" and told them to remain vigilant.[10]

In contrast, several case studies of local camps reveal a relationship between personnel and prisoners that was based less on hatred and more on informal networks or the whims of specific Gulag bosses. In Alan Barenberg's detailed study of Vorkutlag, we see a shift during the war from a relatively lax application of the regulations to a much more regimented approach, in part due to the needs of the war effort. One of the main reasons for the change, however, was the appointment of M.M. Mal'tsev as camp commander. Mal'tsev ruled Vorkutlag much like a fiefdom and saw prisoners as a resource for extracting coal, and thus punished and rewarded on the basis of output.[11] As Barenberg writes, "On the whole, Mal'tsev's management techniques suggest that directors of prison camps behaved largely in the same manner as officials did throughout the Soviet Union, combining official authority with less formal activities like patronage in order to accomplish their goals."[12] Some prisoners benefited from Mal'tsev's leadership, while others did not.

Viola's study of the special settlements, which makes excellent use of local sources from the North and from Western Siberia, includes a wealth of material on centre-periphery relations. The picture that emerges is far more complex than that presented in Ivanova's work.[13] At the local level, the Gulag officials who ran the special settlements were essentially "Soviet company men" who, for all practical purposes, "*were* Soviet power" in a given settlement. Viola notes that they were often unqualified for the enormous tasks of running the settlements, tasks made more difficult by high turnover and personnel shortages. However, they had complete power over their jurisdictions, and this led to abuses.

Underscoring the importance of individual decision-making at the local level, Fyodor Mochulsky's memoir of his time as a Gulag boss includes numerous instances when he was able to intervene directly to make important changes that had an impact on prisoners' lives. For example, he describes temporarily falsifying official work-norm data so that prisoners would have time to build proper barracks for themselves, and another instance when he allowed the less physically fit prisoners to set snares near the camp, so that during "the whole bleak winter, every person, including all of the prisoners, had partridge meat every day."[14] In both of these cases, Mochulsky ignored regulations, and thus risked punishment, although we must keep in mind that Mochulsky always paints his actions in a positive light, and remains silent about the ways in which his actions may have had a negative impact on prisoners.

Dietrich Beyrau's recent comparison of the Gulag and Nazi concentration camps underscores the ordinariness of Gulag staff within the Soviet context. Like Ivanova, he highlights the unattractiveness of Gulag positions, but he also further explores the implications of the some of the hardships faced by Gulag staff. For example, he notes that, for the Gulag, "the distance among guards, camp personnel, and prisoners was usually not as great as the distance in German camps. The lower-level personnel and guards had to rely on additional income. Thus corruption chains formed between criminals and prisoner staff, including exiles working in camp industries or camp personnel."[15]

Thus, what these more focused studies of Gulag officials and staff highlight is the significant impact that individual camp commanders and administrators could have on the lives of prisoners, regardless of camp regulations, due to informal relationships and networks. These more focused studies, in effect, downplay the role of ideology in the day-to-day Gulag operations. Ivanova herself even likens the relationship to that of a serf owner and his serfs, arguing that the arbitrariness and self-serving actions (and even, at times, acts of kindness) of local Gulag directors vis-à-vis the prisoners was similar to the serf-lord relationship that had existed in Russia before emancipation in 1861.[16]

These types of individual relationships are not, however, generally evident in statistical information concerning Gulag personnel. Statistically, what is most striking about the Gulag cadres is that the camps faced a constant personnel shortage. While the NKVD had always faced recruitment difficulties for the Gulag system, the war exacerbated the problem: many Gulag personnel left the camps to fight in the Red Army.[17] Recruitment difficulties meant that the practice of using prisoners in administrative positions (and even as guards) never completely ceased, despite repeated efforts from central authorities to limit its extent.[18] Authorities also frequently arrested guards and other camp personnel for various infractions. Prisoners stayed on at the camps as civilians following their release. These occurrences complicate the picture of a strict dichotomy between perpetrator and victim in the Gulag.[19]

At first glance, excavating the motives and attitudes of camp officials seems a daunting, possibly impossible, task. There are very few personal memoirs available from former camp employees, for example,[20] and the information in central archives related to cadres heavily favours statistical data.[21] However, examining the meeting minutes of local camp Communist Party organizations can move us away from analysis based only on statistics.[22] In these meetings, camp cadres discussed a wide variety of topics, from disciplinary measures directed at camp personnel, to the study of the *Short Course of the History of the VKP(b)*, to how to respond to the outbreak of the war, to issues of camp living conditions and economic production. The Communist Party, too, as the "vanguard of the proletariat," provides a crucial lens for assessing the actions and motivations of Gulag cadres and the rationale for the Gulag at the local level. After all, one would expect party members to attach ideological significance to their work; to set examples of how officials and guards were supposed to behave vis-à-vis prisoners; and to lead the camps in economic and cultural matters.

The various Siblag and Novosibirsk Province Camp and Colony Administration party organizations did not see themselves significantly differently from, say, factory party organizations. Emphasis in these meetings fell on the party's role in boosting economic production through raising political awareness and organizing competitions, as well as on various party tasks: membership, discipline, education, selecting members for various committees or conferences, and so on. The party members discussed prisoners relatively infrequently, and the overall picture reveals the prisoners as a resource in plan fulfilment, rather than as "enemies" or as potentially "re-forgeable" individuals. When discussing party propaganda work among non-party members, the stenographic reports and protocols usually refer to the camp *civilian* (*vol'nonaemnye*) population, rather than the prisoners.[23] The language in the documentation changes for a brief period following the German invasion, when the view shifts and there is considerable discussion of the isolation of enemies as the system's main task.

Certainly, too, we find in these documents considerable evidence of abuses of power, bending or ignoring the rules, and utter indifference to the fate of individual prisoners. But the majority of the time, the party organizations concerned themselves more with internal party business and production matters.

Siblag's non-prisoner employees could work in administration, as guards, or in other positions, such as medical staff.[24] While key administrative positions were held by members of the NKVD, most non-prisoner employees were civilians. Complicating the picture, however, prisoners could also hold administrative or guard positions, and many civilian employees were ex-prisoners now employed by the camp. Siblag's many camps, colonies, camp stations, and administrative departments required a large staff. As of February 1941, Siblag employed over 11,000 civilians.[25] The entire prisoner population at Siblag at the time was around 50,000, meaning that non-prisoner Siblag employees were a significant proportion of the camp's workforce.[26] The civilian staff of the Novosibirsk Province Camp and Colony Administration in spring 1942, after the division of Siblag, comprised 6,428 people, a number that was still only 87 per cent of the system's allotted 7,371. Turnover was extremely high at this time, too, with 2,212 new personnel arriving in the first half of 1942, and 2,533 leaving the camp.[27] Just the upkeep of camp cadres cost tremendous sums, a point worth considering when assessing the productive value of forced labour. As noted in chapter 2, Siblag's budget for 1941 allotted 25 million rubles for the upkeep of the guards alone, enough "to build a decent-sized factory [*nemalen'kii zavod*]" according to camp director Kopaev.[28] The ex-prisoners among the civilians often worked in the same positions they had occupied as prisoners, only now for pay and with more freedom of movement. Civilians also worked in the Militarized Guard (*voenizirovannaya okhrana*, or VOKhR), as the NKVD hired many demobilized Red Army soldiers for guard duty.

The Militarized Guard – so called because the guards themselves lived together in barracks and were treated and paid much like soldiers – was the official term for the camp guards. These guards sought to prevent escapes, performed sentry duties, and convoyed prisoners to the work sites but were theoretically not allowed to interact with the prisoners. Mochulsky describes the Militarized Guard as "usually country boys with elementary education."[29] Other guards of a sort, called "supervisors" (*nadzirateli*), enforced camp regimen and ensured that the prisoners were actually working at the work sites, and thus had considerable daily interaction with the prisoner population. The "supervisor" position was a more privileged position than that of the Militarized Guard. Prisoners who were also guards – sometimes referred to as *samookhraniki*, or "self-guarders" – had the same duties as the Militarized Guard and were counted in their ranks.[30]

During the war, prisoners and ex-prisoners continued to hold important positions, even within the camp administration. A Novosibirsk Province Camp and Colony Administration report from October 1942 noted that there had been little attention paid to the selection of staff, which was "littered with all sorts of rascals." In the camp administration alone, the report continued, there were ninety-five workers who had received sentences, including three for murder, ten for absenteeism and lateness, and twenty-one for "abuse of a position of service for mercenary ends."[31]

There were considerable problems with nepotism in hiring practices. Many high-ranking officials had family members working in other departments. Thus, the wife of Shuster, who was leader of the medical department (*sanotdel*), directed a health clinic; the Political Department director Ivanov's son-in-law worked as the deputy director for Corrective-Labour Colony 4, while Ivanov's wife was in the Administrative-Economic Department (AKhO). Twenty relatives of Vol'pov, the head of the Second Department, had arrived in

Novosibirsk – likely as wartime evacuees – along with twenty-two relatives of Shvarts, the director of the Novosibirsk camp. Vol'pov and Shvarts managed to secure food and living space in Novosibirsk for all of their relatives at a time when many camp specialists – not to mention others in the city – went without lodging.[32]

Along with unsurprising corruption, what this nepotism highlights is that running the camps could be, at times, a family affair.[33] That many guards and administrators had their families with them or nearby is worth underlining, for it is yet another indicator of the extent of interaction between the Gulag and Soviet society. To cite another Gulag example, when the Tomsk colony for juveniles converted from a furniture to a munitions factory (now with adult prisoners), 134 new personnel, including engineers, were transferred there to help with production. They brought 145 family members with them.[34] In many Gulag camps, guards' family members even slept with them in the barracks due to a lack of housing; these barracks often were in not much better shape than those of the prisoners, and were sometimes even converted prisoner barracks.[35]

Guarding had long occurred on a relatively ad hoc basis, especially in the 1930s. Many prisoners were used as guards, and many thousands of prisoners even travelled to the work site and back without escort (the latter practice remained prevalent throughout the Gulag's existence).[36] In March 1939, top secret NKVD Order 00268 technically removed prisoners from the Militarized Guard, replacing them with civilians. As the Russian scholar Petrov points out, this move, combined with a pay increase, was at first largely successful. By 1 September 1940, prisoners comprised only 0.2 per cent of the Militarized Guard for the Gulag as a whole.[37] This situation did not last for every camp, however, as the disruptions caused by the war and continued recruitment difficulties meant that, in many camps, prisoners made up a large proportion of the Militarized Guard from the war at least until the mid-1950s.[38]

Gulag jobs – particularly guarding prisoners – were hardly prestigious. The general consensus among historians is that the Gulag was a place to which troublesome Chekists could be transferred;[39] NKVD officials who worked outside of the camps tended to receive higher pay than their Gulag counterparts.[40] It is clear that some Gulag guards viewed their position as a punishment.[41] Yet during the war and postwar years, a position in the Militarized Guard, according to Petrov, gained a small measure of prestige, as demobilized Red Army soldiers began to populate its ranks.[42]

Efforts to improve conditions by increasing pay failed to solve personnel shortages. The number of guards within the Novosibirsk Province Camp and Colony Administration, for example, was regularly well below the desired threshold of 9 per cent of the prisoner population.[43] Data for the spring of 1942 show a prisoner population at the Novosibirsk camps and colonies of 50,453.[44] The number of Militarized Guard as of July 1 of that year was 3,025, or roughly 6 per cent of the spring population figure. Data also support the assertion that the Militarized Guard was not comprised of the ideological elite, especially at the camps and colonies of Novosibirsk Province. Only 3 per cent, for example, had party status, while 2.2 per cent were candidate members and 8.8 per cent were Komsomol members.[45]

The Militarized Guard especially, as the main barrier between dangerous criminals, counter-revolutionaries, and Soviet society, in theory had to be politically reliable. Yet they, along with other camp employees, could also be part of the problem. Sidorenko, the deputy director of the Novosibirsk Camp and Colony Administration's Militarized Guard in charge of supply, had earlier directed supply at Dal'stroi and had lost his job there for selling bread and other foodstuffs on the black market.[46] A February 1942 directive from Siblag's Political Department noted that civilian employees and the Militarized Guard often traded goods with both prisoners and the surrounding population, thus facilitating a black market in camp supplies.[47] The Political Department complained that camp clothing was being sold on the black market at great expense to the system, placing the cost in the region in the hundreds of thousands of rubles, and noted that the problem was particularly acute in the urban areas of Novosibirsk and Kemerovo.[48] The Political Department did not offer specific measures to prevent black market activity, merely calling for explanatory work among the Militarized Guard, "concrete measures" (unidentified in the document) to secure the camp's borders, and an end to the squandering of camp resources.[49]

A March 1942 NKVD circular (number 107) worried about "doubtful foreign" (*somnitel'nym chuzhdym*) elements within the Militarized Guard. There were many within the ranks who were either former prisoners or were of suspect background, including those who had previously served in the White armies or were former kulaks, counter-revolutionaries, bandits, or recidivists. The circular called for a purge of these types from the Militarized Guard, even though there were problems attracting cadres at that time.[50] That there may have been significant numbers of personnel with suspect backgrounds is not surprising. Not only were many personnel themselves former prisoners, but some individuals with suspect backgrounds actually sought employment in the camp system out of worry that they might be arrested if they remained in Moscow or other major population centers.[51]

Training for Camp Personnel

Part of the system's personnel issues lay in the generally poor state of training for the guards and other Gulag cadres. In May 1942, Gulag director Nasedkin complained that many riflemen (*strelki*)[52] did not know how to use their rifles, particularly foreign-made models; had poor knowledge of their duties; and ultimately were unable to guard prisoners properly.[53] Nasedkin criticized many camps for not planning training exercises for the guards. He singled out the Novosibirsk Province Camp and Colony Administration as particularly problematic, interestingly, not because some of the bosses were unacquainted with the rules and regulations but because they failed to adapt these rules to specific conditions: "In several camps at UITLK UNKVD for Novosibirsk Province the task of the ongoing training of the Militarized Guard is concerned only with the reading of charters and manuals, without relating [the information] to the concrete reality of the given camp, [and] without practical actions related to the given camp's specific climactic conditions."[54] Thus, their Moscow superiors could admonish Gulag officials both for ignoring regulations and for not adapting those regulations to local circumstances.

A key problem, as the above circular makes clear, was that many Gulag cadres simply were not qualified for the job. The lack of experienced technical personnel certainly contributed to economic difficulties. In a February 1943 letter to Nasedkin, one high-ranking Gulag official explained that one of the reasons for low munitions production at the Tomsk factory and elsewhere was the "lack of cadres who have any experience" in related work.[55] Poor training and lack of qualified personnel were issues in many administrative positions, too. For example, take the educator at the Novosibirsk camp's cultural and educational section (KVCh), in charge of running propaganda campaigns and basic literacy programs for the prisoners: in 1941, the director of Siblag's cultural-educational department (KVO) reported,

> The KVCh inspector of the Novosibirsk camp, Comrade Baranov, is apparently so illiterate that he could not read the newspaper out loud to the

prisoners; and when they asked him at a political discussion, "What is the USA? [*Chto takoe SShA?*]," he was unable to answer and declared, "This is not our concern."[56]

As discussed in chapter 3, at the outbreak of the war, the cultural sections in some Siblag camps were not even staffed, and the cultural facilities – such as they were – acted as storage facilities for the camp.[57] Through most of the 1930s, most Gulag cadres had received no special training outside of their training as NKVD officers.[58] By the late 1930s, there was only one school, located in Kharkov, specifically for the training of Gulag personnel for various positions of responsibility within the camps.[59] For most positions, it was during the war, in 1942 and 1943 – possibly due to the recognition of the need to make the system more professional – that several schools opened up around the Soviet Union to train cadres for specific tasks.[60] By late 1944 there were ten Gulag schools for training cadres of various types.[61] One of these was located at Siblag's headquarters in Mariinsk. It trained gunsmiths (*oruzheinykh masterov*), and while it was one of the Gulag's smallest training facilities in terms of the number of pupils, it was also one of its most intensive, with a six-month course. The Siblag school opened in November 1942 with a three-month course designed to enable participants to repair all types of arms.[62] Elsewhere, schools trained cadres for various leadership positions – including as camp bosses for subcamps and camp stations, cultural-educational section directors, general supply section directors, and lieutenants for the Militarized Guard – and various positions related to the breeding and training of guard dogs.[63]

Authorities reorganized the central Kuibyshev school (relocated from Kharkov) during the war.[64] In September 1944, the Kuibyshev school became the Central Gulag School, designed to prepare leadership cadres (initially 500) in five-month courses.[65] While enrolled in the program, the participants were to receive wages equivalent to their prior position; extra stipends were available for inspectors (*inspektorskogo sostava*)[66] and for accountants. Grading occurred using the traditional five-point system.[67] The wartime emphasis on training, which continued into the postwar years, suggests a growing impetus towards the professionalization of camp cadres. The chaos of the war may have forced the hand of the Gulag and NKVD administrations, as experienced, qualified cadres were now more difficult than ever to find and something had to be done to ameliorate the situation. Beria himself recognized that, despite obvious contributions to key economic sectors, the Gulag's overall operations were extremely costly and inefficient, and thus needed improvements.[68]

A detailed 1940 NKVD circular and booklet concerning the training of camp Second Department (Accounting and Distribution) workers gives an idea of the type of instruction they were supposed to have received.[69] Notably, the booklet states that the camps' purpose is twofold: first, to isolate criminals and secure the interests of state security; and second, to contribute to the economic development of the country. The training was divided into eighteen themes involving numerous courses. The first three themes related to general information about the camps: the first was on camp organization, the second on types of places of confinement, and the third on the structure of the Second Department. Most of the remaining themes had to do with the specific record-keeping tasks of the department. Thus, these themes point to the increased bureaucratization of the system. On paper, the Gulag resembled a modern bureaucratic organization.

Harsh wartime conditions and the mobilization of cadres for the Red Army exacerbated the problem of a lack of sufficient personnel, and worked to prevent the bureaucracy from functioning efficiently. A report on the movement of the peripheral and administrative staff (*nomenklatura upravl. i periferii*) at the Novosibirsk Province Camp and Colony Administration for the first half of 1942 is particularly revealing.[70] Out of a staff listed at around 6,500 for spring of that year, a total of 2,533 of these cadres left the camp during this time, while 2,212 were hired on.[71] As one Siblag prisoner recalled, in 1941 and 1942, "with each passing day there were fewer and fewer young riflemen [*molodykh strelkov*]. They were replaced by old [guards], too old or unhealthy to fight at the Front."[72]

As is clear from table 4.1, over one-third of those who left in the first half of 1942 joined the ranks of the Red Army; slightly over 20 per cent left because of "family circumstances and personal reasons [*lichnomu zhelaniiu*]." Of the thirteen reasons given for vacating a position, negligent or criminal behaviour do not factor heavily, but are prevalent enough to suggest a significant lack of discipline among camp employees. Including every reason on table 4.1 from service discrepancies (*Po sluzhebn. nesootvetstviu*) down to official misconduct (*Za dolzhnostnye prestupl.*), around 17 per cent of those cadres who left the Novosibirsk Province Camp and Colony Administration in the first half of 1942 did so because in one way or another they were not fulfilling their duties. The category of "staff reductions" – curious given that there were

4.1. Administrative personnel departures, Novosibirsk Province Camp and Colony Administration, first half of 1942

Reason for departure	Total number	Number as %
Military service	865	34.3
Family/personal reasons	529	20.5
Staff reductions	253	9.9
Transfers to other camps	250	9.5
Health	196	7.8
Service discrepancies	120	5.1
Failed background checks	109	4.4
Discipline infractions	65	2.5
Violation of 26 June 1940 labour law	49	1.5
Immoral actions	39	1.5
Counter-revolutionary activity	12	1.4
Official misconduct	26	1.0
Death	11	0.4
TOTAL =	2533	100%

Source: GANO f. P-260, op. 1, d. 24, l. 1. Numbers are as reported on the document. Clearly, there are some typos on the document. The percentages add up to 99.8, likely due to rounding. More troubling is the number versus percentage for counter-revolutionary activity. One of these numbers (or both) is incorrect. Other percentage calculations are slightly off, if actual numbers are accurate. Finally, the total adds up to 2,524, not 2,533, as reported.

shortages – may simply indicate restructuring, but it is certainly possible that this category could mask disciplinary infractions or even poor health among the staff.

Notably, of the 2,533 who left, 62.7 per cent had been at their positions for less than a full year and almost 93 per cent for fewer than three years. Clearly, few of these cadres had much experience in their specific positions, which no doubt had a negative impact on efficiency. For the first half of 1942, the incoming contingent had a higher percentage of party members and was better educated than the outgoing contingent, perhaps because many within the incoming contingent were older than those sent to the front. That being said, these new cadres were hardly extraordinary. Party members or candidate members made up only 5 per cent of the incoming contingent, only 2.2 per cent had completed some sort of higher education, and only 7.3 per cent had completed secondary school.[73]

For the entire Gulag, the movement of cadres must have caused huge headaches. In 1944, 14 per cent of all NKVD cadres (91,523 persons) left the NKVD, almost half from the Gulag. The largest proportion (approximately 32 per cent) left for family reasons. Authorities expressed optimism at this, however, because "only" 14.2 per cent had left due to some sort of negligent or criminal activity, while more than 85 per cent left for other reasons, including family, illnesses or age, and Red Army mobilization. In that same year, however, 181,134 persons joined the NKVD. Both the NKVD and the camp system were beginning to replace lost personnel by the last years of the war. Over 80,000 of these new recruits, many of them demobilized Red Army soldiers, went to work in the Gulag.[74] By January 1945 the Gulag as a whole was still showing a staffing shortfall in many areas.[75]

At the Tomsk Provincial Department of Prison Colonies (OITK TO)[76] in the first half of 1945, already after the situation had improved, only 83 per cent of positions were filled (2,162 out of 2,605 workers).[77] Of these 2,162 workers, moreover, almost 78 per cent had worked in the system for fewer than three years. Problems were especially acute where specialists were concerned. The Tomsk Prison Colonies could not find sufficient medical and veterinary staff, and lacked enough skilled engineers. Thus, non-party, poorly educated, unskilled, and inexperienced workers were the norm among wartime Gulag staff in Western Siberia.

The poor living and working conditions for most Gulag cadres are particularly striking. A central directive sent to all leaders of prison camps, administrations for prison camps and colonies, and departments of prison colonies in early 1943 noted that there had recently been cases of serious illness for many within the Militarized Guard, including pellagra, scurvy, dystrophy, and anemia, many of the same diseases prevalent among prisoners and all suggestive of extremely poor nutrition.[78] The directive blamed improper food, and inadequate rest and medical services, but also refused to lay the blame on central authorities, claiming, "The state supplies everything that is necessary so that the riflemen will be in good health, but certain local leaders and commanders have a criminally negligent relationship to the organization of food and rest for the riflemen." There had been three cases of death from pellagra among the Militarized Guard at the Novosibirsk Province Prison Camps and Colonies in January 1943 alone. Guards often worked long hours, too, frequently as many as thirteen to fifteen hours per day.[79] Conditions for prisoners, of course, were much worse.

The Communist Party in the Gulag

While many of the guards and camp personnel seem to have been more or less ordinary Soviet men and women, there were also members of the Soviet ideological elite – the Communist Party – who worked in and ran the Gulag camps. On the whole, however, even the camp party members do not appear to have been motivated overtly by ideological concerns, at least not as far as day-to-day camp operations were concerned.

The party structure in the camp system had been formalized in 1937 with the creation of a Political Department (*Politotdel*) within the Gulag and each of its camps.[80] The party organizations within the Gulag were not large. Almost all directors of individual camps and of the Militarized Guard were party members, but, according to statistics from the mid-1940s, only about 18 per cent of Gulag personnel as a whole were members of either the party or the Komsomol.[81] In a 1943 letter, Ivanov (unidentified in the documentation) complained that the Primary Party Organizations for the Novosibirsk Province Camp and Colony Administration were too small. The letter, written to Maslov, the head of the camp's Political Department, listed eleven Primary Party Organizations, with an average of only nine members each (the largest – the Krivoshchekovsk camp – had twenty-one party members and the smallest – the Novosibirsk Transit Station – had only two).[82] While organizationally small, the party was, for the most part, active within the camp system.

Party activities in the Gulag mirrored party activities within Soviet society at large. While Barnes argues that the *Politotdel* attempted to highlight the dangerous nature of the prisoner population,[83] a reading of the Western Siberian meeting protocols for various camp and colony party organizations reveals a focus on issues of membership and planning for political lectures and discussions. Party business, rather than prisoners, was the priority; the protocols only infrequently mention prisoners. As elsewhere, study of the *Short Course of the History of the VKP(b)* was mandatory for party members, although in practice, just as outside of the camps, not all members were conscientious in their studies.[84] Disciplinary measures, too, frequently came about due to abuse of one's position, alcohol-related incidents, or the misplacing of party identification cards, all of which were common outside of the Gulag.[85] In 1944, for example, the Party Control Commission[86] for the Novosibirsk Province Camp and Colony Administration investigated forty-five party and candidate members. Of the top four reasons for investigation (loss of party documents, abuse of a position of service, connections with prisoners, and drunkenness, respectively) only one, connections with prisoners, related directly to the Gulag.[87]

These disciplinary infractions, particularly the loss of party documents, nevertheless had important connotations when associated with the camps. While discussing two cases of lost party documents at a February 1941 meeting, several party members at Corrective Labour Colony 6 expressed worry that such documents could end up in the wrong hands. As one participant stated, "Because of a lack of vigilance amongst certain communist comrades, party documents may fall into the hands of enemies of the people."[88] The loss of party documents was, however, considered a grave infraction even outside of the camps.[89]

Just as in a factory party committee, many of Siblag's party meetings focused on economic issues. This was especially true of centralized meetings. In January 1942, Siblag held its first all-camp party conference, with party representatives from every camp, colony, and camp department. These conferences continued on an annual basis throughout the war. While not exclusively devoted to production issues (indeed disciplinary and training issues figure prominently), economic output appears to have been the biggest concern. It is through the party's disciplinary activity, however, that we can gain great insight into the history of the "elite" of the camp personnel.

Party members employed in the Gulag were frequently the subjects of disciplinary procedures due to their creating informal networks with prisoners in order to smuggle goods in and out of the camps. The black market flourished in part due to connections between prisoners and camp personnel.[90] These types of connections also went beyond black market arrangements, extending to fraternization and sexual relations.[91] Such infractions were sometimes ignored, but, on the part of party members, were often regarded as an egregious lack of vigilance.

Prisoners at times benefited directly or indirectly from the illicit actions of party members. There are, for example, numerous instances of the disciplining of party members for smuggling alcohol to prisoners and, even, for drinking with the prisoners themselves. In June 1940, at the Zavarzino colony, one Zakharov received a strict reprimand for un-party-like behaviour, which included instances of drinking with prisoners. According to the discussion of his case, he frequently drank with his driver, a prisoner, and also appeared drunk in front of other prisoners.[92] Interestingly, at a January 1940 meeting, Zakharov had accused another official of similar behaviour, noting that this official often took his driver (a prisoner) to the neighbouring village and that they would come back together, drunk. Zakharov may have had some inkling at this meeting that he might face future problems, however, as he was forced to defend the colony's production record against accusations that a group of wreckers was operating within the colony.[93]

Even in the harsher-regimen camps of the region, such connections were common. In February 1940 at Tomasinlag, one party member, Plekhanov, was fired from his job and given a strict reprimand with a warning, in part for binge drinking earlier that year. One incident in particular stands out. His fellow party members accused him of taking, without permission, two prisoners to the local grocer (*produkty*) and then leaving them in town without any surveillance. Plekhanov then allegedly got drunk and brought the prisoners back to the camp, throwing them into the penalty isolator without reason. To top it all off, he took 590 rubles from a prisoner commissary worker (*zakliuchennogo larechnika*), even though he lacked the authority to do so. Five days later, he had still not given the funds back to the camp's financial department. Here we see clear examples of how the authorities' abuses of power could at times help prisoners, while at other times harm them. Two prisoners had the opportunity to move about town unsupervised, which surely must have been a welcomed reprieve from camp conditions; later, however, the camp official punished them through no fault of their own, and the same official then allegedly stole prisoner funds. Plekhanov, moreover, got off rather lightly: he was not, at this point in any case, expelled from the party or criminally charged, although he did lose his position.[94]

The frequency of these types of infractions is difficult to assess. In March 1941, the head of Siblag's Political Department described the need to liquidate all instances of illicit connections between civilian workers, guards, and prisoners. In 1940, for Siblag as a whole, he reported that authorities had uncovered thirty-seven cases of illicit connections between guards and prisoners and thirteen cases of guards living with women prisoners.[95] While clearly an affront to the rules and regulations governing the camps, these numbers are not high, given the size of the camp: Siblag's prisoner population was 40,275 as of 1 January 1940 and 43,857 on 1 January 1941.[96] Nevertheless, the numbers were high enough to catch Moscow's attention. The Gulag's central Political Department listed Siblag as one of four camps "where connections between civilian workers and prisoners have become common occurrences."[97] It is also likely that reported cases were only the tip of the iceberg. After all, the memoir literature is filled with descriptions of corrupt officials, some of whom used other prisoners for their personal gain. A prisoner of Siblag in the early 1940s, for example, remembers that the head of the camp's Third Department – certainly a party member due the Third Department's important role in internal surveillance – conducted strict surveillance work with the help of some prisoners, who would steal from others without fear of disciplinary measures.[98]

The authorities consistently blamed connections with prisoners, drunkenness, and other disciplinary infractions on a lack of vigilance and a lack of party activities. In a report on the political condition of the guards at the Zavarzino colony in February 1940, the head of the guards (a party member) complained of numerous instances of illicit connections between guards and prisoners. Several party members linked this immoral behaviour directly to a lack of political-educational work and the party's failure to raise the guards' cultural level.[99] Poor party work, both in relation to other personnel and to the prisoners themselves, not only led to numerous regimen infractions but also had a direct impact on economic output, as party work was seen as a key part of labour mobilization (and, conversely, as a scapegoat for problems). For example, at a February 1941 Siblag party meeting, the party blamed the unfulfilled economic plan on poor party work, arguing that the party had not worked hard enough to mobilize the camp or to prevent improper behaviour. They downplayed more obvious problems, such as the lack of sufficient fuel.[100]

Yet it is hardly surprising that party matters were stressed over seemingly more practical ones. Indeed, the improper behaviour and lack of sufficient vigilance of its members undermined the party's role as the vanguard of the proletariat and its educative function within the camps. If party members did not behave morally, or with sufficient attention to mobilization and other matters, then how could one expect guards, much less prisoners, to do the same?

Most of the disciplinary examples above deal with the 1939–41 period of partial wartime activity. Did the German invasion of 22 June 1941 change party discipline within the camps? On 25 June, just three days after the invasion, the Primary Party Organization of Siblag's Asinovo camp (formerly part of Tomasinlag) held a closed meeting to discuss Foreign Affairs Minister Viacheslav Molotov's radio address from 22 June.

The meeting's discussion centred on the need to prevent illicit interaction between the prisoners and the surrounding population, and on the party's important role in this endeavour. The head of the party organization, Petrov, began by saying, that "now, like never before, it [was] necessary to mobilize the Party-Komsomol and union organizations for the guarding of prisoners in the zones and at the work sites," and that party members needed to be examples of excellent workers. In the ensuing discussion, one participant, Pantileeva, pointed out that just like the Red Army, they, too, were dealing with a "barbaric enemy." Pantileeva gave an example of a woman in the nearby town whose husband was serving his sentence in the camp. She worried that the prisoner, who worked at the Forestry combine (*Lesokombinat*), would be able to see his wife: "In this regard we comrades must be tactful [*chutkim*] and vigilant, or else the prisoners working outside of the camp will talk with free citizens [*s vol'nymi grazhdanami*]." As one solution, they decided to make sure that the number of prisoners sent to work would be in proportion to the number of guards available. As party members, they were clearly conscious of their vanguard role. Later in the discussion, Pantileeva stated that a communist must "stand a head taller" than non-party members, and pointed out that it had been wrong to replace a Komsomol member with a non-party member in a leadership position. One participant, Gorskii, put it simply: he argued that enemies were now conducting "enemy work" (*vrazheskuiu rabotu*) and that a strong home front would always defeat the enemy. He noted, rather ominously, that special settlers, intent on defeating the Soviet Union, surrounded them.[101]

References to prisoners and special settlers as enemies of the Soviet Union are surprisingly infrequent in these meeting protocols, and seem to be confined mostly to the period following the 22 June 1941 invasion, as the example above illustrates. Indeed, one of the first post-invasion orders concerning the Gulag, issued on 22 June itself, forbade those sentenced under especially dangerous provisions of the criminal code – including terror, spying, Trotskyism, and banditry (but not murder) – from leaving the camps, even after their terms expired. This decree affected many thousands of prisoners across the Gulag. Many individual camps also unilaterally ended certain privileges (on 22 June, for example, Ustvymlag in the Komi Republic banned all correspondence and newspapers).[102]

Yet even at the Asinovo camp meeting, discussed above, not all participants viewed the prisoners only with suspicion. While discussing the need for increased vigilance, Comrade Egorov emphasized the contributions that prisoners could make to the war effort, especially through forestry work and defence production. The party should focus, he argued, on using the workforce more efficiently.[103] Egorov's focus on economic production was echoed a few days later by Siblag's director, Kopaev, who in a lengthy document outlined Siblag's preparation for war, noting in particular that those prisoners in contract camps were the key source of labour for defence-related construction, and calling directly on the camp to raise the production and labour-use rates of prisoners. Only after outlining Siblag's actual and potential contributions to wartime mobilization did Kopaev focus on vigilance, particularly on the need to prevent escapes.[104]

Even though there was general agreement among the Siblag administration that party discipline had to improve if the economic and political needs of the home front were to be met, if anything the situation became worse. Escapes increased following the war's outbreak. Disciplinary infractions spiked, too. At a closed party meeting of the Asinovo Primary Party Organization on 23 March 1942, in a response to a directive from the Gulag's Political Department's complaints about poor party work, the Asinovo party organization found that it, too, had many problems. In the first half of 1941, there had been fifty-two cases of infractions, while in the second half 103 cases – an almost 100 per cent increase following the outbreak of the war. There were four times as many disciplinary measures for drunkenness (admittedly from a low starting point – three in the first half of 1941 to twelve in the second).[105] This could be partially due to increased vigilance in punishing improper behaviour, but given the chaos of the first years of the war, when many camp personnel left to fight on the front and supplies were severely disrupted, it is likely that party discipline actually worsened, at least until the war's latter half.

The illegal flow of goods in and out of the camp continued. At the same meeting, the party organization discussed the file of party member V.N. Pantiukhov, a Militarized Guard division leader, who was caught stealing food products and giving them to his daughter. A search found 1.7 kilograms of stolen millet, 800 grams of butter, and one kilogram of macaroni, at a time when camp supplies were beginning to dwindle. The organization then voted to exclude Pantiukhov from the party and transfer his file to judicial organs (v sud).[106]

Importantly, too, party members could also be blamed and punished for the worsening conditions in the camps. In January 1942, the Party Control Commission of Siblag's Political Department decided to give N.F. Korostel', the secretary of the Akhpunsk camp's party organization, a strict reprimand with a notation in his file. The commission also recommended that he be removed from his position as party secretary.[107] The recommendation related not to the abuse of power but to Korostel's "negligent relation to duties." The control commission noted that Akhpunsk had incredibly poor living conditions: the bathhouse and disinfection chamber (*dezokamera*) were not working properly, resulting in a massive lice problem; food distribution was poorly organized and foodstuffs often stolen; prisoner complaints and petitions were ignored; prisoners were beaten; and ill prisoners were forced to work, dying as a result. All of these problems had caused a massive increase in mortality. Two hundred and fifteen prisoners died in November 1941, out of a prisoner population of 4,723 (a staggering 4.5 per cent of the prisoner population in just one month, well before camp mortality rates reached their peak). On an annual basis, this would mean a mortality rate of over 50 per cent at the camp, many times above the Gulag average. Criminal proceedings had already opened against the director, Bekshaev, at the time of the control commission's report.

If some personnel emphasized that prisoners were enemies, while others spoke of them as a potential resource for the war effort, much of the tone of the party documentation is neutral where prisoners are concerned. The stenographic reports and meeting minutes usually refer to camp inmates simply as prisoners. They use the abbreviated form of the Russian word for prisoner – *zakliuchennyi*, which is *z/k* (or *z/k, z/k* for the plural). Likely, then, the word used at the various meetings most often was the abbreviated *zek*, a potentially dehumanizing term. The *zeks* became, in a sense, a subspecies within the Soviet world and were often, as we know, treated that way after release, when they had difficulties in finding employment, housing, and so on.[108] In part, though, the use of this language may simply show that many camp authorities saw the Gulag as a normal prison system, regardless of the fact that it was located within a highly abnormal Soviet context. The term "enemies of the people," or even simply "enemies," comes up only rarely when applied to prisoners.

Although camp cadres rarely referred to prisoners as enemies, at least in official documents, their statements often reveal an extreme indifference to prisoner welfare. The worst of this rhetoric supports the contention that camp authorities viewed *zeks* as less than human. In 1941, Kopaev emphasized the need,

> to break some of our workers of the rotten theory [*gniluiu teoriiu*] of the impossibility of using invalids in light work in the manufacture of consumer

goods ... We have 9,000 invalids and around 15,000 persons suitable to light labour [and] the maintenance of invalids costs us 11 million [rubles] per year; therefore, the task of using invalids in the manufacture of consumer goods should save us 6–7 million rubles of public funds.[109]

Were it not for the invective, "rotten theory," the above statement might be mistaken for an impulse towards bureaucratic efficiency. Clearly some camp personnel (if not the commander himself) recognized the need to improve the health of invalids by keeping them away from manual labour.[110]

Local orders to divert prisoners to various construction sites and other projects suggest that authorities thought of prisoners as a resource in fulfilling economic tasks. As discussed in chapter 2, the Provincial Party Committee, for example, regularly ordered Kopaev to transfer large numbers of prisoners to specific defence enterprises, such as the large Novosibirsk complex, Combine 179. These types of orders demonstrate little room or concern for the individual prisoner, who becomes just a number. This is an example of the bureaucratic mechanism at its worst: the need for a timely completion of an important factory complex resulted in a complete lack of concern for the welfare of those involved. As usual, when discussing a system as complex as the Gulag, however, the issue is more complicated. We have already noted that individual relationships between prisoners and camp personnel could make a large difference in the lives of some prisoners.

The final word on prisoner-personnel relations should be given to the prisoners themselves. How did inmates at Siblag and the Novosibirsk Province Camps and Colonies feel about those who ran the camps? To some degree, the picture is not black and white even from the prisoners' point of view. Certainly cases of reported abuses are the norm, rather than something exceptional. Sergei Vladimirov, who spent ten years in Siblag from 1942 to 1952 and wrote his memoir under the pseudonym V. Belousov, vividly describes an incident when a guard killed a young prisoner who had been fishing, and the prisoners gathered around, threatening to beat the guards. The local camp's boss, Major Zvantsev, whom the prisoners had nicknamed "The Boar," objected to the prisoners' complaints:

"You are thinking of rebelling?" he shouted. "To the cooler [*kartsere*] with you! I'll send you to the tower! Bastards [*Svolochi*]! ... Disperse!"
    From the crowd could be heard in response:

"Murderers! They've killed [*zagubili*] the boy!"

"For a little fish … a person died [*pogib*]!"

"A person?" roared The Boar, "There aren't any here! Here are enemies of the people, traitors of the Motherland, bandits, crooks [*zhuliki*]. The dregs of humanity, scum [*mraz'*], riff-raff [*podonki*], that's who is here!"[111]

There are positive memories of some camp officials, too, although these certainly stand out as exceptional. Evsei Moiseevich L'vov, a prisoner at the Siblag agricultural camp of Orlovo-Rozovo in the early 1940s, had great respect for the camp's boss, F.I. Kazachenko,[112] who apparently had tremendous knowledge of animal husbandry. L'vov writes, "And to this day former Orlovo-Rozovians [*orlovo-rozovtsy*] recall F.I. Kazachenko with kind words. He was strict and fair, a true Party-man, faultlessly honest, and cultured [*kul'turn*] in all essences."[113] L'vov was not, as he himself suggests, the only former prisoner to remember Kazachenko this way. Sof'ia Sergeevna Potresova recalls Kazachenko telling her and her fellow inmates, "We don't consider you to be prisoners, but only temporary detainees [*vremenno zaderzhannymi*]."[114] What these various prisoner impressions highlight, then, is that the personalities and decisions of individual camp bosses – as opposed to bureaucratic directives from Moscow – were key to the camp experience.

Ordinary Soviets

Overall, the wartime camp personnel in Western Siberia is noteworthy for its ordinariness. While there were no doubt camp officials who were ideologically motivated, most camp personnel were not party members, and even those who were party members often behaved as if ideology did not matter.[115] In some ways there was a certain banality, then, to the actions of these guards and camp party members.

Indeed, one is tempted to argue that Gulag cadres were not that different from other Soviet bureaucrats. In her classic study, *Eichmann in Jerusalem*,[116] Hannah Arendt posited that Eichmann, a high-level Nazi bureaucrat, was complicit in the Holocaust not because of anti-Semitism or because he was a sociopath – she presents him as a relatively normal person – but because he abdicated moral responsibility to Hitler/the Nazi state, that is, he was just following orders. For Arendt, although there was nothing peculiar about Eichmann, Eichmann's choice was an individual one, and thus his abdication of moral responsibility did not actually absolve him of that responsibility. Arendt referred to this as the "banality of evil," and thus suggests that any of us might have acted similarly under a similar system.[117]

Yet although there was a certain "banality" to many Gulag cadres, the tendency of Gulag officials to flout the rules and, occasionally, to form informal networks with prisoners, shows that they were not simply cogs in a bureaucratic machine, following orders without considering the consequences.[118] They were looking out for their own self-interest, too.

The evidence from the party documents from the Western Siberian Gulag, as well as other materials pertaining to the camp personnel, suggests that, for the most part, those who worked in the camps were "ordinary" Soviet men and women. They were, generally, poorly educated, and even from within the NKVD they were not from the elite. While motivations are almost impossible to discern, the presence of informal practices and networks and the absence of a focus on the prisoners as enemies suggests that ideology was not a major factor in the actions of camp personnel. Based on Communist Party meeting minutes, it seems that many camp personnel approached their work in the Gulag administration in a similar way to personnel of any other Soviet institution. It is only right after the outbreak of the war that the documentation under review for this chapter reveals a temporary focus on the prisoners as dangerous enemies. At this time, some personnel invoked a patriotic response, calling for the need to defend the Soviet Union from enemies on the home front, or even leaving the camps to serve on the battlefront. Yet the rhetoric of prisoners as an internal enemy faded as the war progressed.

Despite the ordinariness of the Gulag personnel, it is crucial to understand that the Soviet Union during the Stalin era – and especially during the war – was itself quite extraordinary: extraordinarily violent, and in an extraordinary state of mobilization.[119] Little value was placed on the lives of individuals. Indeed, there is a cruel indifference to the lives of prisoners either explicit or implied in many of the party organization documents. Thus, the ordinariness of the personnel did not make the Gulag any less deadly.

The Gulag was an undesirable place to work. Many personnel, like Mochulsky, were no doubt sent to work in the camps with little choice in the matter. Others may have chosen to do so due to difficulties in finding employment elsewhere. Many were former prisoners whose best chance at employment likely was in the camps, or who had little choice but to stay on and work in the camps, often conducting work similar to what they had done as prisoners. Demobilized soldiers made up another large contingent of Gulag personnel. The institution was deadly and violent, but those who worked for the institution were decidedly ordinary. Perhaps many of them truly believed they were part of a struggle for a much larger cause, but they more likely saw the Gulag as their place of employment and tried to do their best to make the situation work for them. That very few personnel went out of their way to help the prisoners; that many others were cruel and sadistic; and that most appear to have been indifferent to the extreme suffering of the camp system suggests that violence had been normalized in Soviet society. To be an ordinary Soviet, in other words, meant to participate either directly or indirectly in a system of extraordinary violence.

The camp systems of Western Siberia emerged from the war having contributed to Soviet victory. The highly efficient, bureaucratic system that existed on paper was no match for the corrupt system based on informal practices that existed in the camps themselves. Yet, Soviet victory appeared as an endorsement of the Soviet system. Is it possible to measure the success of the Gulag at war? Was its success due to its part in the full mobilization of the Stalinist system or to the flexibility of its informal practices? How, in other words, can we assess the Gulag's role in Soviet victory?

5 The Gulag's Victory

It is undeniable that the forced sacrifice of Gulag prisoners, including those of Western Siberia, contributed to the war effort. Ex-prisoners fought at the front, often in the most extreme conditions. In the camps, prisoners worked on almost every aspect of the wartime economy and produced foodstuffs, uniforms, and military equipment and munitions in significant quantities, even as conditions deteriorated to the worst recorded levels. Although the sacrifice was forced, and involved suffering on an almost unprecedented scale, Gulag prisoners gave their lives, through their labour, for the war effort. Can we say that Soviet victory in the Second World War, the Great Patriotic War, was the Gulag's victory?

The answer to this question involves a discussion of the nature of the Stalinist forced labour system in light of the war, as well as an understanding of what happened to the system following the Second World War. This chapter thus explores the Gulag in a more comparative context and ends with a section on the postwar fate of Siblag and the other camps of Western Siberia.

The Gulag and the War: A Comparative Perspective

While some studies of the Gulag have made underdeveloped comparisons to slavery, and more recent works have attempted to situate Stalin's Gulag within either a global history of concentration camps or a global history of convict labour and prisons, there is no scholarly consensus on how to explain the Gulag within its global context. Ultimately, a comparison is useful for underscoring the peculiarities of the wartime Gulag. The Soviets, unlike most wartime belligerents, did not place more emphasis on systems of forced labour – particularly camp-like systems – in the context of the war.

The first book-length scholarly analysis of the Gulag, the 1947 publication *Forced Labor in Soviet Russia* by Dallin and Nicolaevsky, frequently refers to prisoner labour as akin to slavery, although the comparison is not developed in any systematic way.[1] Many studies from the 1950s and 1960s continued this trend, even emphasizing the comparison in their titles (e.g., *The Soviet Slave Empire* or *Stalin's Slave Camps*), but not developing the comparison except for an emphasis on the cruelty of forced labour in both cases.[2] The first real systematic study of the Gulag as a system of forced labour was Swianiewicz's 1965 book, *Forced Labour and Economic Development*, which argued that an economic rationale, sometimes unbeknownst to the actors themselves, was behind much of the camp system's expansion under Stalin.[3] He compared collectivization and dekulakization, for example, to the British enclosure process of the eighteenth century, because in both cases mass numbers of peasants found themselves displaced or pushed off the land and into the cities, in search of work. The Soviet case differed due to the huge number of arrestees, whose forced labour then served as a check on wage inflation during industrialization. As Swianiewcz's critics have pointed out, however, this interpretation leaves little room for the clearly political motivations behind much of the Gulag's expansion, including the pacification of the countryside.[4]

More recent studies focusing on forced labour have done so as either a point of comparison with other types of convict labour or a window into the Stalinist industrialization process. Marcel van der Linden, for example, argues that the main impetus for the Gulag's expansion lay in the needs of the industrializing state, when resources such as timber and gold were crucially important.[5] Paul Gregory emphasizes that authorities chose the locations of most Gulag camps, particularly the more remote ones, based on economic considerations, although his work as a whole argues that political motivations played the main role in the creation and expansion of the system.[6] James Harris's study of the Urals region points to local officials who sought to expand the local camp system in order to have a ready supply of forced labour.[7] Despite these apparent uses of forced labour, many scholars have emphasized the extreme inefficiency of prisoner labour in the Stalinist system, a point reinforced in the present study.[8] On the more explicitly comparative side, Christian de Vito and Alex Lichtenstein's edited volume, *Global Convict Labour*, situates the Gulag within a broader history, dating back hundreds of years, of the use of some type of prisoner labour.[9] On prisoner labour, Jeffrey Hardy has argued that an approach that condemns prisoner labour in the Soviet Union without also discussing prisoner labour in other contexts is misleading (when, after all, it is allowed in both the 13th Amendment of the US Constitution and in the UN Standard Minimum Rules for the Treatment of Prisoners, adopted in 1955). He also demonstrates that many of the post-Stalin penal reforms that fundamentally changed the Gulag followed a similar trajectory to that of other European penal systems.[10]

Looming large over the broader comparison with other systems of forced labour or even other penal systems, is the comparison with the camps of Nazi Germany. Scholars who have developed a more theoretical approach to the concentration camp often use the Nazi camps as the basis for their respective theories and then broaden this to include other systems, like the Gulag. So, for example, Tzvetan Todorov's exploration of morality in the camps includes frequent reference to Gulag memoirs.[11] Giorgio Agamben's focus on biopolitics as key to understanding the concentration camp is based primarily on the Nazi camps, but he occasionally applies these ideas to the Soviet Union in passing.[12] Perhaps most prominently, Hannah Arendt's early, but still influential, *Origins of Totalitarianism* makes a more systematic comparison between the Nazi and Soviet camp systems, although this is not the main focus of her book. She argues that both camp systems were fundamental for securing compliance among the non-camp populations, and also acted as a laboratory where "everything is possible," and were thus key for the existence of the totalitarian system. For her, the Nazi camps were "hell" and the Gulag "purgatory," mostly due to the less systematic nature of death in the Stalinist camps.[13]

More recently, historians Dietrich Beyrau and Alan Barenberg have separately conducted more focused comparisons of the two systems. Beyrau's study is part of a larger work that seeks to situate the Gulag not in a global framework of convict labour, but within a global framework of mostly twentieth-century concentration camps, while Barenberg's is part of an anthology related to the global history of slavery.[14] Beyrau notes many similarities between the two systems, arguing that the "camps were embedded in the transformation of society – the development of the apartheid society in Germany and in German-controlled Europe and in the formation of a society organized according to stratified rights in the USSR." However, he points to key differences between the two systems, arguing that one's status as a prisoner was more "fluid" in the case of the Soviet Union, and that, unlike in German camps, Soviet prisoners and their guards often came from the same milieu.[15] Barenberg also notes a key difference that may help explain the issue of social distance: except for POWs, those used in forced labour in the Soviet Union were primarily Soviet citizens, while in the case of Germany during the Second World War, the forced labourers were primarily non-German citizens.[16]

The complexity of the system, particularly the overlapping economic, political, and ideological motivations behind Gulag operations, make easy comparison difficult. Yes, the Gulag was a system of mass incarceration, but it was also part of mass mobilization and a place of mass death, particularly during the war. One of the most intriguing possible frameworks for understanding the Gulag comes from a phrase Steven Barnes uses in his key work, *Death and Redemption*. He states that the Gulag "was both a concentration camp and a penal system," arguing that this made it both similar to, and distinctive from, both types of institutions.[17] He explores characteristics the Gulag shared with other modern penal systems, in particular the idea of rehabilitation, while also demonstrating the shared characteristic of the concentration camp, mass death. The characterization of the Gulag as both a prison and a concentration camp (rather than either/or), provides a starting point for comparison. Barnes views the Gulag's main purpose as weeding out or reforming individuals as part of a broader attempt to transform society, a process shared by other modern states.

Barnes' arguments relate closely to those of Zygmunt Bauman, in his now classic work, *Modernity and the Holocaust*. Bauman argues that the violence of the Nazi death camps (he does not deal with the significant, less systematized genocidal violence on the Eastern Front) progressed naturally from the bureaucratic structures, population politics, and interventionist policies of the Nazi regime, characteristics shared, to some degree, with all "modern" states. Bauman developed the idea of the modern state as the "gardening state," cultivating certain characteristics and weeding out others.[18] Bauman's arguments have heavily influenced a strand within the historiography of the Stalin era that views the Soviet system as emblematic of modernity, with elements such as large bureaucracies, major state-driven population shifts, a propensity to categorize and track individuals, and increased surveillance.[19] Stephen Kotkin, moreover, argues that the mass mobilization and mass politics of the Stalin era were part of a European "interwar conjuncture," not that dissimilar from that occurring in other modernizing states.[20]

What was the nature of the Stalinist bureaucratic system as it pertained to the Gulag? As we have seen, Siblag and nearby camps as well as special settlements developed in an ad hoc manner, both before and during the war, only rarely achieving stated goals and frequently beset with inefficiencies. No doubt seeking to standardize and streamline Gulag operations, the NKVD increasingly sought to codify camp regimen and practices. In the period from 1939 to June 1941, when the Soviet Union was in a state of partial wartime mobilization, the NKVD issued a flurry of regulations governing most aspects of camp life. These regulations dealt with such issues as ration regimes, discussed in chapter 2, censorship, and the day-to-day functioning of the camps.

As noted in chapter 1, the first Soviet Corrective-Labour Code of 1924 had placed considerable emphasis on rehabilitation.[21] Although this code also speaks of isolation and deterrence as goals of punishment, the rehabilitative aspect of incarceration is front and centre. Later regulations, however, have little to say about issues of correction, re-education, or re-forging. For example, the August 1939 NKVD operational order no. 00889 included the massive "Temporary Instruction on Regimen," which attempted to regulate most aspects of camp life and death through 152 regulations, some of which included subsets of rules. The first three regulations read as follows:

1. Confinement regimen for prisoners in corrective-labour camps is determined by the present instruction and must ensure:
   a. The reliable isolation of criminals, sentenced for crimes stipulated by the criminal code;
   b. The organization of orderly upkeep of prisoners in the camp, ensuring the most effective use of the prisoners' labour.
2. For the purposes of ensuring state security those sentenced for counter-revolutionary crimes are sent, as a rule, to camps located in remote areas.
   With regards to prisoners sentenced for counter-revolutionary crimes apply a strengthened regimen.
3. Prisoners of corrective-labour camps are distributed to camp stations ... that are organized close to the work sites.[22]

There is no mention of re-education in the 1939 instruction at all, even though the instruction contains 152 rules (some with subsets of further rules) covering almost all aspects of camp life, from daily schedules, to punishments, to privileges, to death and release. Even a 1940 regulation on the tasks of the cultural-educational department, which logically should focus on re-education, is unclear on exactly this point. According to this document, cultural-educational work in the corrective-labour camps and colonies had a dual purpose: "a) re-educating prisoners, sentenced for petty [*bytovye*] and administrative [*dolzhnostnye*] crimes on the basis of highly-productive, socially-useful labour"; and "b) making the most effective and efficient use of the labour of all prisoners on production for the fulfilment and over-fulfilment of production plans." Thus re-education, according to this regulation, was technically available only to those with relatively light sentences, but even here the emphasis was on economic output.[23]

Rehabilitation, a key link with modern penology, was de-emphasized (though never abandoned) as the Stalin era progressed and the Gulag expanded. Despite this, however, other modern concerns – including increased bureaucratization and regimentation, as well as continued tracking of individual prisoners – are clearly visible in the Gulag regulations for the years immediately preceding the Second World War. The *intention* of these rules conforms to a modern ethos concerning the rational ordering of society. The *result* of many of them, however, was increased inefficiency and an entrenchment of informal practices.

We have already seen in chapter 2 that ration regimes were nearly impossible to follow. The war exacerbated supply problems, but the regulations themselves were onerous enough to ensure non-compliance, especially given understaffing and frequent personnel turnover. Rations were not the only area where official regulations were virtually impossible for individual officials to follow. The documents regarding censorship in the camps are similarly problematic. In late 1939, the NKVD issued detailed instructions for camp censors.[24] The instruction required censors to use seven different forms, depending on the circumstances, and also to enlist the help of the Third Department if the prisoners' letters contained certain information.[25] According to the regulations, there was only one censor for every 1,300–1,500 prisoners in subcamps, and one censor per subcolony, regardless of the number of prisoners. In colonies with fewer than 800 prisoners, moreover, the censor was also in charge of the sending and receiving of packages and organizing prisoner meetings with relatives.[26] Given the low educational levels of camp personnel generally, as well as chronic staff shortages, issues discussed in greater detail in chapter 4, it is difficult to imagine that censors would fill out each necessary form in each case. Recent scholarship regarding camp correspondence confirms this assessment, revealing that certain prisoners evaded censorship with the help of informal networks, but also that officially censored letters did not always black out sensitive information.[27]

By making many rules overly bureaucratic or nearly impossible to follow, the Gulag bureaucracy encouraged inefficiency, corruption, and a flaunting of the rules. In his study of the Victorian prison, Richard Ireland notes that, due to understaffing, rules could actually lead to arbitrariness, rather than create more predictability:

> Clearly the introduction of a rule of silence into a gaol in which it had not been used before was likely to increase the number of cases of rule-breach which called for punishment. Moreover, since it is a rule easy to breach and, in an understaffed institution at any rate, almost impossible to enforce absolutely, it may necessitate a degree of tolerance and/or the danger of arbitrary enforcement.[28]

The Gulag faced similar issues. Given the detail and paperwork involved with some of the rules and regulations, and the general inefficiency of the system and chronic staff shortages, rules were arbitrarily enforced, whether intentionally or not.[29] Ultimately, while attempting to foster centralization and greater uniformity, the bureaucratization of the system helped to entrench informal practices prevalent in the camps. Local authorities often found it easier to ignore the rules, creating their own systems or fiefdoms, than to follow the rules to the letter. Prisoners, for their part, also created networks and practices that circumvented rules and regulations.

While modern on paper and very much concerned with issues of "modernity," including population politics, institutionalized power, and mass mobilization, the Gulag and its host of informal practices point to more traditional methods of power negotiation, from exchanging favours, to patronage, to petitioning. Thus, while the Gulag was part of the Soviet Union's drive towards modernization, it both reinforced and in many ways created more traditional practices, reminiscent of "neo-traditionalism," as outlined by such scholars as Terry Martin, resurrecting the argument from Ken Jowitt.[30] According to Martin, neo-traditionalism is a type of modernization, but a modernization that entrenches informal practices that are akin to more traditional, less bureaucratized pre-modern power relationships. At the very least, Soviet modernity was a particular type of modernity, one that mimicked and even developed characteristics of Western modernity (bureaucratization, mass politics, social welfare, information gathering, biopolitical concerns), while nevertheless relying on a wide array of informal practices.[31] A version of modernization, and even a type of hyper-modernity, was always the goal, but on-the-ground operations frequently undermined this goal.

During the Second World War, there was a greater emphasis on professionalization on paper, as dedicated training facilities appeared in numerous Gulag camp systems in order to train personnel. At the same time, on-the-ground practices continued to function haphazardly, at best, as incredibly high personnel turnover meant most of the staff was poorly trained. High prisoner turnover due to death and release, combined with supply problems exacerbated by the war, meant that the Gulag, in practice, relied on informal practices to function.

In the postwar period, the trend towards greater bureaucratization continued. The 1947 "Instruction on Regimen for Prisoners at Corrective-Labour Camps and Colonies of the MVD" points to important postwar changes in the system. Of note, both the 1939 instruction for corrective-labour camps and a similar 1940 instruction for corrective-labour colonies had been "temporary" instructions on regimen. In 1947, these "temporary" instructions were combined into one, single, regimen manual, with the word "temporary" removed from its title. Under "General Provisions," the instruction notes that camps should hold prisoners with sentences greater than three years, while prisoners with shorter sentences should be sent to colonies. This, however, is one of the few differences listed between the two types of incarceration. The 1939 and 1940 instructions had differed somewhat in their language on the locations of camps. The 1940 instruction on colonies had noted the possibility of locations within urban areas, while the 1939 instruction on camps had called for their locations to be removed from population centres. The 1947 instruction uses the same language for both, however, merely stating that they should be located "as close as possible to the place of work and separated from population centres [*punktov*]."[32]

The differences between corrective-labour camps and colonies should thus not be exaggerated, particularly in the postwar years. As of 1 January 1951, for example, prisoners serving five-to-ten-year sentences made up the largest number of prisoners in *both* the camps and the colonies (58.8 and 46.3 per cent, respectively), and in *both* the camps and colonies the next-largest group was made up of prisoners serving three-to-five-year terms (14.2 and 19.5 per cent).[33]

The 1947 instruction reinstates the emphasis on re-education that had been mostly missing since the early 1930s, stating that camp regimen was meant to isolate prisoners, prevent escapes, ensure discipline, ensure the re-education of prisoners on the basis of their labour, ensure the correct organization of prisoners' labour, and ensure that prisoners lived in appropriate conditions.[34] Propaganda on the transformation of the prisoner had focused on a patriotic response to the war and a duty to work hard in order to defeat the enemy, but postwar regulations reveal a reversion to pre-war ideas of rehabilitation, although the early rhetoric of "re-forging" is not used. In all, the document is much more detailed than either the 1939 or 1940 instruction. It includes a total of 338 rules, many also with subsections, suggesting a continued drive towards greater regulation and an increase in the bureaucratization of the camp system.

In key respects, neither "modernity" nor "neo-traditionalism" adequately describes the Stalinist camp system. Whatever their reliance on informal networks, both Stalinism in general and the Gulag in particular were far from traditional. The Stalinist mobilization state attempted to transform society radically, and a focus on neo-traditional practices risks missing this radical element of Stalinism. Stalinism relied on total, mass mobilization, epitomized in many respects by both the Gulag and the Second World War. Subsuming the system under the term "modernity" is also problematic, however, for it tends to de-emphasize what was peculiar to the Stalinist system. The term "modernity" accounts for the increased bureaucratization and record keeping, and the propensity for categorization, rationalization, and so on that we see in the Gulag, but it does not adequately cover the plethora of informal practices that operated on the ground.

If the scholarship on modernity offers unclear answers to the question of the Gulag's place in comparative perspective, recent writing on wartime concentration camps might prove more fruitful. The Gulag, however, fits only marginally into Giorgio Agamben's currently fashionable argument surrounding the concentration camp and war.[35] For Agamben, the concentration camp occurs as modern states use the pretext of war and/or emergency to place certain unwanted citizen-subjects and/or groups into a "state of exception," where they are confined in a liminal legal state in that they are defined by their extralegal status, thus existing outside of the law, but only in relation to the law. Agamben bases much of his argument on the work of interwar German political theorist Carl Schmitt, who had argued, in his 1922 *Political*

Theology, that the sovereign is "he who decides the exception" and that, therefore, the exception is central to the operation of the modern state.[36]

Soviet authorities did not present the Stalin-era Gulag as something exceptional, at least not at first; indeed, it was supposedly a model of humane penal reform. Notably, Agamben draws a clear distinction between the camp as the space of exception, and the place of confinement, which operates within the legal system.[37] Gulag inmates were charged and convicted (however harsh the laws and/or the interrogation methods) of crimes that violated Soviet law. In other words, they were not extralegal; they had, in the eyes of the state, in any case, committed illegal acts. There is admittedly a grey area for Article 58ers. As the "counter-revolutionary" set of crimes, Article 58 was not outside of the law in Agamben's sense, and in some respects included activities that were classified as criminal just about everywhere, such as treason, espionage, and terrorism. The arbitrary use and abuse of Article 58, however, clearly sets Stalinism apart from nations that operated under the rule of law, however. (One clear recent example of camp punishment completely outside the law is the Guantanamo Bay camp as part of the "war on terror," which, at least according to the US government, exists outside of international law regarding the treatment of POWs, and also outside of US domestic law.)[38] Furthermore, authorities tried most Article 58 cases via NKVD troikas, rather than in the regular courts, so certainly the Article 58 convictions should be considered extrajudicial. A case can also be made that Stalinism itself operated within a state of exception even if, unlike Nazi Germany, that state of exception was not legally proclaimed.[39]

Nevertheless, no doubt the special settlements come closer to a space of exception in Agamben's meaning. Here were groups of people – first peasants, and later ethnic groups like the Volga Germans – forced to resettle in remote areas, restricted in their rights, but not formally charged with anything. Their punishment was outside the law. But perhaps most importantly for our purposes, unlike other twentieth-century wartime belligerents, such as the British during the South African War or the Nazis during the Second World War, the Soviet Union appears to have placed less emphasis on repressive measures like the Gulag *during* the war than it had beforehand (or afterwards).

Thus, we can question the extent to which the Second World War in the Soviet Union actually represented the "pursuit of purity," as Amir Weiner argues, or whether the Soviet state used the war as a pretext to define and exclude "the exception," as Agamben's arguments concerning the concentration camp suggest.[40] Weiner argues that the war created a "totalization of categories and practices against internal enemies," but the pragmatic – if deadly – mobilization of both prisoners and special settlers suggests that these categories were flexible.[41] The Gulag, moreover, decreased in population during the war, dropping from approximately 1.9 million prisoners on 1 January 1941, to a low of 1.2 million prisoners on 1 January 1944.[42] As shown in chapter 2, even if we include the time from August 1939 to June 1941, it would be hard to argue that the Soviet state relied *more* on the Gulag during the war than it did during peacetime. As mentioned, the Gulag's economic contribution during the war was similar, proportionately, to its pre-war contribution.[43] In Western Siberia specifically, the prisoner contingents increased during the war, but for war-related production, the mobilization of other human resources was more important than Gulag labour, and local authorities exhibited a pragmatic approach to forced labour contingents.

The Soviet state did not use the war as a pretext to expand a repressive camp system except, once again, if we focus on the special settlements. In contrast to the camps, the settlements saw a dramatic increase in population, although it was a population in flux. In June 1939, the settlements for the entire Soviet Union housed 990,473 people, mostly so-called former kulaks, who had been exiled during collectivization.[44] By October 1945, the settlements had grown to almost 2.2 million people, a number that included approximately 687,000 Volga Germans, 607,000 former kulaks, 406,000 Chechen and Ingush deportees, 195,000 Crimean Tatars, and tens of thousands of several other ethnic groups, including 80,000 Kalmyks.[45] The numbers themselves speak of incredible upheaval and ethnic cleansing of many areas in the European parts of the Soviet Union, especially considering that large numbers of deportees did not survive the war. Even here, however, the situation is far from clear-cut. During the war, authorities reinstated the citizenship rights of many former kulaks.[46] Many thousands of special settlers from Novosibirsk Province and elsewhere were mobilized to fight in the Red Army, too.[47] So while the wholesale exile of certain suspect ethnic groups during the war, such as the Volga Germans and Kalmyks, appears to confirm Agamben's hypothesis and to support Weiner's argument, the special settlements at the same time relaxed some of the repression towards peasants more generally. The Volga Germans, moreover, although experiencing devastating loss of life, became relatively integrated into the local economies of places like Western Siberia and Kazakhstan, in part because their labour was in high demand.[48] They were removed from their homeland, but they were not completely excluded.

In *Stalin's Genocides*, Norman Naimark examines the wholesale deportations of certain ethnic groups, plus other repressive campaigns, to conclude that Stalin's Soviet Union, like Hitler's Germany, engaged in genocide.[49] He takes a broader definition of genocide than that of the United Nations, one that includes not only the destruction of ethnic groups, but also of groups targeted due to class or political beliefs. This allows Naimark, for example, to conclude that the de-kulakization campaigns were genocidal. Yet even if we allow Naimark the broadened definition of genocide, a definition that has some basis in the post–Second World War debates concerning such crimes, the wartime Gulag does not appear to reinforce Naimark's points, at least in Western Siberia. While certain groups were violently removed from their homelands, they were then at least partially integrated into new areas, and there were always ways in which local economic considerations appear to have superseded ideological concerns.

One could argue that the harsh labour laws of the war created another wartime state of exception. These laws, however, were clumsily enforced – many workers sentenced for absenteeism, for example, could not be found, and thus were never sent to the camps. These laws also existed alongside policies towards religion and even the cultural elite that suggest a partial relaxation of repressive measures.[50] Stalin's partial rapprochement with the Orthodox Church, his focus on patriotic (as opposed to communist) symbols in order to rally the people, and the relaxation of repression against intellectuals all suggest a pragmatic approach to wartime mobilization, a pragmatic approach that is mimicked in the total war effort of the Western Siberian Gulag.

The pragmatic approach to the war, as far as the Gulag was concerned, tells us something important about the Gulag's place within the Stalinist system and in its broader, comparative perspective. The Gulag formed and developed due to particular features of the Soviet Union under Stalin, features that were informed more by past and contemporary practices in Russia than by external considerations. Nicholas Wachsmann points to the key domestic reasons for the development of the Nazi camp system, and the Soviet camp system tells a similar story.[51] Yes, Trotsky was aware of the camp system developed by the British in the South African War, and likely saw some sort of camp system as a useful tactic in the Russian Civil War, but the system as it developed under Stalin was much different from the early camps of the pre-Stalinist period.[52] The Gulag became "Stalin's Gulag" – and not simply the "Russian" Gulag or even the "Soviet" Gulag – for two main reasons. First, the scale of mass mobilization, at enormous cost in human life, was peculiar to the Stalinist system. Second, the ad hoc, hyper-bureaucratized nature of the Gulag necessarily encouraged informal practices (black markets, exchanges of favours, a flouting of the rules, and a fudging of the data) that are another characteristic of the Stalinist system. The Gulag was thus Stalin's for both planned and unplanned reasons.

Despite its similarities with other, modern prison systems in terms of a stated focus on rehabilitation, deterrence, and punishment, as well as a similarity with other, modern concentration camps in terms of its spatial organization and extraordinarily harsh conditions, the peculiarities of the Gulag mean that we should understand its development in the Russian, particularly Stalinist context. Like pre-revolutionary Russia, the Gulag was a system of penal camps and exile that involved hard labour and included both criminal and political prisoners. As discussed in chapter 1, the Gulag provided an apparent solution to two long-standing questions of Russian history: the exploitation of underused resources and the pacification of the peasantry. The Soviets even reintroduced the dreaded tsarist-era *katorga* punishment during the Second World War, for the harshest of the Gulag camps. This long-standing type of Russian punishment, however, changed considerably under the telescoped development and total mass mobilization of the Stalin era. The Gulag dwarfed its tsarist predecessors in terms of scale, economic production (however inefficient), and death. It was a key cog in Stalinist modernization, a type of modernization that attempted to create a well-ordered, rationalized system, but due to inefficiencies and impossible-to-enforce rules, instead created a system based on informal activities, whereby virtually everyone was breaking some type of rule or regulation.

Within the Stalin era of 1928–53, moreover, the wartime Gulag points to a need to understand specific periodization. Despite a relaxation of certain repressive measures, it was during the war that the Gulag was characterized by mass death. Official statistics place well over half of Gulag deaths in the relatively short period from June 1941 to May 1945, and memoirists certainly highlight the war years as particularly harsh. Also distinctive of the wartime Gulag was the propaganda, which clearly attempted to encourage a sense of patriotism among prisoners rather than encouraging a sort of individual communist transformation, as had been the case with the "re-forging" campaigns of the 1930s. Finally, and especially if we consider the whole period from 1939 to 1945, we see significant emphasis in bureaucratization and professionalization, an emphasis that only partially masked the incredible turnover in prisoners and personnel and the extreme inefficiencies of wartime supply.

Despite its inefficiencies and mass death, the Gulag successfully mobilized to aid in the total war effort to defeat Nazi Germany, thus confirming, as far as the state was concerned, Stalinist mass mobilization as an effective way to organize society. The Gulag was fully integrated into this mobilization state, not only on the macro level of economic planning and propaganda campaigns but also on more micro levels of interaction between prisoners and non-prisoners at defence enterprises and other work sites.

The interactions and inefficiencies mark the Gulag as peculiar within a comparative context of both prisons and concentration camps. Yes, black markets and other informal practices have pervaded both institutions in many contexts, and the trading of smuggled goods and the exchange of favours was certainly an important aspect of survival even in places like Auschwitz.[53] Yet both modern prisons and other iterations of the concentration camp place greater emphasis, in practice, on the isolation of unwanted populations than the wartime Gulag did. The Soviet state lacked either the resources or the willpower – or both – to enforce the strict isolation of prisoners from society, and unescorted prisoners and contract prisoners in defence enterprises regularly had opportunities to interact with non-prisoners, especially in many of the corrective-labour colonies, which tended to be located within urban centres. As a growing body of scholarship has demonstrated, the Gulag was not an archipelago, separated from the mainland of Soviet society, but was a key component of Soviet society and Stalinist mobilization, one end of a spectrum of labour and mobilization that helped carry the Soviet Union to victory in the Second World War.[54]

The contrasts with systems like the Nazi camp system are clearer than any similarities. While both Nazi Germany and the Soviet Union may have had "high modernist" goals in their attempts to make populations legible and to order society along bureaucratic, rational lines, in practice we see two very different systems.[55] The Nazis only belatedly tried to include unwanted populations in the total mobilization effort, and without much success. While the work of Christopher Browning has shown that many ordinary men participated in the atrocities of the Holocaust, the Nazi camps themselves relied largely on what should have been the ideological elite, the SS, to run and staff the camps, at least until late in the war.[56] The Gulag, as we have seen, was staffed for the most part with relatively ordinary Soviet men and women, few of whom were Communist Party members, and some of whom were even former (or future) prisoners of the camps.

The Postwar Gulag

If the wartime Gulag in comparative context reveals certain peculiarities – a de-emphasis in certain repressive measures, as well as a full integration into the war effort – the postwar camp system is also unusual, in that, instead of opting for a relaxation of repressive measures, the authorities instead increased the size and severity of the system.

The local Gulag shaped the postwar landscape in many areas of the Soviet Union's home front. Regions like Vorkuta, for example, developed largely as a result of the home front contributions of Gulag labour, and then began a long and gradual shift from a focus on prisoner to non-prisoner labour in the postwar period, particularly after Stalin's death.[57] Even in Western Siberia, where many cities and towns were already well developed before the war, the Gulag nevertheless had tangible effects on the landscape. The accelerated growth of Combine 179, for example, stimulated the creation of a densely populated urban area on Novosibirsk's left bank, and the combine itself converted into a major machine-parts factory in the postwar period. The Chkalov Aviation Factory remains an important defence enterprise in Novosibirsk to this day. Gulag prisoners played a role in the development and densification of areas on the outskirts of Tomsk, such as Zavarzino. And, of course, prisoners and special settlers helped further the expansion of many of the region's key industries, including agriculture, forestry, and coal mining.

Postwar Western Siberia itself encountered many of the hardships of other areas of the Soviet Union that had not been under direct occupation: overcrowding, hastily developed wartime infrastructure, and a lack of direct investment as authorities concentrated on the reconstruction of areas directly devastated by the war.[58] Western Siberia experienced a brief economic downturn but recovered relatively quickly, reaching its 1945 production levels by 1948.[59]

Yet the direct contribution of the Gulag, both to victory and to the development of Western Siberia, is difficult to assess. It is possible that the counting numbers – x shells, y airplanes, etc. – made the difference in the war. From mid-1941 to early 1943, when the threat was at its greatest and much of the country was in complete disarray, the Gulag appeared to offer a steady supply of labour to deal with the needs of the war, and thus an assurance that production would not cease. However, that simple summary hides a multitude of inefficiencies.

As we saw in chapter 2, forced labour was important in the region but also costly, inefficient in terms of lives lost, labour use, and upkeep (including the upkeep of personnel), and ultimately surpassed by non-prisoner labour, both in the form of evacuees and the mobilization of underutilized local populations. Gulag labour may have been helpful, but certainly the evidence points to ways in which the same production could have been achieved at a much lower cost, in terms of both money and lives. That the Gulag was a place of mass death during the war is indisputable, but it did not need to be. Thus, the story of Stalin's Gulag at war underlines the tragedy of the system: in huge numbers, the system sacrificed the lives and the health of the prisoners, a sacrifice that no doubt made a difference but was unnecessary and has remained largely unnoticed. It is clear that resources could have been used more efficiently.

But does it matter if prisoner labour was efficient? On the one hand, arguably the prime goal, in the end, is victory. On the other hand, clearly in the Gulag's case, where lives were at stake, if victory could have been achieved more efficiently and with less loss of life without the large forced labour network, then the Gulag's victory was no doubt a victory marred by the institution's function as a place of mass death, mass death that was far removed from the bloodlands of Poland, Ukraine, and Belarus.[60] And if it was a victory accompanied by mass death and a reaffirmation of the Stalinist version of total mobilization, then surely it was a victory that, despite bringing the natural feelings of relief and pride at surviving a very real existential threat, was a double-edged sword. For many, particularly within the forced labour network, the system became even crueler, as sentences were lengthened and mass incarceration continued. As Steven Barnes argues, the postwar Gulag emerged as a "new circle of hell" due to the implementation of even harsher punishments and regimes, exemplified by the so-called special camps, established in 1948.[61] Alexopoulos, too, argues that the postwar period saw the worst camp conditions, conditions that authorities attempted to mask.[62]

Due to deaths and the inefficiencies, Soviet victory was the Gulag's victory not so much for the Gulag's direct contributions to the war effort – although these were not negligible, as we have seen – but because Soviet victory confirmed the importance of the total mobilization state, a system Stalin had launched with his First Five Year Plan, and a system that achieved victory in the Great Patriotic War.

Robert Dale has recently argued that the postwar Soviet Union differed from its European counterparts in at least one crucial respect. "In the Soviet Union, however," Dale writes, "the war's aftermath did not bring about a release from wartime obligations and constraints, but rather new demands and objectives: remobilization rather than demobilization."[63] Total mobilization was one of the key foundations of the Stalinist system, the Soviet Union emerged victorious in the war in part because of that total mobilization, and Stalin was not about to abandon the system after the war. Remobilization was in order, and after a large amnesty to celebrate victory, remobilization meant, for the Gulag, the expansion of the system.

In some respects, the Gulag operated more efficiently in the postwar period. Despite a spike in 1946, the authorities made relative improvements in preventing escapes.[64] There was a mass amnesty of non-political prisoners in 1945, when over 1 million prisoners were immediately freed or received reductions to their sentences. In Novosibirsk Province, 86.3 per cent of those freed were from the region, and many local inhabitants blamed the released prisoners for a postwar spike in crime.[65] Following the amnesty, the Gulag's population grew steadily, reaching the peak figure for its entire existence in the early 1950s and then levelling off until after Stalin's death.[66] NKVD (from March of 1946 the MVD, *Ministerstvo vnutrennykh del*, or Ministry of Internal Affairs)[67] and Gulag officials made a concerted effort to improve production, too, by offering incentives such as wages for labour and the reinstatement of workday credits by 1950/1951.

In part, however, the postwar work incentives may have resulted from the Gulag's failures rather than any perceived success. Beria recognized that the Gulag was hardly cost-effective, and thus took steps to reform the system before Stalin's death.[68] The speed with which authorities partially dismantled aspects of the Gulag following Stalin's death attests to the disillusionment among Soviet leadership with using prisoner labour as a means to help the economy, and a desire to shift away from total mobilization as the defining feature of the Soviet system.

The postwar Gulag was a paradox. Central authorities increasingly understood its ineffectiveness but, at the same time, undertook measures that caused an expansion of the MVD's forced-labour empire. During this time, the Soviet criminal justice shifted towards longer sentences for both political and non-political crimes, resulting in an increase in the average prisoner population.[69] Indeed, although the Gulag prisoner population reached its peak during this time, the total numbers arrested and sentenced per year from around 1948 to 1953 were among the lowest in the Stalin era.[70]

Peter Solomon describes the postwar criminal justice system as one that relied even less on law and more on administrative regulations; became more arbitrary by relying increasingly on "secret regulations and laws"; and used "unusual severity" to punish non-political crimes.[71] The official 1 January figures show the Gulag reaching a peak population of 2,561,351 prisoners on 1 January 1950, and remaining around 2.5 million until Stalin's death. Siblag's postwar peak was in 1947 (41,075), but for Western Siberia as a whole – which now housed quite a few camp systems – the peak was approximately 163,000 in 1952.[72]

There were other changes in the Gulag during the postwar period. A rise in tensions between national minority groups occurred. Indeed, some accounts have pointed to "clans," formed along national lines in the postwar years, with the most powerful and cohesive from the former Baltic countries and Ukraine.[73] Also, animosity between criminal gangs within the camps and the politicals (Article 58ers) became more prevalent in the postwar years. There seems to have been more "rebelliousness" and better organization among those sentenced under Article 58. Solzhenitsyn notes that many Article 58ers in the postwar period really had nothing to lose, as the extremely long sentences, often in strict-regimen "Special Camps," meant that authorities' threats of additional punishments were almost meaningless.[74] The MVD's network of special settlements continued to be quite extensive in the postwar period, but settlements now mostly housed exiled national minority groups, as opposed to peasants, continuing a trend from the war.[75] For many of the original waves of peasant special settlers, their rights had been restored, and even if they continued to live in their place of exile, they were no longer labelled special settlers. Of the Western Siberian exile groups, the Kalmyks were only able to return to their homeland in 1957, while the Volga Germans were never allowed to return, although both groups recovered from initial devastating losses. Many of the surviving borderland deportees from eastern Poland and the Baltics were able to return in the immediate postwar years.[76]

As before the war, prisoners in the Gulag under non-political sentences comprised the large majority of the camp prisoner populations, although for a brief period following the 1945 amnesty, the number of "counter-revolutionaries" in the corrective-labour *camps* (not including corrective-labour *colonies*) exceeded half of all prisoners for the first and only time in the Gulag's history.[77] If one takes into account all Gulag prisoners, even in this brief period there was not a majority of Article 58ers. In any case, the proportion of counter-revolutionaries quickly dropped. In 1948, for example, less than a quarter of prisoners had sentences under Article 58.[78] The majority of the Gulag's prisoners were criminals and violators of harsh labour laws and laws concerning socialist property.

The Gulag in Western Siberia saw a proliferation of postwar camps, a process that began during the war. The pre-war Siblag was now four separate camp administrations: Siblag, administered from Mariinsk; the Novosibirsk Province Camp and Colony Administration, administered from Novosibirsk; the Department of Corrective-Labour Colonies of Tomsk Province (OITK TO), administered from Tomsk; and the Department of Corrective-Labour Colonies of Kemerovo Province (OITK KO), which became the Kemerovo Province Camp and Colony Administration (UITLK KO) in 1949. What is more, two relatively large camp complexes – Sevkuzbasslag and Iuzhkuzbasslag – were founded in Kemerovo Province in 1947, both focusing on forestry and both part of the Main Administration of Forestry Camps (GULLP: *Glavnoe upravleniia lagerei lesnoi promyshlennosti*). One of the larger postwar complexes in the region was Voroninlag, formed in 1949 (originally called Construction site 601 and ITL) out of two colonies of the Tomsk Province Labour Colony Department. Rounding out the picture are the Tomsk Corrective-Labour Colony, a small camp that existed from 1946 to 1949; Kamyshlag, located in Kemerovo, founded in 1951 as the region's only strict-regimen "special camp"; Kamenlag, in Novosibirsk, (originally named Construction site 600 and ITL); Arlichevleg, which existed in the early 1950s in Kemerovo Province; and Tom'-Usinksii ITL and ITL Kemerovozhilstroia, both small camps in Kemerovo Province in the late 1940s.[79]

The Gulag carried out diversified economic activities in the region, although each separate camp system tended to be fairly specialized. In his memoir, one former prisoner describes postwar Siblag as being "like an enormous state farm, with all kinds of agricultural production and support services."[80] Overall, the Western Siberian Gulag mirrored production activities for the Gulag as a whole. Of the 2.2 million Gulag prisoners at the end of 1947, over 700,000 worked in agriculture and the manufacture of consumer goods; over 500,000 were contracted out to non-MVD enterprises; and around 273,000 worked in forestry.[81] These were the three most common categories for Gulag labour in the postwar years, and the three most common in Western Siberia as well.[82] Aside from agriculture, contract work, and forestry, prisoners in Western Siberia worked in construction, smelting, wood- and metalworking, textiles, road and railroad repair, and even furniture manufacture.

As had been the case both before and during the war, local camp authorities had to deal with unusually unhealthy prisoner contingents in comparison with many other regions, lending weight to the recent argument that authorities masked the horrendous camp conditions partially by keeping healthy prisoners in priority camps, and unhealthy contingents in non-priority areas.[83] A lengthy procurator's report about the Novosibirsk Province Camp and Colony Administration for the first half of 1947 notes that plans had been unfulfilled for contract work and that the problem was growing more acute as the year progressed. One contributing factor was the "updating" of the contingent through out-transfers and the Decree (*Ukaz*) from 10 January 1947.[84] The following year saw even greater difficulties with unfit prisoners at the camps and colonies of the Novosibirsk Administration, which is not surprising, given famine conditions within the Soviet Union, which probably resulted in around 1 million deaths in the country as a whole.[85] In January 1947, 55.4 per cent of the contingent was either unable to work or could perform only light work; invalids, included here, made up 7.9 per cent of the total contingent. By March 1948, 71 per cent of the contingent was suitable for either light work or no work at all, with invalids comprising 18 per cent of the total.[86] These numbers are especially shocking, given that authorities only reluctantly placed prisoners in the invalid or light-work categories. The procurator delineated three reasons for the poor health of the prisoners: first, an interruption in food supply "so that the given nourishment is biologically not enough and the caloric content of the daily ration is lowered" (bureaucratic speak for starvation); second, massive problems with overcrowding, which led to poor living conditions; and, third, the transfer, by order of the Gulag, of around 17,000 mostly able-bodied prisoners out of the camp to higher priority camps.[87] Furthermore, the Novosibirsk Province Camp and Colony Administration had received many "seriously ill [*tiazhelo bol'nikh*]" prisoners from Iuzhkuzbasslag and from contingents in transit through the area.[88]

Another prime example of the region's struggle to retain its able-bodied prisoners comes from 1951. As part of the effort to place strict-regimen *katorga* prisoners into separate camps, the Gulag ordered Siblag to send 493 physically fit strict-regimen prisoners to Vorkutlag, a high-priority camp located in the far north of European Russia. The Gulag also ordered the transfer of 837 invalids under strict regimen from the Tomsk area camp of Voroninlag to Siblag. Thus, as had been common practice in the 1930s and during the war, the prisoners in poor physical condition remained in the region, while a healthy contingent departed.[89]

Aside from dealing with the poor health of the prisoner contingent, camps in the area continued to face issues of inefficiency and porous borders. Despite efforts at increased bureaucratization and specialization, informal practices remained prevalent. The postwar period saw concerted efforts by camp authorities to root out corruption and patronage networks among prisoners, efforts often thwarted by unreliable informants and the not infrequent complicity of camp staff.[90] Camp borders simply could not restrict the flow of goods and people in the ways that the authorities hoped. Continued black market activity within the camps of the region and the remarkable frequency of illicit contact between men and women in the camps highlight the persistence of informal practices.

One of the more egregious examples of black market activity occurred from August 1946 to January 1947, just as the postwar famine was beginning. Prisoners in relevant bureaucratic positions – shipping/receiving and accounting – within the Novosibirsk Province Camp and Colony Administration managed to make connections with "local speculators" to sell foodstuffs produced at the camp on the black market. They got away with selling a "market value" sum of over 80,000 rubles worth of foodstuffs, mostly bread (at least 300 kg per month over this period). No doubt their black market activity benefited themselves and perhaps their friends in the camps, but clearly the sale of such large quantities of bread, at a time when many in the region's camp system were on the brink of starvation, had a negative impact on the lives of many prisoners. These sorts of activities, nevertheless, help underscore the degree to which informal networks and practices could impact camp life.[91]

The prevalence of sexual activity in the camps also highlights the importance of informal practices. Despite rules designed to limit and even, at times, prohibit contact between male and female prisoners, pregnancies were common in the camps, and most camp systems built maternity wards, nurseries, and so on, providing a type of structural support for this illicit activity. In practice, conditions were generally terrible for pregnant and nursing mothers – as well as their babies – but this did not stop sexual activity from occurring.[92] As I have argued elsewhere, coercion and force was frequently involved, but camp sexual activity could also be based on love, desire, or a practical exchange of sex for food or protection. A 1952 inspection of Siblag revealed 377 pregnancies on the day of an inspection, and complained that not only did men and women work together in the fields, but that there were even men living in women's camp stations and vice versa.[93]

In the postwar period, then, the regime had difficulties enforcing its rules. Yet clearly, at least from 1945 to 1953, authorities doubled down on the Gulag as part of the Soviet mobilization state, increasing the size of the system in terms of both numbers of prisoners and numbers of camps. When Stalin died in 1953, amnesties and uncertain reforms vastly changed the camp system in Western Siberia. Releases and reforms shrunk the regional camp system considerably. Quite simply, Stalin's death brought an end to Stalin's Gulag; the idea of a system in a constant state of total mobilization no longer seemed necessary.[94]

Abandoning total mobilization did not mean an end to prisoner labour. There was an important shift, however, to a focus on vocational training and a reaffirmation of the educational aspects of labour. While prisoners remained involved in industries like agriculture and forestry, and some camp bosses continued to emphasize output, most hard, manual labour was abandoned or minimized in favour of training, and prisoners no longer found themselves mobilized as part of major infrastructure projects. In short, prisoner labour in the post-Stalin years came to resemble, more closely, prisoner labour in other countries. And, certainly, mass death was no longer a defining feature of the prison camps, as camp death rates dropped to below national averages.[95]

Conclusion

Stalin's Gulag at war was an institution of both total war and mass death. Prisoners struggled to survive, particularly in the harshest years of 1942 and 1943. This was especially true of Western Siberia, where the camps were not prioritized and not located in the most remote or the harshest climactic conditions of the Soviet Union but nevertheless experienced mortality rates well above average. Prisoners relied on relatives, resorted to violence, worked their way into more privileged positions, and formed black market connections with other prisoners or staff in order to survive. Personnel, too, relied on informal networks to improve their own situations. Both frequently professed a patriotism that seems unusual, given the harshness of the conditions, but perhaps understandable in the context of total war, where prisoners could hope for early release to fight on the front, and some personnel initially called for renewed vigilance against perceived internal enemies. Nevertheless, even the Communist Party within the Gulag downplayed ideology during the war, focusing instead on economic production.

The Gulag in Western Siberia produced, or helped to produce, artillery shells, airplanes, uniforms, foodstuffs, and other equipment that were important for the front, perhaps even crucial. Prisoners and special settlers also worked in forestry, construction, and mining in the region, all industries crucial for regional development at a time when the region was one of the most important industrial areas of the home front. Yet their overall contribution, despite Soviet victory in the war, has a tragic element to it. Stalin's Gulag at war was tragic not only because of the lives lost, but, as home front mobilization in Western Siberia has revealed, also because much of this production was overshadowed by mobilization of underused populations *outside* of the Gulag, who participated in the mass mobilization of the Second World War without nearly the cost in health and lives experienced by Gulag prisoners. To put it bluntly, as a tool of mass mobilization, the Gulag was largely unnecessary, and its contributions could have easily been made up other ways. That the contributions of Gulag prisoners have largely been overlooked, moreover, adds to the tragic circumstances. Prisoners sacrificed, without choice, their health and their lives, experiencing almost unimaginable suffering, yet this sacrifice is largely forgotten.

Epilogue

Memory, Stalin's Gulag, and the Great Patriotic War

The post-Stalin Gulag was hardly an unambiguous move towards a more humane system. Soviet prison camps, and Soviet criminal justice, remained harsh, even with improved conditions and less emphasis on forced labour.[1] The Soviet public, too, when limited public discussion of the Stalinist camps arose in response to the publication of Aleksandr Solzhenitsyn's *One Day in the Life of Ivan Denisovich* in 1962, reacted with suspicion towards Solzhenitsyn's hero.[2] An ambivalent, or perhaps conflicted, attitude towards the camps has continued to the present, exacerbated by a renewed emphasis on the memory of the war as a time of heroic struggle, a memory that does not have much room for the Gulag. Still, that the memory of the Gulag exists alongside the memory of the war, even in official discourse, is a point that needs further exploration.

As is well known, Vladimir Putin has promoted the memory of Soviet victory in the Second World War as a source of pride and a foundation for modern Russian patriotism. Even the dramatic experiences of his parents during the war have become a part of Putin's personal narrative.[3] The 9 May Victory Day is one of the main holidays of the year, and commemorations of the war have grown larger, and arguably more symbolically significant, over the course of Putin's rule. As Elizabeth Wood writes, "By making World War II the central historical event of the twentieth century, Putin and his handlers have chosen an event of mythic proportions that underlines the unity and coherence of the nation, [and] gives it legitimacy and status as a world power."[4] Not surprisingly, the Gulag's role in Soviet victory is not part of the official discourse, as it potentially undermines that story of unity. The mass death of the wartime Gulag, after all, was caused not by Nazi Germany but by Soviet policies and practices.

If the Gulag has not been part of the official memory of the Second World War, however, that does not mean there is no room for memory of the camp system in Putin's Russia. While the Gulag's role as part of any official collective memory began as early as the publication of Solzhenitsyn's Ivan Denisovich story, it was not until the late 1980s, under Gorbachev's glasnost policy, that considerable room opened up for discussion of Stalinist repression. The late 1980s also saw the publication of many Gulag memoirs and the founding of the Soviet Union's first NGO, the Memorial Society, which sought to preserve the memory of Stalinist repression. Initially, Memorial pushed for a Gulag memorial in the centre of Moscow and succeeded in placing a stone from the Solovki camp in the square across from the Lubianka, the headquarters for the KGB and its predecessors.[5] Gulag memoirs continued to appear in large numbers in the early 1990s and then publications slowed. The profoundly difficult economic issues of the post-Soviet transition left little space or energy for an in-depth discussion of the horrors of the camps. Still, organizations like the Memorial Society, Vozvrashchenie, and the Sakharov Centre continued to publish and collect memoirs and other materials related to Stalin-era repressions. At the same time, as the Putin era began, Russian scholarly activity on the Gulag increased considerably, and has continued seemingly unabated.[6]

While Putin's gradual acquisition of control of the media is well documented, as is his seeming desire to control narratives about the Soviet past, the Gulag specifically occupies an ambiguous place. On one hand, two high-production television mini-series based on works by Solzhenitsyn and Shalamov have appeared on state-sponsored Russian television.[7] The work of Memorial has finally come to fruition – in conjunction with city and federal authorities – in the opening of a major Gulag museum in Moscow, and a large Gulag monument was unveiled in October 2017, right on the outskirts of downtown Moscow, near a high-traffic area.[8] In 2015, moreover, Prime Minister Dmitrii Medvedev signed a policy on perpetuating the memory of victims of political repression, which states that "Russia cannot develop the rule of law or secure moral leadership ... without first perpetuating the memory of the victims of Soviet repression."[9] On the other hand, both Memorial and the Sakharov Centre have been targets of recent laws meant to crack down on NGOs with foreign connections, and the main post-Soviet Gulag museum, Perm' 36, in 2015 underwent a bizarre transition, whereby it was initially slated to be shut down, but then reworked as a Gulag museum with a more positive spin, particularly concerning Stalin's role in the modernization of the country. The new Perm' 36 even weaves Gulag memory with that of the war, emphasizing the Gulag's role in helping to achieve victory.[10]

The ambiguity in the Putin-era collective memory of the Gulag points to Russia's complex relationship with its Soviet past, as well as the complexity of the Gulag itself. If commemorative activity is generally meant to "strengthen the feeling of community and solidarity among those who commemorate,"[11] one can easily see how the memory of the Gulag could undermine Putin's narrative of the Second World War, a narrative that is meant to evoke pride and strength. However, another one of Putin's pillars of support lies in his close relationship with the Orthodox Church. The Orthodox Church certainly remembers the Gulag – particularly the Gulag of the 1930s – for its extreme repression, specifically directed against clergy, monks, and other believers. As Zuzanna Bogumił, Dominique Moran, and Elly Harrowell have recently argued, the Orthodox Church and the Memorial Society have competed to establish a collective memory related to Soviet-era repression, and the Church's narrative has gained more traction because it fits better within Putin-era nationalism than Memorial's narrative, which is based more in liberal notions of human rights.[12] As the case of the Perm' 36 museum shows, moreover, there may be some room to discuss the Gulag in the context of the war, as far as the system played a role in Soviet victory.

Some have argued that the frequently blurred distinctions between perpetrator and victim in the Gulag have created an inability to deal with the past constructively, and thus the ambiguous relationship to Stalinism today has less to do with current political calculations than with the nature of Stalinism itself. As Maria Tumarkin notes, almost everyone (or their families) in Russia today was involved in the Soviet state to some degree, making it difficult to condemn the perpetrators and honour the victims.[13] For Alexander Etkind, the lack of a coherent narrative about the past has created a "warped mourning" of repression, a past that haunts the Russian present. Etkind writes that, "in Russia, a land where millions remain unburied, the repressed return as the undead. They do so in novels, films, and other forms of culture that reflect, shape, and possess people's memory."[14] He argues that the "soft memory" of memoirs and oral stories needs to be anchored in "hard memory" of monuments, museums, and burial sites that can recognize the victims.[15] Still, the ability to recall the Stalinist past in a coherent narrative is not an easy task. The "past was *itself* ambivalent," suggests

Xenia Cherkaev in her critique of Etkind's call for a clearer narrative.[16] Collective memory of the Gulag, for both political and historical reasons, thus remains contested memory and is likely to remain that way for quite some time.

In terms of Western Siberia in particular, where many inhabitants are themselves descendants of former exiles (from both the imperial and Soviet periods) or former prisoners, there is also an ambivalent relationship with the repressive aspects of the region's history. The only museum in the region devoted to issues of Stalinist repression – the Memorial Museum NKVD Remand Prison in Tomsk, affiliated with the Tomsk Local Studies (*kraevedcheskii*) Museum – has faced numerous obstacles over the years, including insecure funding and a decrease in operating space due to the encroachment of commercial enterprises. Although it is one of the most visited museums in Tomsk, not everyone is happy with the current state of affairs. In November 2016, vandals spray-painted a red bust of Stalin onto the "Sorrow Stone" monument in the square next to the museum, a monument dedicated to "those slain on Tomsk lands during the years of Bolshevik terror." The police at first refused to investigate, claiming the stone, with its accompanying arch, was neither an official monument nor of cultural significance, and thus could not be protected. In March 2017, following a concerted effort by the museum staff to raise public awareness, the stone was finally recognized as a monument of cultural significance, and thus subject to legal protection. Given the uncertainties of the Gulag's place in collective memory, however, these types of battles seem likely to reoccur.[17]

Stalin's Gulag at war was a site of mass mobilization and mass death that ultimately contributed to Soviet victory in the Second World War. For the Gulag and its prisoners, this was a Pyrrhic victory at best, however. On net balance, did the Gulag contribute to the conditions of victory more than it subtracted from them? In certain respects, this question is impossible to answer. The direct aid to the battlefront and the home front from the Gulag was considerable, and perhaps necessary for victory. The Soviet Union barely survived a true existential threat, and the Gulag played its part in the war effort. Yet as the overall picture of mobilization in Western Siberia confirms, Soviet authorities could have achieved such production without the camp system and its enormous costs in terms of health and lives. Victory, moreover, confirmed the perceived effectiveness of Stalinist total mobilization, and ensured the existence and expansion of the forced-labour network in

6.1: The Tomsk "Sorrow Stone" and monument, Photograph by the author,
August 2016.

the postwar period. Stalin and his advisors chose to enhance the repressive features of total mobilization, extending Gulag sentences and becoming more arbitrary in the application of criminal justice. Soviet victory was the Gulag's victory precisely because, for all its inefficiencies, victory ensured the continued reliance on the Gulag as a fully integrated part of the Stalinist system, and the Gulag itself epitomized the system's ability to allocate human resources to projects deemed necessary.

The contributions of the Gulag's prisoners on the home front have largely been forgotten, removed from an official memory of the war that focuses on national unity and strength. But Stalin's Gulag at war was an important part of the Soviet total war effort, and despite its inefficiencies and the myriad responses of both prisoners and personnel, it achieved its main wartime goal: to help achieve victory, no matter the staggering cost.

Notes

Introduction

1 The Ob' River runs through the city of Novosibirsk at only 86 metres above mean sea level. The city itself varies in elevation. Its high right bank is around 160 metres and its lower left bank is around 110 metres elevation. The Ob' has its origins in the Altai Mountains, and winds its way 5,410 kilometres to the Ob' Gulf. See Google Earth and *Encyclopaedia Britannica*, accessed 4 May 2017, https://www.britannica.com/place/Ob-River.

2 Wilson T. Bell, "Tomsk Regional Identity and the Legacy of the Gulag and Stalinist Repression," in Edith Clowes, Ani Kokobobo, and Gisela Erbsloh, eds., *Russia's Regional Identities* (London: Routledge, 2018), 206–25.

3 For more on resistance to the Bolsheviks during the Civil War, see N.G.O. Pereira, *White Siberia: The Politics of Civil War* (Montreal: McGill-Queen's University Press, 1995).

4 Richard E. Lonsdale, "Siberian Industry before 1917: The Example of Tomsk Guberniya," *Annals of the Association of American Geographers* 53, no. 4 (1963): 479–93, esp. 482.

5 Here and throughout: I use the term "camp" or "colony" to describe the subcamps of the region's main camps (although occasionally I use the term, "subcamp," to avoid confusion). The Russian term for these sub-camps (*podrazdelenie*, literally, "subdivision") conveys a somewhat different meaning in Russian than in English. Most camps housed the camp administration in a town or urban centre, with the actual prison camps and colonies scattered around the region. The prisoners themselves tended to refer to these subunits as camps. Most of these camps, in turn, were divided into several smaller camps called "stations" (*punkty*). Thus, a camp

like Siblag had its administration in Mariinsk for most of the war, but had subcamps and colonies located in many parts of the region, and many of these camps and colonies had their own stations, too (see figure 0.1).

6 V.V. Alekseev and Z.G. Karpenko, "Razvitie narodnogo khoziastvo," in V.V. Alekseev et al., eds., *Rabochii klass Sibiri v period uprocheniia i razvitiia sotsializma* (Novosibirsk: Nauka, 1984), 148.

7 Amir Weiner, *Making Sense of War: The Second World War and the Fate of the Bolshevik Revolution* (Princeton, NJ: Princeton University Press, 2001); Steven A. Barnes, *Death and Redemption: The Gulag and the Shaping of Soviet Society* (Princeton, NJ: Princeton University Press, 2011).

8 Unlike other concentration camps, it is not clear that the Gulag during the Second World War functioned as part of the "state of exception," in Giorgio Agamben's sense of the phrase: Agamben, *State of Exception*, trans. Kevin Artell (Chicago: University of Chicago Press, 2005). See chapter 5 of the present study for a more comparative analysis.

9 Timothy Snyder, *Bloodlands: Europe between Hitler and Stalin* (New York: Basic Books, 2010); Norman Naimark, *Stalin's Genocides* (Princeton, NJ: Princeton University Press, 2011).

10 Nikolaus Wachsmann, *Kl: A History of the Nazi Concentration Camps* (New York: Farrar, Straus and Giroux, 2015), esp. 157–63, 403–27 (quotation 158).

11 For more on key differences (and some similarities) between Gulag and Nazi camp personnel, see especially Dietrich Beyrau, "Camp Worlds and Forced Labor: A Comparison of the National Socialist and Soviet Camp Systems," trans. Nicole Eaton, in Michael David-Fox, ed., *The Soviet Gulag: Evidence, Interpretation, Comparison* (Pittsburgh: University of Pittsburgh Press, 2016), 224–49, esp. 235–8 and 246–8. See also Wachsmann, *Kl,* esp. 108–15, 155–7, 361–3.

12 Zygmunt Bauman, *Modernity and the Holocaust* (New York: Columbia University Press, 1989), 77.

13 For a recent argument that Gulag deaths were the result of intentional policies to exploit prisoners, see Golfo Alexopoulos, "Destructive-Labor Camps: Rethinking Solzhenitsyn's Play on Words," *Kritika: Explorations in Russian and Eurasian History* 16, no. 3 (2015): 499–526, as well as her *Illness and Inhumanity in Stalin's Gulag* (New Haven, CT: Yale University Press, 2017).

14 Wachsmann, *Kl,* 6 and 240–89. Wachsmann estimates that 2.3 million people spent time in the concentration camps (not including the death camps) between 1933 and 1945, with over 1.7 million deaths. Most of these deaths were during the war. The Gulag's official statistics reveal roughly the same number of total deaths from 1930 to 1953, but with a total number of prisoners likely around 18 million over that same period.

15 Snyder, *Bloodlands*, xiii.
16 Barnes, *Death and Redemption*, 116. For more on Gulag mortality, see Alexopoulos, *Illness and Inhumanity*.
17 For more on the Soviet Union and Nazi Germany as "violent societies," see Christian Gerlach and Nicholas Werth, "State Violence – Violent Societies," in Michael Geyer and Sheila Fitzpatrick, eds., *Beyond Totalitarianism: Stalinism and Nazism Compared* (Cambridge: Cambridge University Press, 2009), 133–79.
18 See also Wilson T. Bell, "Was the Gulag an Archipelago? De-Convoyed Prisoners and Porous Borders in the Camps of Western Siberia," *The Russian Review* 72, no. 1 (2013): 116–41.
19 Edwin Bacon, *The Gulag at War: Stalin's Forced Labour System in the Light of the Archives* (New York: New York University Press, 1994), 24. On 1 January 1941, only 22 per cent of Gulag prisoners were in corrective-labour colonies. By 1 January 1944, this figure was 44 per cent, and by 1 January 1945 over half (51 per cent) of Gulag prisoners were in colonies. Prisoners in colonies would remain at least half of the Gulag's prisoner population until partway through 1948. While most books do not address the corrective-labour colonies, one partial exception is O.V. Kornilova's study of the building of the Moscow-Minsk highway, a pre-war project that used prisoners from both corrective-labour camps and colonies. See O.V. Kornilova, *Kak stroili prevuiu sovetskuiu avtomagistral' (1936–1941 gg.)* (Smolensk: Svitok, 2014). Alexopoulos also addresses the colonies in her *Illness and Inhumanity*, showing that they often had particularly harsh conditions, since authorities kept healthy prisoners in priority camps.
20 For more on the relationship between the special settlements, the Gulag, and the NKVD, see the introduction to Gosudarstvennyi arkhiv Rossiskoi federatsii (GARF) f. 9479, op. 1. There had been an attempt in 1933 to reorganize the system with a separate Main Administration of Labour Settlements, but the settlements remained under the Gulag's direction at this time. See N.V. Petrov, "Vvedenie," in N.V. Petrov and N.I. Vladimirtsev, eds., *Istoriia Stalinskogo Gulaga*, vol. 2, *Karatel'naia sistema: struktura i kadry* (Moscow: Rosspen, 2004), 29.
21 During the war, authorities counted three camp administrations as agricultural camps – Siblag, Karlag, and Srednebellag – but counted a total of 414 agricultural subcamps operating within larger camp systems. See p. 52 of V.G. Nasedkin's report on the Gulag during the war: GARF f. 9414, op. 1, d. 68, l. 53. (Nasedkin joined the ranks of the security police in 1921 and directed the Gulag from February 1941 until September 1947.) For more, see the online version of N.V. Petrov and K.V. Skorkin, eds., *Kto rukovodil NKVD? Spravochnik* (Moscow: Zven'ia, 1999), accessed 7 May 2017,

http://old.memo.ru/history/NKVD/kto/biogr/index.htm. Steven Barnes's
Gulag research focuses on Karlag. See Barnes, *Death and Redemption*.

22 Oleg Khlevniuk, *The History of the Gulag: From Collectivization to the Great
Terror*, trans. Vadim A. Staklo (New Haven, CT: Yale University Press,
2004), 331–4.

23 Khlevniuk, *The History of the Gulag*, 178.

24 V.N. Uimanov, *Penitentsiarnaia sistema Zapadnoi Sibiri (1920–1941 gg.)*
(Tomsk: Izd-vo Tomskogo Universiteta, 2011); V.N. Uimanov, *Likvidatsiia
i reabilitatsiia: politicheskie repressii v Zapadnoi Sibiri v sisteme bol'shevistskoi
vlasti (konets 1919–1941 g.)* (Tomsk: Izd-vo Tomskogo Universiteta, 2012);
S.A. Papkov, *Stalinskii terror v Sibiri, 1928–1941* (Novosibirsk: Izdatel'stvo
Sibirskogo Otdeleniia RAN, 1997); S.A. Krasil'nikov, *Serp i molokh:
Krest'ianskaia ssylka v Zapadnoi Sibiri v 1930-e gody* (Moscow: Rosspen,
2003).

25 For examples, see R.S. Bikmetov, "Siblag v gody Velikoi Otechestvennoi
voiny," *Vestnik Kemerovskogo gosudarstvennogo universiteta* 61, no. 3
(2015): 110–15; S.A. Papkov, "'Kontrrevoliutsionnaia prestupnost' i osobennosti ee podavleniia v Sibiri v gody Velikoi Otechestvennoi voiny
(1941–1945)," in S.A. Papkov and K. Teraiama, eds., *Ural i Sibir' v Stalinskoi
politike* (Novosibirsk: Sibirskii khronograf, 2002), 205–23; I. M. Savitskii,
"Formirovanie kadrov oboronnoi promyshlennosti Novosibirskoi oblasti
v gody Velikoi Otechestvennoi voiny," in V.A. Isupov et al., eds., *Zapadaia
Sibir' v gody Velikoi Otechestvennoi voine (1941–1945 gg.)* (Novosibirsk:
Nauka, 2004), 3–35.

26 For examples, see V.P. Danilov and S.A. Krasil'nikov, eds., *Spetspereselentsy
v Zapadnoi Sibiri, 1939–1945* (Novosibirsk: Ekor, 1996); L.I. Gvozdkova and
A.A. Mit', eds., *Prinuditel'nyi trud: Ispravitel'no-trudovye lageria v Kuzbasse
(30–50e gg.)*, 2 vols. (Kemerovo: Kuzbassvuzizdat, 1994); and V. Maksheev
and Aleksandr Solzhentsyn, eds., *Narymskaia khronika, 1930–1945: Tragediia
spetspereselentsev: Dokumenty i vospominaniia* (Moscow: Russkii put', 1997).

27 Bacon, *The Gulag at War*, 39, 123–44.

28 Anne Applebaum, *Gulag: A History* (New York: Doubleday, 2003); Barnes,
Death and Redemption; Alan Barenberg, *Gulag Town, Company Town: Forced
Labor and Its Legacy in Vorkuta* (New Haven, CT: Yale University Press,
2014); Khlevniuk, *The History of the Gulag*.

29 Leonid Borodkin and Simon Ertz, "Coercion vs. Motivation: Forced Labor
in Norilsk," in Paul Gregory and Valery Lazarev, eds., *The Economics of
Forced Labor: The Soviet Gulag* (Stanford: Hoover Institution Press, 2003),
79–80.

30 Ertz also argues that, by the mid-to-late 1930s, "the Gulag administration
had evolved in the minds of top Soviet leaders from an organization that

supplied prisoner labour to an administration that could, on its own, carry out complex construction projects of the highest priority"; see Simon Ertz, "Building Norilsk," in Gregory and Lazarev, eds., *Economics of Forced Labor*, 133. David Nordlander has come to a similar conclusion for the camps of Kolyma, where "economic rather than political needs were paramount." David Nordlander, "Magadan and the Economic History of Dalstroi in the 1930s," in Gregory and Lazarev, eds., *Economics of Forced Labor*, 107.

31 Barenberg, *Gulag Town, Company Town*, 44.

32 A good overview can be found in Bacon, *Gulag at War*, 72–7.

33 After all, scholars such as Ivanova and Khlevniuk have shown that re-sources spent on the camps drained resources from the front and, po-tentially, from other projects. See, for example, Oleg Khlevniuk, "The Economy of the OGPU, NKVD, and MVD of the USSR, 1930–1953: The Scale, Structure, and Trends of Development," in Gregory and Lazarev, eds., *Economics of Forced Labor*, 63–5; and Galina Ivanova, *Labour Camp Socialism: The Gulag in the Soviet Totalitarian System*, trans. C. Flath (Armonk, NY: M.E. Sharpe, 2000), 69–125, esp. 86, 104.

34 Ivanova, *Labour Camp Socialism*, 76, 86, 96.

35 Golfo Alexopoulos, "Amnesty 1945: The Revolving Door of Stalin's Gulag," *Slavic Review* 64, no. 2 (2005): 274–306. The NKVD and the USSR Procurator Directive 185 from April 1942 ordered Article 58ers to remain in the camps, even after their terms had ended, for the duration of the war. For an example, see the following prisoner file: Gosudarstvennyi arkhiv Tomskoi oblasti (GATO) f. R-1151 op. 1 d. 319, esp. l. 119.

36 Steven A. Barnes, "All for the Front, All for Victory! The Mobilization of Forced Labor in the Soviet Union during World War Two," *International Labor and Working-Class History* 58 (2000): 242.

37 Alexopoulos, "Amnesty 1945," 303.

38 See Barnes, "All for the Front," 252, and Barnes, *Death and Redemption*, esp. 107–54.

39 Alexopoulos, "Destructive-Labor Camps" and *Illness and Inhumanity*.

40 See Gosudarstvennyi arkhiv Novosibirskoi Oblasti (GANO) f. P-260 op. 1 d. 24 ll. 40–41ob. By 1 April 1943, 51 per cent of the camp contingent was unable to work due to poor physical condition. Given Alexopoulos's argument concerning labour categories – that even those deemed physi-cally fit for heavy labour were generally in poor physical condition – a very high percentage of the prisoner contingent in Western Siberia was likely on the verge of death at this time. See Alexopoulos, "Destructive-Labor Camps."

41 Lennart Samuelson, *Plans for Stalin's War Machine: Tukhachevskii and Military-Economic Planning, 1925–1941* (New York: St. Martin's Press, 2000).

42 For more, see chapter 5 of the present work, as well as Wilson T. Bell,
    "The Gulag and Soviet Society in Western Siberia, 1929–1953" (PhD diss.,
    University of Toronto, 2011), esp. 112–62.

43 Alena Ledeneva, *Russia's Economy of Favours:* Blat, *Networking and Informal
    Exchange* (Cambridge: Cambridge University Press, 1998); see also Sheila
    Fitzpatrick, *Everyday Stalinism: Ordinary Life in Extraordinary Times: Soviet
    Russia in the 1930s* (New York: Oxford University Press, 1999). For issues of
    blat and corruption as they pertain specifically to the Gulag, see also James
    Heinzen, "Corruption in the Gulag: Dilemmas of Officials and Prisoners,"
    Comparative Economic Studies 47 (2005): 456–75. Heinzen focuses on the
    years 1945–53.

44 J. Otto Pohl, *The Stalinist Penal System: A Statistical History of Soviet
    Repression and Terror, 1930–1953* (London: McFarland & Company, 1997),
    40.

45 Asif Siddiqi, "Scientists and Specialists in the Gulag: Life and Death in
    Stalin's *Sharashka,*" in David-Fox, ed., *The Soviet Gulag*, 87–113 (quotation
    104).

46 GARF f. 9414, op. 1, d. 68, l. 10.

47 Barenberg, *Gulag Town, Company Town*, 9.

48 Along with Barenberg's *Gulag Town, Company Town*, see Oleg Khlevniuk,
    "The Gulag and the Non-Gulag as One Interrelated Whole," trans. Simon
    Belokowsky, *Kritika: Explorations in Russian and Eurasian History* 16, no. 3
    (2015): 479–98, and Bell, "Was the Gulag an Archipelago?" for more on
    interaction between the Gulag and Soviet society.

49 Kate Brown, "Out of Solitary Confinement: The History of the Gulag,"
    Kritika: Explorations in Russian and Eurasian History 8, no. 1 (2007): 67–103,
    esp. 77.

50 Amy Knight, *Beria: Stalin's First Lieutenant* (Princeton, NJ: Princeton
    University Press, 1993).

51 For more on the key role the collectivization/de-kulakization played
    in the growth of the Gulag, see John L. Scherer and Michael Jakobson,
    "The Collectivisation of Agriculture and the Soviet Prison Camp System,"
    Europe-Asia Studies 45, no. 3 (1993): 533–46, and Lynne Viola, *The Unknown
    Gulag: The Lost World of Stalin's Special Settlements* (New York: Oxford
    University Press, 2007).

52 For more on illicit interactions between men and women in the camps, see
    Wilson T. Bell, "Sex, Pregnancy, and Power in the Late Stalinist Gulag,"
    Journal of the History of Sexuality 24, no. 2 (2015): 198–224.

53 See, in particular, the bibliography compiled by Sarah J. Young, "Selected
    Bibliography of Gulag Narratives and Secondary Sources," *Gulag Studies*

7–8 (2014–2015): 110–40. Young has a more extensive version of this bibliography on her website, accessed 4 May 2017, http://sarahjyoung.com/site/gulag-bibliography/. For publications based largely on prisoner correspondence, see Orlando Figes, *Just Send Me Word: A True Story of Love and Survival in the Gulag* (London: Allen Lane, 2012), and Arsenii Formakov, *Gulag Letters*, trans., ed., and with an introduction by Emily D. Johnson (New Haven, CT: Yale University Press, 2017).

1 Ready for Total War?

1 Iosif Berger, *Krushenie pokoleniia. Vospominaniia*, trans. I. Berger (Florence: Aurora, 1973), 102.
2 For the text of the 482-page report, see Rossiskii gosudarstvennyi arkhiv ekonomii (RGAE) fond 7486, opis' 10, delo 5, beginning with list 1.
3 For more on Western Siberia as a "frontier" for the Soviet Union, see David Shearer, "Mastering the Soviet Frontier: Western Siberia in the 1930s," in Eva-Maria Stolberg, ed., *The Siberian Saga: A History of Russia's Wild East* (Frankfurt am Main: Peter Lang, 2005), 159–72. See also Kate Brown, "Out of Solitary Confinement: The History of the Gulag," *Kritika: Explorations in Russian and Eurasian History* 8, no. 1 (2007): 67–104, esp. 89.
4 RGAE f. 7486, op. 10, d. 5, l. 3.
5 RGAE f. 7486, op. 10, d. 5, l. 4.
6 This was the name of Stalin's article relating to the need for increased collectivization rates. See Lynne Viola, *The Unknown Gulag: The Lost World of Stalin's Special Settlements* (New York: Oxford University Press, 2007), 21–2.
7 For key data on Siblag, see *Sistema ispravitel'no-trudovykh lagerei v SSSR, 1923–1960: Spravochnik*, comp. M.B. Smirnov, ed. N.G. Okhotin and A.B. Roginskii (Moscow: Zven'ia, 1998), 391–3. [Henceforth cited as *Sistema*]
8 This is the basic argument set forth in John L. Scherer and Michael Jakobson, "The Collectivisation of Agriculture and the Soviet Prison Camp System," *Europe-Asia Studies* 45, no. 3 (1993): 533–46. See also Lynne Viola, V.P. Danilov, N.A. Ivnitskii, and Denis Kozlov, eds., *The War Against the Peasantry, 1927–30*, vol. 1 of *The Tragedy of the Soviet Countryside*, trans. Steven Shabad (New Haven, CT: Yale University Press, 2005); V.P. Danilov, R.T. Manning, and L. Viola, eds., *Tragediia sovetskoi derevni: kollektivizatsiia i raskulachivanie: dokumenty i materialy v piat' tomakh, 1927–1939*, 5 vols. (Moscow: Rosspen, 1999); and Lynne Viola, *Peasant Rebels under Stalin: Collectivization and the Culture of Peasant Resistance* (New York: Oxford University Press, 1996), and *The Unknown Gulag*.

9 For more on the telescoped development of Soviet institutions, see Peter Holquist, *Making War, Forging Revolution: Russia's Continuum of Crisis, 1914–1921* (Cambridge, MA: Harvard University Press, 2002).

10 Much of the information presented here on Siberia's pre-revolutionary development comes from W. Bruce Lincoln, *The Conquest of a Continent: Siberia and the Russians* (Ithaca, NY: Cornell University Press, 2007).

11 Yuri Slezkine, *Arctic Mirrors: Russia and the Small Peoples of the North* (Ithaca, NY: Cornell University Press, 1994).

12 Willard Sunderland notes that Peter the Great was the first tsar to "view acquiring territorial knowledge as an intrinsically valuable pursuit." Sunderland, "Imperial Space: Territorial Thought and Practice in the Eighteenth Century," in Jane Burbank, Mark von Hagen, and Anatolyi Remnev, eds., *Russian Empire: Space, People, Power, 1700–1930* (Bloomington: Indiana University Press, 2007), 33–66, esp. 33–4.

13 Steven G. Marks, *Road to Power: The Trans-Siberian Railroad and the Colonization of Asian Russia 1850–1917* (Ithaca, NY: Cornell University Press, 1991), esp. 222–6. Interestingly, Marks views the development of the Trans-Siberian Railway as almost "belong[ing] more to the Soviet period than to the tsarist" (225) because of the relationship of the centralizing state to the economy and the overall inefficiencies of the project.

14 Lincoln, *Conquest of a Continent*, 259. In some years, the number of Siberian immigrants was around half a million.

15 Daniel Beer, "Penal Deportation to Siberia and the Limits of State Power, 1801–1881," in Michael David-Fox, ed., *The Soviet Gulag: Evidence, Interpretation, Comparison* (Pittsburgh: Pittsburgh University Press, 2016), 173–98.

16 See Andrew Gentes, "Katorga: Penal Labor and Tsarist Siberia," in Stolberg, ed., *Siberian Saga*, 73 and 85. The Stalinist regime even resurrected the term, *katorga*, for its strict-regimen camps, in April 1943, despite the fact that *katorga* had been one of the most hated practices of the Tsarist regimes. For more, see Steven A. Barnes, "All for the Front, All for Victory! The Mobilization of Forced Labor in the Soviet Union during World War II," *International Labor and Working-Class History* 58 (Fall 2000): 251–2.

17 Abby M. Schrader, "Unruly Felons and Civilizing Wives: Cultivating Marriage in the Siberian Exile System, 1822–1860," *Slavic Review* 66, no. 2 (2007): 230–56 (quotation 236).

18 Schrader, "Unruly Felons," 237. For more on Tsarist-era *katorga* and exile, see Daniel Beer, *The House of the Dead: Siberian Exile under the Tsars* (New York: Alfred A. Knopf, 2017); and Sarah Badcock, *A Prison without Walls? Eastern Siberian Exile in the Last Years of Tsarism* (Oxford: Oxford University Press, 2016).

19 Siberian dairy products, in particular, were considered luxury goods in parts of Western Europe in the years before the First World War. See Eva-Maria Stolberg, "The Genre of Frontiers and Borderlands: Siberia as a Case Study," in Stolberg, ed., *Siberian Saga*, 19.

20 Richard E. Lonsdale, "Siberian Industry before 1917: The Example of Tomsk Guberniya," *Annals of the Association of American Geographers* 53, no. 4 (1963): 479–93, esp. 482. There is debate over the living conditions of factory serfs. For the Urals, where factory serfs worked in huge numbers in the pre-emancipation period, the general consensus is that living and working conditions were terrible. See, for example, William Blackwell, *The Beginnings of Russian Industrialization, 1800–1860* (Princeton, NJ: Princeton University Press, 1968), 155–63. However, Thomas Esper, who looked more closely at archival materials and first-hand accounts of the metallurgical industries in the Urals, concluded that factory serfs there were relatively well off, both in comparison to field serfs in European Russia and even in comparison to factory workers in similar industries in Western Europe at the time. See Thomas Esper, "The Condition of the Serf Workers in Russia's Metallurgical Industry, 1800–1861," *The Journal of Modern History* 50, no. 4 (1978): 660–79.

21 Richard Hellie, "The Economy, Trade and Serfdom," in Maureen Perrie, ed., *The Cambridge History of Russia*, vol. 1, *From Early Rus' to 1689* (Cambridge: Cambridge University Press, 2006), 539–58.

22 There is debate about the actual situation in the Russian countryside in the years between emancipation and the First World War. Wheatcroft concludes, "The growth in peasant unrest over this period [1880s–1914] was probably more a consequence of the decline in governmental authority, regional problems, and the specific problems of wage laborers, than any increase in overall peasant destitution." Stephen G. Wheatcroft, "Crises and the Condition of the Peasantry in Late Imperial Russia," in Esther Kingston-Mann and Timothy Mixter, eds., *Peasant Economy, Culture, and Politics of European Russia, 1800–1921* (Princeton, NJ: Princeton University Press, 1991), 128–74, esp. 166.

23 Only a small number of peasants actually left the commune. See David Moon, *The Russian Peasantry, 1600–1930: The World the Peasants Made* (London: Longman, 1999), 351. See also Yanni Kotsonis, "The Problem of the Individual in the Stolypin Reforms," *Kritika: Explorations in Russian and Eurasian History* 12, no. 1 (2011): 25–52, for more on the motivations behind the reforms.

24 For more, see N.G.O. Pereira, *White Siberia: The Politics of Civil War* (Montreal: McGill-Queen's University Press, 1995) 156–71, 175. The Siberian peasantry, while hardly fond of the Whites, tended to be suspicious

of (and at times hostile towards) the Bolsheviks as well. For a discussion of peasant resistance to Bolshevik rule in Siberia, see also V.M. Suverov and E.V. Suverov, "Povstancheskoe dvizhenie v Sibiri. 1920–1923 gg.," in S.V. Makarchuk, ed., *Sibir': XX vek* (Kemerovo: Kuzbassvuzizdat, 1997), 53–60. See also John Channon, "Siberia in Revolution and Civil War, 1917–1921," in Alan Wood, ed., *The History of Siberia: From Russian Conquest to Revolution* (London: Routledge, 1991), 158–80, esp. 161.

25　Pereira, *White Siberia*, 161.

26　The extent of that "prosperity" is, of course, debatable. Moshe Lewin notes that "Soviet rural 'capitalism' barely existed," although the birth rate in the countryside during the period of the New Economic Policy (NEP) increased, helping the country recover from the disastrous Civil War. See Moshe Lewin, *The Making of the Soviet System: Essays in the Social History of Interwar Russia* (New York: The New Press, 1994), 213–15. NEP brought economic recovery to parts of the countryside. By 1926, Siberia's grain yield exceeded pre-war figures. See Lincoln, *Conquest of a Continent*, 320.

27　See Vladimir Lenin, *The Development of Capitalism in Russia* (Moscow: Foreign Languages Publishing House, 1956), esp. chap. 2.

28　There is considerable debate over the extent of economic stratification among the peasantry in the pre-revolutionary countryside. For more, see Robert E. Johnson, "Family Life-Cycles and Economic Stratification: A Case-Study in Rural Russia," *Journal of Social History* 30, no. 3 (1997): 705–31; and Teodor Shanin, *The Awkward Class: Political Sociology of Peasantry in a Developing Society: Russia 1910–1925* (Oxford: Clarendon Press, 1972).

29　Franklyn D. Holzman, "The Soviet Ural-Kuznetsk Combine: A Study in Investment Criteria and Industrialization Policies," *The Quarterly Journal of Economics* 71, no. 3 (1957): 368–405 (quotation 368).

30　Stephen Kotkin, *Magnetic Mountain: Stalinism as a Civilization* (Berkeley: University of California Press, 1995), 39.

31　Kotkin, *Magnetic Mountain*, 399n12.

32　See Viola et al., eds., *War Against the Peasantry*; and Viola, *Peasant Rebels under Stalin*, 13–44.

33　This is David Moon's argument. See Moon, *The Russian Peasantry, 1600–1930*.

34　Anne Applebaum, in *Gulag: A History* (New York: Doubleday, 2003), 47, notes that peasants comprised the vast majority of Gulag prisoners throughout the 1930s.

35　The show trials commonly associated with the Great Terror were a separate phenomenon from the mass operations. For a discussion, see Paul Hagenloh, *Stalin's Police: Public Order and Mass Repression in the USSR, 1926–1941* (Baltimore: Johns Hopkins University Press, 2009), 410–11n105.

See also "Document 170: NKVD operational order [no. 00447] 'Concerning the punishment of former kulaks, criminals and other anti-Soviet elements,' 30 July 1937" in J. Arch Getty and Oleg V. Naumov, eds., *The Road to Terror: Stalin and the Self-Destruction of the Bolsheviks, 1932–1939* (New Haven, CT: Yale University Press, 1999), 473–80. See also Brown, "Out of Solitary Confinement," esp. 98–9.

36 See Applebaum, *Gulag*, 47; and, for an excellent discussion of the internal passports, Hagenloh, *Stalin's Police*, 119–32. Stalin's obsession with the countryside and agricultural production also underscores the importance of the peasant question to Stalin-era development. See R.W. Davies, "Stalin as Economic Policy-Maker: Soviet Agriculture, 1931–36," in Sarah Davies and James Harris, eds., *Stalin: A New History* (Cambridge: Cambridge University Press, 2005), 121–39.

37 See James R. Harris, "The Growth of the Gulag: Forced Labor in the Urals Region, 1929–31," *The Russian Review* 56, no. 2 (1997): 265–80. For another example of an argument showing a move from a repressive to an economic rationale, see Edwin Bacon, *The Gulag at War: Stalin's Forced Labour System in Light of the Archives* (New York: New York University Press, 1994). Bacon argues that the Gulag gradually took on an economic rationale as authorities attempted to make the camps self-sufficient and use the increasing number of prisoners at their disposal.

38 The Andreev Commission was created by the Politburo in March 1931 to administer kulak operations. For more, see Viola, *Unknown Gulag*, 96–7, 114–15, 128–9.

39 Rossiskii gosudarstvennyi arkhiv sotsial'no-politicheskoi istorii (RGASPI) f. 17, op. 162, d. 9, ll. 176–8.

40 See, for example, Sheila Fitzpatrick, *Everyday Stalinism: Ordinary Life in Extraordinary Times: Soviet Russia in the 1930s* (New York: Oxford University Press, 1999).

41 This has prompted some scholars and others to conclude that the concentration camp was fundamental to Soviet rule. See, for example, Applebaum, *Gulag*, 5–10. Applebaum notes that the "Red Terror was crucial to Lenin's struggle for power. Concentration camps, the so-called 'special camps,' were crucial to the Red Terror" (8).

42 Aidan Forth, "Britain's Archipelago of Camps: Labor and Detention in a Liberal Empire, 1871–1903," in David-Fox, ed., *The Soviet Gulag: Evidence, Interpretation, Comparison* (Pittsburgh: Pittsburgh University Press, 2016), 199–223.

43 Richard Pipes's examination of Lenin's unpublished writings notes, "As far as Lenin's personality is concerned, we note, first and foremost, his utter disregard for human life, except where his own family and closest

associates were concerned." See Richard Pipes, ed., *The Unkown Lenin: From the Secret Archives* (New Haven, CT: Yale University Press, 1996), 9.

44 Many scholars have argued that the experiences of the Civil War had a profound effect on later Soviet practices. See, for example, Sheila Fitzpatrick, *The Russian Revolution*, 2nd ed. (Oxford: Oxford University Press, 1994), 68–92; and Donald J. Raleigh, *Experiencing Russia's Civil War: Politics, Society, and Revolutionary Culture in Saratov, 1917–1922* (Princeton, NJ: Princeton University Press, 2002).

45 Some scholars emphasize the basic inevitability of Stalinist repression. Martin Malia, for example, traces a direct link from Marxist-Leninist ideology to Stalinist. See Malia, *The Soviet Tragedy: A History of Socialism in Russia, 1917–1991* (New York: The Free Press, 1994), esp. 1–3, 16–17, 52. Malia's link between ideology and repression is evident in such statements as, "It was the all-encompassing pretensions of the Soviet utopia that furnished what can only be called the 'genetic code' of the tragedy" (16).

46 Michael Jakobson, *Origins of the GULAG: The Soviet Prison-Camp System, 1917–1934* (Lexington: University Press of Kentucky, 1993), 5.

47 For more, see Peter H. Solomon, *Soviet Criminal Justice under Stalin* (Cambridge: Cambridge University Press, 1996), 26–30.

48 Sheila Fitzpatrick argues that, instead of basing class on economic factors, the Bolsheviks inadvertently through their policies "ascribed class," that is, made class dependent on the state, much as the tsarist regimes had done (with a different hierarchy, of course). See Fitzpatrick, "Ascribing Class: The Construction of Social Identity in Soviet Russia," in Sheila Fitzpatrick, ed., *Stalinism: New Directions* (London: Routledge, 2000), 20–46.

49 Solomon, *Soviet Criminal Justice*, 30.

50 The Cheka (or VChK – *Vserossiiskaia chrezvychainaia komissia po bor'be s kontrrevoliutsiei i sabotazhem* – All-Russian Special Commission for Combating Counter-revolution and Sabotage) was meant to be a temporary security force to fight counter-revolution following the Bolshevik takeover of 1917. It was the precursor for other internal security-police forces, sometimes referred to as the "secret police." "Secret" may be a misnomer, as the Cheka, in particular, operated relatively openly. See, for example, Fitzpatrick, *Russian Revolution*, 77.

51 Jakobson, *Origins of the GULAG*, 70: here he notes that the *Glavnoe upravlenie mest' zakliucheniia* (GUMZ), the NKVD's prison agency in the 1920s, attempted to destroy ideas of re-education while still speaking in those terms. Note, however, that Jakobson's sources heavily favour the NKIu point of view, and there is evidence to suggest that some within the NKVD

took ideas of re-education seriously in the 1920s. See the review by Peter
H. Solomon Jr., in *Slavic Review* 54, no. 1 (1995): 190–2.

52 The OGPU was created in 1923 out of the Russian NKVD as an all-union
organization responsible for state security. In 1934, the newly formed all-
union NKVD came into existence and reabsorbed the OGPU. For more,
see Hagenloh, *Stalin's Police*.

53 The initial proposal came in April 1929. See Applebaum, *Gulag*, 50. There
is also a good discussion in Oleg Khlevniuk, *The History of the Gulag: From
Collectivization to the Great Terror* (New Haven, CT: Yale University Press,
2004), 24–39. See also Hagenloh, *Stalin's Police*, 62–5, 149–61.

54 Document no. 9, "Ispravitel'no-Trudovoi Kodeks RSFSR [16 October
1924]," in A.I. Kokurin and N.V. Petrov, eds., *GULAG (Glavnoe upravlenie
lagerei) 1918-1960* (Moscow: Materik, 2002), 30–56.

55 Kokurin and Petrov, eds., *GULAG*, 30.

56 Kotkin, *Magnetic Mountain*, esp. 230–5.

57 Shearer, "Mastering the Soviet Frontier," 163.

58 See N.Ia. Gushchin, "Demograficheskoe razvitie sovetskoi Sibiri," in R.S.
Vasil'evskii and N.Ia. Gushchin, eds., *Istoricheskaia demografiia Sibiri: sbornik
nauchnykh trudov* (Novosibirsk: Nauka, 1992), 125.

59 See Nick Baron, "Conflict and Complicity: The Expansion of the Karelian
Gulag, 1923–1933," *Cahiers du Monde russe* 42, no. 2–4 (2001): 615–48,
esp. 628. Here Baron discusses the lack of patience for voluntary settlement schemes.

60 Khlevniuk, *History of the Gulag*, 339.

61 RGASPI f. 17, op. 3, d. 815, ll. 17–19.

62 Applebaum, *Gulag*, 56.

63 Khlevniuk, *History of the Gulag*, 24.

64 Oleg Khlevniuk, "Vvedenie," in Khlevniuk, ed., *Istoriia Stalinskogo Gulaga*,
vol. 3, *Ekonomika Gulaga* (Moscow: Rosspen, 2004) 26. [Henceforth cited as
ISG, 3]

65 See Alan Barenberg, *Gulag Town, Company Town: The Gulag and Its Legacy in
Vorkuta* (New Haven, CT: Yale University Press, 2014).

66 Gosudarstvennyi arkhiv Rossiskoi federatsii (GARF) f. 9479, op. 1, d. 3, ll.
23–4. Iagoda's proposal has also been published in English translation. See
Document 6: "G.G. Yagoda's proposals to convert camps into colonization
settlements 12 April 1930," in Khlevniuk, *History of the Gulag*, 23–5. See
also Viola, *Unknown Gulag*, 4–5.

67 Kate Brown argues that this incident confirmed for authorities that
independent prisoner colonies would not work. She writes, "Most important, the Nazino tragedy discredited Iagoda's notion of flourishing,

self-sufficient, penal settlements on the frontier. Instead of self-reliant, the settlers became emaciated dependents or victims of violence." See Brown, "Out of Solitary Confinement," 92. For more detail on the tragedy, see Nicholas Werth, *Cannibal Island: Death in a Siberian Gulag*, trans. Steven Rendall (Princeton, NJ: Princeton University Press, 2007). The exiles were "socially harmful elements," many of them peasants who had fled the countryside and had been living in Moscow and Leningrad.

68   Robert Eikhe was an Old Bolshevik. He had been a party member from 1905 and served as secretary of the Western Siberian Party Committee in the 1930s. From 1937 to 1938 he was the People's Commissar of Agriculture. He was arrested in 1938 and shot in 1940. See Khlevniuk, *History of the Gulag*, 347.

69   See Werth, *Cannibal Island*, esp. 106–7, 120, 121–70; Sergei Krasil'nikov *Serp i Molokh: Krest'ianskaia ssylka v Zapadnoi Sibiri v 1930-e gody* (Moscow: Rosspen, 2003), 99–107; and A.V. Bol'shakova, Sergei Krasil'nikov, and B.P. Trenin, eds., *Nazinskaia tragediia: Iz istorii zemli Tomskoi: Dokumental'noe nauchnoe izdanie* (Tomsk: Nauka, 2002).

70   For a brief summary of the relationship between the special settlements, the Gulag, and the NKVD, see the introduction to Gosudarstvennyi arkhiv Rossiskoi federatsii (GARF) f. 9479, op. 1. See also N.V. Petrov, "Vvedenie," in Petrov and N.I Vladimirtsev, eds., *Istoriia Stalinskogo Gulaga*, vol. 2, *Karatel'naia sistema: struktura i kadry* (Moscow: Rosspen, 2004), 29. [Henceforth cited as *ISG*, 2]

71   I.I. Dolgikh directed this department from 1930 until 1938. Dolgikh would go on to have a long career within the Gulag and the NKVD and later MVD. Following his work at Siblag (where, it should be noted, he was one of the longest-tenured senior administrators), he later was the director of Viatlag, Ivdel'lag, and Iuzhkuzbasslag (another West Siberian camp) and also spent time as vice-director for the administration for prisoners of war and internees of the MVD. See Krasil'nikov, *Serp i Molokh*, 181.

72   There were special settlements located all over the region, including close to population centres (particularly in the Kuznestk Basin), but the majority of the settlements were located in remote areas to the north, particularly Narym. See Shearer, "Mastering the Soviet Frontier," 163.

73   Werth, *Cannibal Island*, 23.

74   Indeed, when the seven new forestry camps were founded in 1937 (reformed in a different configuration as the Administration of Camps of the Forestry Industry (ULLP) in 1939, there was only one in Western Siberia, Tomasinlag, despite the region's vast forests. See Khlevniuk, *History of the Gulag*, 178.

75 RGASPI f. 17, op. 162, d. 10, ll. 51–4.
76 See, for example, GARF f. 9479, op. 1, d. 30, ll. 6, 7–8.
77 See also Shearer, "Mastering the Soviet Frontier," esp. 170.
78 For the figures, see table 4 and table 7 of V.N. Zemskov, *Spetsposelentsy v SSSR, 1930–1960* (Moscow: Nauka, 2005), 24–5 and 40–1. For more on the restoration of rights, see Viola, *Unknown Gulag*, 150–9.
79 Table 8 of Zemskov's *Spetsposelentsy v SSSR* (43) indicates that about one-third of the special settlers in 1938 were children under the age of fourteen.
80 For more on the 1938 special settlement population, see Zemskov, *Spetsposelentsy v SSSR*, 33.
81 GARF f. 9479, op. 1, d. 3, ll. 81–5.
82 GARF f. 9479, op. 1, d. 16, l. 12. For more on the severe living conditions in the special settlements, see Viola, *Unknown Gulag*, esp. 132–41.
83 I.I. Dolgikh, quoted in Krasil'nikov, *Serp i molokh*, 177. See also note 71, above, for more on Dolgikh.
84 For information on living space in the camps, see GARF f. 9414, op. 1, d. 328, l. 19; GARF f. 9414, op. 1, d., 469, l. 159; Document no. 94, in A.B. Bezborodov, I.V. Bezborodova, and V.M. Khrustalev, eds., *Istoriia Staliniskogo Gulaga*, vol. 4, *Naselenie Gulaga: chislennost' i usloviia soderzhaniia* (Moscow: Rosspen, 2004), 217–18; and Gosudarstvennyi arkhiv Novosibirskoi oblasti (GANO) f. R-20, op. 1, d. 404, l. 9 and GARF f. 9414, op. 1, d. 469, l. 159. The special settler living space information comes from GARF f. 9479, op. 1, d. 12, l. 41.
85 GARF f. 9479, op. 1, d. 29, ll. 7–8.
86 GARF f. 9479, op. 1, d. 30, l. 19.
87 Kotkin, *Magnetic Mountain*, 161.
88 These figures come from the document "Iz statisticheskikh prilozhenii k otchetnomu dokladu SIBLaga OGPU ob itogakh khoziastvennogo osvoeniia spetspereselentsami Naryma za period s maia 1931 po iiun' 1932 g.," in Danilov and Krasil'nikov, eds., *Spetspereselentsy v Zapadnoi Sibiri 1931–33* (Novosibirsk: Nauka, 1992), 288–9.
89 The 26,709 deaths represent approximately 6.5 per cent of the total number of special settlers in the region at one point or another during the year, or approximately 10.3 per cent of the average number of settlers during that year. The numbers come from Zemskov, *Spetsposelentsy v SSSR*, 24–5.
90 GARF f. 9479, op. 1, d. 35, ll. 1–4. Note that by this time, while most settlers lived in heated homes or barracks, 12 per cent still resided in earthen dugouts (*zemlianki* and *poluzemlianki*).
91 GARF f. 9479, op. 1, d. 30, l. 19: a memorandum (*dokladnaia zapiska*) from Matvei Berman, the director of the Gulag, to Iagoda, regarding the state of special settlements in Narym.

92 S.A. Krasil'nikov, "Spetspereselentsy, spetsarteli i spetsorgany: mekhanizmy i rezul'taty spetskolonizatsii severa Zapadnoi Sibiri v 1930-e gg.,"
in L.I. Borodkin, P. Gregori [Paul Gregory], and O.V. Khlevniuk, eds.,
GULAG: Ekonomika prinuditel'nogo truda (Moscow: Rosspen, 2005), 279–316,
esp. 287, 291. This type of comparison – between conditions and economic
activity inside the Gulag and out – is lacking in the historiography, and
Krasil'nikov's work represents a step in the right direction.

93 Berman had a connection to Western Siberia. He had been the chair of the
Tomsk Cheka from 1920–3 and thus played a role in the Bolshevik victory
in Siberia during the Civil War. He held various posts within the OGPU,
rising to the position of deputy director of the OGPU's camp administration in July 1930 and director of the Gulag in June 1932. He received
numerous awards, including the Order of Lenin in 1933 for his role in the
construction of the White Sea–Baltic Canal and the Order of the Red Star in
1937 for the construction of the Moscow-Volga Canal. He was arrested in
December 1938 and shot in March 1939. For more, see Kokurin and Petrov,
eds., *GULAG*, 804.

94 Viola, *Unknown Gulag*, 157.

95 For Iagoda's letter and the TsIK's response, see GARF f. 9479, op. 1, d. 29,
ll. 10–11.

96 Viola, *Unknown Gulag*, 157.

97 GARF f. 9479, op. 1, d. 35, l. 5. See also Viola, "'Tear the Evil from the
Root': The Children of the *Spetspereselentsy* of the North," *Studia Slavica
Finlandensia* 17 (2000): 34–72.

98 R.S. Bikmetov, "Uchastie spetskontingenta v formirovanii infrastruktury
gorodov Kuzbassa v 1930-e – 1950-e gg.," in Iu. V. Kupert and K.V. Fadeev,
eds., *Problemy urbanizatsii vostochnykh regionov Rossii v XIX-XX vv.* (Tomsk:
Izd-vo TGASU, 2007), 132–42, particularly 133–4.

99 *Sistema*, 392. Note that I use the term "at least" because the exact number
is difficult to know: there are small gaps for which information is unavailable. The longest-serving director during this period was the first, M.M.
Chuntonov, who held the position for just over two years from September
1929 to October 1931 and again for over two years from February 1934
to April 1936. Chuntonov was also the director of Karlag from 1932
(exact date unknown) to August 1933 and of the Baikalo-Amurskii ITL
(BAMLag) from August 1933 to February 1934, and the acting (*vrid.*) director of Belbaltlag for July and August 1937. Given that August 1937 is his
last listed employment within the Gulag, in all likelihood he was arrested
during the Great Terror. See *Sistema*, 153, 163, 285, 392.

100 Note that in 1934 the official term for the settlements became "labour settlements" and their inhabitants "labour settlers" (*trudposelentsy*), although they were still often referred to as special settlers (*spetsposelentsy*), a term that came back into official use in 1944 for the de-kulakized peasants. See Viola, *Unknown Gulag*, 199n4.

101 GARF f. 9401, op. 1a, d. 6, l. 95: "Ob organizatsii Upravleniia lagerei, trudposelenii i mest zakliucheniia UNKVD ZSK" (7 August 1935).

102 GARF f. 9401, op. 1a, d. 35, l. 4: *NKVD Prikaz no. 00871: O reorganizatsii Siblaga NKVD i upravlenii OITK UNKVD po Novosibirskoi oblasti* (29 July 1939).

103 See *Sistema*, 392n5. UITLK NSO (Siblag) remained the administrative body for the area camps until spring 1942, when it was divided into two separate administrations: UITLK NSO in Novosibirsk, made up mostly of the camps and colonies involved in contract work, and Siblag in Mariinsk, made up mostly of camps engaged in agricultural work. For more, see chapter 2 of the present study. For the purpose of simplification, I refer to the camp system as Siblag for the period prior to the 1942 split.

104 For examples of orders from local party organizations, see especially chapter 2 of the present study.

105 GARF f. 9401, op. 1a, d. 6, l. 131.

106 *Sistema*, 204. For more on Gornoshorlag, see the discussion later in this chapter.

107 *Sistema*, 482–3. These "refugees" were from territories annexed by the Soviet Union at the outbreak of the Second World War in Europe. For more, see the discussion of resistance in chapter 3 of the present study.

108 See S.A. Papkov, *Stalinskii terror v Sibiri, 1928–1941* (Novosibirsk: Izd-vo Sibirskogo Otdeleniia Rossiiskoi Akademii Nauk, 1997), 130; and GANO f. P-260, op. 1, d. 1 [Protokol partiino-khoziastvennogo aktiva UITLK UMVD po NSO], l. 5. Unfortunately, I was unable to find out specific information about the involvement of the Antibes camp at the expo.

109 Papkov, *Stalinskii terror v Sibiri*, 134–5.

110 Document 13, "Dokladnaia zapiska zamestitelia predsedatelia OGPU G.G. Iagody I.V. Stalinu ob itogakh khoziastvennoi deiatel'nosti lagerei za 1932 i pervyi kvartal 1933 g. Ne ranee 26 apr 1933," *ISG*, 3:96. Iagoda's plan for prisoner colonies had not failed completely by this time, either, although the focus had shifted to ex-prisoners. He informed Stalin that as of 1 January 1933 there were twelve "colonization settlements" with a total population of 6,062 people (3,570 ex-prisoners and their family members). Siblag was one of five camps to run these types of settlements,

tied to specific "industrial enterprises," unnamed in the documentation. See Document 13, *ISG*, 3:106.

111   For camp mortality rates during the Stalin era, see Applebaum, *Gulag*, 582–3.

112   V.M. Molotov was a member of the Bolshevik Central Committee from 1921–57, and the Politburo from 1926–57. From 1930–41 he was Chair of the Council of People's Commissars (SNK, or *Sovnarkom*). See Getty and Naumov, *The Road to Terror*, 605.

113   RGASPI f. 17, op. 162, d. 13, l. 132 (pt 18, prot 120 O stroitel'stve Baikalo-Amurskoi magistrali [proekt predlozhenii] PB ot 16.10.32g pr. No 119, p. 21). Two of these projects, the Moscow-Volga Canal and firewood for Leningrad and Moscow, were located in the very heart of European Russia, and only two (the BAM and Kolyma) were east of the Urals.

114   Leonid Borodkin and Simon Ertz have concluded that unfit prisoners were rarely sent to Arctic camps such as Norilsk. See Borodkin and Ertz, "Coercion vs. Motivation: Forced Labor in Norilsk," in Paul Gregory and Vasily Lazarev, eds., *The Economics of Forced Labor: The Soviet Gulag* (Stanford: Hoover Institution Press, 2003), 79–80.

115   Golfo Alexopoulos, *Illness and Inhumanity in Stalin's Gulag* (New Haven, CT: Yale University Press, 2017), 189.

116   The most famous Siblag memoir is that of Anna Larina, Nikolai Bukharin's widow. This was published in English in 1993 as *This I Cannot Forget: The Memoirs of Nikolai Bukharin's Widow*, trans. Gary Kern, intro. Stephen Cohen (New York: W.W. Norton, 1993). Her, memoir, however, mostly focuses on Bukharin, rather than her time in the camps. The large memoir database (now around 1,600 memoir texts or excerpts) housed by the Sakharov Center (http://www.sakharov-center.ru/asfcd/auth/) does not contain many memoirs devoted to Siblag. A database search for Siblag on 5 May 2017 revealed seventy-one publications about or by former prisoners that mention Siblag (226 results, but many of these were repeats). Of the seventy-one former prisoners, only thirty spent time in the camp (others mention it in passing, or simply refer to Siberian camps, but did not spend time in Siblag), and only sixteen spent time in Siblag during the war. Not all of these memoirs are available on the site, either. The Memorial Society archives in Moscow contained only seven Siblag accounts when I was there for my doctoral research in 2004–5: eight files for seven separate memoirs: Memorial f. 2, op. 1, dd. 56, 84, 97; Memorial f. 2, op. 2, d. 14, 27–28, 48; Memorial f. 2, op. 3, d. 28.

117   Beer, "Penal Deportation to Siberia," 177–8.

118 See GARF f. 9401, op. 1a, d. 6, l. 125 (NKVD prikaz no. 00356, "O nepori-adkakh v Sibirskom Ispravitel'no-Trudovom Lagere NKVD," 25-go sen-tiabria 1935).

119 G.M. Ivanova, "Kadry GULAGa," in I.V. Dobrovol'skii and G.M. Ivanova, eds., *GULAG: ego stroiteli, obitateli i geroi: Rossiia po dorogam fa-natizma i muchenichestva* (Moscow: Mezh.obshchestvo prav cheloveka, 1998), 47.

120 One of the few scholars to discuss the issue of Gulag contract labourers in any detail is Donald Filtzer, *Soviet Workers and Late Stalinism: Labour and the Restoration of the Stalinist System after World War II* (Cambridge: Cambridge University Press, 2002), esp. 15–17, 23–4.

121 Quite early on, Soviet authorities realized that using the special settlers in forestry could benefit the regime, especially in remote areas. See Viola, *Unknown Gulag*, 60–1.

122 See Michael Mancini, *One Dies, Get Another: Convict Leasing in the American South, 1866–1928* (Columbia: University of South Carolina Press, 1996); and Alex Lichtenstein, *Twice the Work of Free Labor: The Political Economy of Convict Labor in the New South* (London: Verso, 1996).

123 Document 18, "Dokladnaia zapiska nachal'nika finansovogo otdela NKVD SSSR L.I. Berenzona narkomu vnutrennikh del SSSR G.G. Iagode ob izlishkakh rabochei sily v lageriakh" (10 Jan 1935), *ISG*, 3:115–16.

124 An NKVD operational order concerning the prevention of escapes, from November 1940, notes that "brigades of prisoners, working at contract sites and other places, where there is the possibility of personal con-tact [*obshchenie*] with the civilian population, must undergo thorough searches at the gates [*na vakhtakh*]." GARF f. 9401, op. 1a, d. 60, l. 41. For more on instances of non-prisoners working alongside Gulag prisoners see Filtzer, *Soviet Workers and Late Stalinism*, 145; and Document 39, on the isolation of prisoners at Ukhta-Pechora, in Khlevniuk, *History of the Gulag*, 121. Contracted prisoners were not the only ones who worked side by side with non-prisoners. This practice was common in the scientific re-search camps called *sharashki*. See Asif Siddiqi, "Scientists and Specialists in the Gulag: Life and Death in Stalin's *Sharashka*," in David-Fox, ed., *The Soviet Gulag*, 93.

125 As quoted in Khlevniuk, *History of the Gulag*, 244.

126 Document 18, *ISG*, 3:115–16.

127 Document 20, "Dokladnaia zapiska narkoma vnutrennikh del SSSR G.G. Iagody I.V. Stalinu o rabote lagerei v 1934 g. i o plane rabot na 1935 g.," in *ISG*, 3:123.

128 *Sibirskaia perekovka*, 27 January 1945, *The GULAG Press 1920–1937* (Leiden, The Netherlands: IDC Publishers, 1999), fiche 485.

129 "Work refusal" covered several possible types of prisoners. Some of the "work refusers" may have been members of criminal gangs, who tended to run their own affairs. Some were simply too ill to work but were not awarded invalid status.

130 Document 27, "Ob"iasnitel'naia zapiska nachal'nika GULAG I.I.Plinera k svodke o trudovom ispol'zovanii zakliuchennykh v lageriakh NKVD za mai 1938 goda," *ISG*, 3:144–5. For more on Sazlag – Sredneaziatskii ITL, see *Sistema*, 399. All three were centred in the more southerly regions east of the Urals (Siblag in Novosibirsk; Karlag in Karaganda, Kazakhstan; and Sazlag in Tashkent, Uzbekistan), making transport somewhat easier, but where one might expect healthier prisoners than in the far north, where weather conditions were much harsher. Given the practice of sending healthier prisoners to priority camps, it is not clear what is meant by a "surplus" in this case, other than a general acknowledgment that these camps suffered from overcrowding. In any case, the practice of sending unhealthy contingents to Siblag likely contributed to the high proportion of idle days at Siblag.

131 GARF f. 9401, op. 1a, d. 15, ll. 111–12.

132 Memorial f. 2, op. 2, d. 14, l. 88.

133 See Ertz and Borodkin, "Coercion vs. Motivation: Forced Labor in Norilsk," esp. 79–80, where they note that Norilsk received mostly healthy contingents.

134 Alexopoulos, *Illness and Inhumanity*, esp. 183–207.

135 N.I. Ezhov had been a party member from 1917. He became the deputy commissar for agriculture in 1930 and from 1936–8 – the period of the Great Terror – he directed the NKVD. He was arrested in April 1939 and shot in 1940. For more see Khlevniuk, *History of the Gulag*, 357, and J. Arch Getty and Oleg V. Naumov, eds., *Yezhov: The Rise of Stalin's "Iron Fist"* (New Haven, CT: Yale University Press, 2008).

136 This is the argument of S.A. Papkov. See Papkov, *Stalinskii terror v Sibiri*, 135.

137 See David J. Dallin and Boris I. Nicolaevsky, *Forced Labor in Soviet Russia* (New Haven, CT: Yale University Press, 1947), 215. Here they write that "living conditions were exceptionally bad" at Siblag.

138 See O. Fel'tgeim", "Konets ssylki," *Annales contemporaines/Sovremennyia zapiski* 68 (1939), 413. From his description, it is unclear what activities the prisoners were engaged in for the first three months.

139 Berger, *Krushenie pokoleniia*, 102.

140 See Document 9, "Letter from worker S. I. Verkhoturov to V.M. Molotov, 5 June 1932," in Khevniuk, *History of the Gulag*, 38–9.
141 This particular letter resulted in an inspection of the camp (by Siblag authorities). The report, not surprisingly, supported the camp's directors. See Khlevniuk, *History of the Gulag*, 39.
142 Tsentr dokumentatsii noveishii istorii Tomskoi oblasti (TsDNI TO) f. 80, op. 1, d. 139, l. 22.
143 TsDNI TO f. 80, op. 1, d. 163, l. 49.
144 According to V.V. Kondrashin, there are no reliable data for Western Siberia's population during the famine, but he notes that the population of the region "hovered on the brink of depopulation [*balansirovalo na grani depopuliatsii*]." See V.V. Kondrashin, *Golod 1932–1933 godov: tragediia rossiskoi derevni* (Moscow: Rosspen, 2008), 191.
145 Sergei Alekseevich Sidorov, *Zapiski sviashchennika Sergiia Sidorova: S pril. ego zhizneopisaniia, sost. docher'iu, V. S. Bobrinskoi* (Moscow: Pravoslav. Sviato-Tikhonov. Bogoslov. In-t., 1999), 240.
146 The need for a psychological connection to family members outside the camps is particularly well illustrated in Arsenii Formakov, *Gulag Letters*, ed., trans., and intro. Emily D. Johnson (New Haven, CT: Yale University Press, 2017).
147 N.I. Sats, *Zhizn' – iavlenie polosatoe* (Moscow: Novosti, 1991), 332.
148 The Russian: "*Umri ty segodnia, i ia – zavtra.*" N.N. Boldyrev, "Zigzagi sud'by," in *Pozhivshi v GULAGe: Sbornik vospominanii*, comp. Aleksandr Solzhenitsyn (Moscow: Rus. put', 2001), 73–140, esp. 93–5. This slogan was common throughout the Gulag.
149 See Ananii Semenovich Gebel', "Kratkie epizody ternistigo puta s 1937 (iiun') do 1956 g. (ianvar')," Memorial f. 2, op. 2, d. 14, ll. 94–9.
150 Applebaum, *Gulag*, 227.
151 It is also not clear that, in reality, the regime actually focused much attention on cultural-educational activities. Nick Baron reports that at the Belomor canal camp in 1936, the authorities devoted 323,000 rubles to cultural-educational work, or roughly 2.7 per cent of the camp budget. In the forestry camps of the region, less than 1 per cent of the funds devoted to prisoner upkeep went towards cultural-educational activities. See Nick Baron, "Production and Terror: The Operation of the Karelian Gulag, 1933–1939," *Cahiers du Monde russe* 43, no. 1 (2002): 139–79, esp. 152.
152 See "Na futbol'nom pole," *Sibirskaia perekovka*, 12 August 1934, *The GULAG Press*, fiche 462. For more on soccer in the camps see, Steven Maddox, "Gulag Football: Competitive and Recreational Sport in Stalin's

System of Forced Labor," *Kritika: Explorations in Russian and Eurasian History*, forthcoming.

153 For her description of cultural activities at Siblag in the late 1930s, see Sats, *Zhizn' – iavlenie polosatoe*, 327–40 (quotations 329, 334). The ellipses in the final quotation are in the original. Sats was transferred to Temlag in 1939 and later Rybinskii camp. She was "released" in August 1942 (at the end of her five-year sentence) but continued to work in a camp cultural club until the following year. She was involved in theatre for the rest of her life, was rehabilitated in the 1950s, and even won the Lenin Prize in 1982. She died in 1993 in Moscow.

154 For more information on this camp, see Veronica Shapovalov, ed., *Remembering the Darkness: Women in Soviet Prisons* (Lanham, MD: Rowman & Littlefield, 2001), 238–9nn1–2.

155 For more on Larina, see Paul Gregory, *Politics, Murder, and Love in Stalin's Kremlin: The Story of Nikolai Bukharin and Anna Larina* (Stanford: Hoover Institution Press, 2010).

156 For Larina's time in the Tomsk camp, see Larina, *This I Cannot Forget*, esp. 42–51.

157 Nina A. (Lekarenko) Noskovich, "Vospominaniia 'pridurka,'" *Neva*, no. 4 (2001): 165–83 (quotation 169).

158 Larina was arrested in September 1937. She first arrived in Siberia in February 1938, but from the end of 1938 through 1941 was back in Moscow, first in the Lubianka prison and then in the Butyrka prison. From 1942–56 she then was back in Siblag: first at the Iask camp, then in a harsh-regimen camp station of the Iskitimsk camp, and then in administrative exile in Novosibirsk Province.

159 Larina, *This I Cannot Forget*, 49. Previous quotation comes from 43.

160 Kseniia Dmitrievna Medvedskaia, "Life is Everywhere," in Shapovalov, *Remembering the Darkness*, 225–41 (quotation 233).

161 The Nazi-Soviet Pact, often referred to as the Molotov-Ribbentrop Pact, after the foreign ministers of the Soviet Union and Germany, respectively, was ostensibly a non-aggression pact signed on 23 August 1939. Secret protocols attached to the pact called for the division of Poland and the Baltic countries between the USSR and Nazi Germany should war break out between Poland and Germany. On 1 September, Germany invaded Poland. Soviet troops entered eastern Poland on 17 September in order to secure their territory as outlined in the pact's secret protocols. The text of the pact and the attached protocols has been widely published. For example, see The Avalon Project: Documents in Law, History and Diplomacy, accessed 31 March 2017, http://avalon.law.yale.edu/20th_century/addsepro.asp.

162 As of January 1940, GULZhDS consisted of eleven camp systems, most in Siberia but some west of the Urals. Some of the GULZhDS conducted roadwork, too. Viazemlag, for example, was a large camp where prisoners worked on the Moscow-Minsk highway. Gornoshorlag's budget for 1939 (approximately 22 million rubles) was on the low side for the railroad camps. Viazemlag had a budget of over 100 million. Viazemlag's population in late 1938 was almost 40,000, while on 1 January 1939 it had a prisoner population of 27,420, giving it approximately 3,650 rubles/prisoner (1 January population). Gornoshorlag's population on 1 January 1939 was 11,670, or only approximately 1,885 rubles/prisoner. See *Sistema*, 204 and RGAE f. 7733, op. 36, d. 202, ll. 130, 119.

163 For more on railway work at the Akhpunsk division, see Document no. 1 "Ob"iasnitel'naia zapiska k otchetu stroitel'stva Gorno-shorskoi zhel. dor. za 1936 god (9 Akhpunskoe otdelenie Siblaga NKVD)" in L.I. Gvozdkova and A.A. Mit', eds., *Prinuditel'nyi trud: Ispravitel'no-trudovye lageria v Kuzbasse (30-50-e gg.)* (Kemerovo: Kuzbassvuzizdat, 1994), 2: 11–21.

164 Ronald Grigor Suny, *The Soviet Experiment: Russia, the USSR, and the Successor States* (Oxford: Oxford University Press, 1998), 238.

165 I.D. Makarov directed Gornoshorlag for its entire existence. He later directed Sevdvinlag in Arkhangel'sk Province from 1941–3, Altailag in the Altai Territory from 1943–5, and Angrenlag in Tashkent from 1945–6. It is unclear what happened to him after this. See *Sistema*, 204, 385, 141, and 147.

166 See Document no. 15, "Prikaz nachal'nika Gornoshorskogo ITL NKVD SSSR o premirovanii lichnogo sostava," 6 November 1940, Gvozdkova and Mit', *Prinuditel'nyi trud*, 2: 52.

167 For the creation of the ULLP, see GARF f. 9401, op. 1a, d. 32, l. 141: NKVD Operational Order no. 00205: *Ob organizatsii v sisteme GULAGa NKVD Upravleniia lesnoi promyshlennosti*, 9 March 1939. One of the Gulag's deputy directors, I.T. Sergeev, was named the director for the newly created ULLP. This was part of a trend towards economic specialization. By the early 1940s, the NKVD established separate main administrations for camps of railroad construction (GULZhDS), hydrotechnical construction (Glavgidrostroi), airfield (*aerodromnogo*) construction (GUAS), mining-metallurgical enterprise construction (GULGMP), highway construction (GUShosDor), and several others. See N.V. Petrov, "Vvedenie," *ISG*, 2: 38–9, for a complete list.

168 Khlenviuk, *The History of the Gulag*, 178.

169 Two forestry camps – Sevkuzbasslag and Iuzhkuzbasslag – were founded in the region in 1947 as part of the Main Administration of Forest Industry Camps, GULLP.

170 On Tomasinlag, see Gosudarstvennyi arkhiv Tomskoi oblasti (GATO) f. R-1152, op. 1, pages 1–3 of the description in the opis'.

171 GARF f. 9401, op. 1a, d. 39, l. 72: *Prikaz no. 0112 "O doiatel'nosti Leningradskogo proektno-izyskatel'skogo biuro upravleniia lesnoi promyshlennosti GULAGa NKVD SSSR,"* 7 May 1939.

172 GATO f. R-1152, op. 1, d. 4 [Doklad o rabote i proizvodstvennykh perspektivakh Tomsk-Asinovskogo lageria NKVD ot 20 maia 1939 goda], l. 15.

173 GATO f. R-1152, op. 1, d. 1 [AKT ot 27/VII - 1939 goda o vypolneniia proizvodstvennoi programmy Kashtakovskogo OLP], ll. 9–10.

2 Total War, Total Mobilization

1 Gosudarstvennyi arkhiv Novosibirskoi oblasti (GANO) f. P-4, op. 34, d. 171, l. 81.

2 Aleksandr Isaevich Solzhenitsyn, *The Gulag Archipelago 1918–1956: An Experiment in Literary Investigation*, vol. 2, trans. Thomas P. Whitney (New York: Harper & Row, 1975), 131.

3 Note that the wartime slogan "All for the Front, All for Victory!" was common on the Soviet home front, including the Gulag.

4 *Miny* can mean mines or mortar shells, and the misspelling in the first word is somewhat confusing.

5 Mikhail Gregor'evich Gorbachev, unpublished memoir, Tomsk Memorial Society archives, pages not numbered. This excerpt is from the third notebook in the file, and is riddled with spelling errors, which have not been included in the translation. Note that most of the Tomsk Memorial Society archives have been transferred to the Archive of the Tomsk Oblast' Kraevedcheskii Muzei, but remained in cataloguing as of my last visit (summer 2016).

6 Anne Applebaum, *Gulag: A History* (New York: Doubleday, 2003), 349. Here she notes that surviving a colony in "western Russia" did not require much of an adjustment, compared to the distant camps. For a counterargument, see Golfo Alexopoulos, *Illness and Inhumanity in Stalin's Gulag* (New Haven, CT: Yale University Press, 2017), esp. 183–207. Mortality rates are discussed in greater detail later in this chapter.

7 Roger Chickering, "Total War: The Use and Abuse of a Concept," in Manfred Boerneke, Roger Chickering, and Stig Forster, eds., *Anticipating Total War: The German and American Experiences* (Cambridge: Cambridge University Press, 1999), 26. For a discussion of the concept in the Soviet context, see Chris Bellamy, *Absolute War: Soviet Russia in the Second World War* (New York: Alfred A. Knopf, 2007), 16–38. He uses "total war" to

mean the total mobilization of industry and society for the war effort, distinguishing it from "absolute war," which includes the targeting of civilians and a goal of the complete destruction of the other side. See also Mark von Hagen, "New Directions in Military History, 1900–1950: Questions of Total War and Colonial War," *Kritika: Explorations in Russian and Eurasian History* 12, no. 4 (2011): 867–84.

8 The NKVD order creating this division (Order no. 0116, 7 April 1942) can be found at Gosudarstvennyi arkhiv Rossiskoi Federatsii (GARF) f. 9401, op. 1a, d. 117, ll. 26–7.

9 Steven A. Barnes, *Death and Redemption: The Gulag and the Shaping of Soviet Society* (Princeton, NJ: Princeton University Press, 2011), 111.

10 There are no available 1 January prisoner population estimates for UITLK NSO for 1943 and 1944, although a May 1942 figure shows 50,423 prisoners at UITLK NSO and an April 1943 figure 46,895. I base my 1 January estimates on these figures (1 January 1943 as roughly midway between the two, 1 January 1944 a little bit lower than the April 1943 figure).

11 Nicholaus Wachsmann, *Kl: A History of the Nazi Concentration Camps* (New York: Ferrar, Straus and Giroux, 2015), 627.

12 GARF f. 9414, op. 1, d. 42, ll. 60–2 (a July 1941 letter from deputy NKVD director Chernyshov to Beria, discussing the evacuation of prisoners).

13 The 750,000 prisoners came from 27 ITLs and 210 ITKs. See J. Otto Pohl, *The Stalinist Penal System: A Statistical History of Soviet Repression and Terror, 1930–1953* (London: McFarland, 1997), 16.

14 For the "Revised estimate" in table 2.1, consider that on 1 January 1940, Tomasinlag and Gornoshorlag were still in existence, and on 1 January 1941, Gornoshorlag still existed. In May 1942, Siblag was split into two camps: Siblag and UITLK NSO. Then, in 1943 and 1944, some of the Siblag and UITLK NSO camps were transferred to the newly formed OITK KO and OITK TO of Kemerovo Oblast' and Tomsk Oblast', respectively. Thus, what Siblag was at the outbreak of the war became four camp systems by the end of the war.

15 M.B. Smirnov, N.G. Okhotin, and A.B. Roginskii, eds., *Sistema ispravitel'no-trudovykh lagerei v SSSR, 1923–1960: Spravochnik* (Moscow: Zven'ia, 1998), 391. Indeed, although *Sistema* is otherwise an excellent source of information on the camps, it lacks detailed information about locally administered camps and colonies.

16 Danila S. Krasil'nikov, "Lageria i kolonii na territorii Novosibirskoi Oblasti v gody Velikoi Otechestvennoi voiny (1941–1945)" (Diplomnaia rabota, Novosibirsk State University, 1999), 44.

17 I.S. Kuznetsov et al., eds., *Novonikolaevskaia guberniia – Novosibirskaia oblast': 1921–2000: Khronika. Dokumenty* (Novosibirsk: Sibirskoe otd. RAN, 2001), 146.

18 GARF f. 9414 op. 1 d. 1978 l. 35.

19 See the 13 June 1941 ammunition plan for the NKVD. GARF f. 9414 op. 1 d. 1978 ll. 1–2.

20 GANO f. P-260 op. 1 d. 1 l. 58.

21 Kuznetsov et al., eds., *Novonikolaevskaia guberniia – Novosibirskaia oblast'*, 138. The Siberian Military District was administered from Novosibirsk, and in 1941 included Novosibirsk Province (including present-day Tomsk and Kemerovo Provinces), Omsk Province, Altai Territory, and Krasnoiarsk Territory.

22 Asif Siddiqi, "Scientists and Specialists in the Gulag: Life and Death in Stalin's *Sharashka*," in Michael David-Fox, ed., *The Soviet Gulag: Evidence, Interpretation, and Comparison* (Pittsburgh: University of Pittsburgh Press, 2016), 87–113, esp. 104.

23 For more on Combine 179, see I.M. Savitskii, "Sozdanie v Novosibirske krupneishego v Sibiri tsentra oboronnoi promyshlennosti v gody Velikoi Otechestvennoi voiny," in S.A. Papkov and K. Teraiama, eds., *Ural i Sibir' v Stalinskoi politike* (Novosibirsk: Sibirskii khronograf, 2002), 192–204.

24 S.A. Papkov, *Stalinskii terror v Sibiri, 1928–1941* (Novosibirsk: Izdatel'stvo Sibirskogo Otdeleniia Rossiiskoi Akademii Nauk, 1997), 133–4.

25 This comes from a report on the work of Siblag's Cultural-Educational Department for the first half of 1943. See GARF f. 9414, op. 1, d. 1452, l. 155.

26 See R.S. Bikmetov, "Siblag v gody Velikoi Otechestvennoi voiny," *Vestnik Kemerovskogo gosudarstvennogo universiteta* 61, no. 3 (2015): 110–15, for more on Siblag's wartime agricultural production.

27 GARF f. 9401, op. 1a, d. 107, l. 192.

28 Wilson T. Bell, "Was the Gulag an Archipelago? De-Convoyed Prisoners and Porous Borders in the Camps of Western Siberia," *The Russian Review* 72, no. 1 (2013): 116–41, esp. 127.

29 For another example, see the case Georgii Strelkov, an Article 58er in Pechora, who before his arrest had headed the Minusazoloto Gold-Mining trust in Krasnoiarsk. During the war at the Pechora camp, he led a re-search lab and was allowed to live in that lab and wear a suit rather than prison garb. See Orlando Figes, *Just Send Me Word: A True Story of Love and Survival in the Gulag* (London: Allen Lane, 2012), 57.

30 GANO f. P-4, op. 33, d. 503g, l. 161. Emphasis added.

31 GARF f. 9414, op. 1, d. 1461, l. 196. See also Steven A. Barnes, "All for the Front! All for Victory! The Mobilization of Forced Labor in the Soviet Union during World War Two," *International Labor and Working-Class History* 58 (2000): 239–60.

32 D.S. Krasil'nikov, "Lageria i kolonii na territorii Novosibirskoi oblasti," 89–90.

33 For this report, see S.A. Krasil'nikov et al., eds., *Nasha malaia rodina: Khrestomatiia po istorii Novosibirskoi oblasti, 1921–1991* (Novosibirsk: Ekor, 1997), 282–5.

34 See discussion later in this chapter.

35 Applebaum, *Gulag,* 349.

36 Bell, "Was the Gulag an Archipelago?" esp. 132–7.

37 For Alin's account of work and life at Chkalov Aviation Factory 153, see D.E. Alin, *Malo slov, a goria rechen'ka…: Nevydumannye rasskazy* (Tomsk: Volodei, 1997), esp. 127–38.

38 Tzvetan Todorov, *Facing the Extreme: Moral Life in the Concentration Camps* (New York: Henry Holt, 1996), 36.

39 Alin, *Malo slov, a goria rechen'ka…*, 135–8 (quotation 137).

40 See A.I. Kokurin and N.V. Petrov, eds., *GULAG (Glavnoe upravlenie lagerei) 1918–1960* (Moscow: Materik, 2002), 476–9.

41 I use "hyper" here in the same sense as Mikhail Epstein in "The Dialectics of *Hyper*: From Modernism to Postmodernism," in M. Epstein, A.A. Genis, and S.M Vladiv-Glover, eds., *Russian Postmodernism: New Perspectives on Post-Soviet Culture*, 2nd ed. (Providence, RI: Berghahn Books, 2015), 23–50. Here Epstein discusses "hyper" in various contexts (hypertextuality, hypersexuality, hypersociality) as both an exaggeration of reality and a pseudo-reality.

42 For comparative purposes, convicts in Victorian England received less food than Gulag prisoners were supposed to have received. The convict diet in the 1870s consisted of between 616 g and 810 g of bread per day, 389 g/day of potatoes, and 132 g/day of meat. There was, however, more day-to-day variety in food servings in the English prisons. See Richard Ireland, *"A Want of Order and Good Discipline": Rules, Discretion and the Victorian Prison* (Cardiff: University of Wales Press, 2007), 204–5.

43 For a description of the soup, see Applebaum, *Gulag*, 288.

44 Aleksandr Klein, *Kleimenye, ili, Odin' sredi odinokikh: Zapiski katorzhnika* (Syktyvkar: n. pub., 1995), 144.

45 For more on the punishment of local camp officials, see chapter 4 of the present study.

46 As Wachsmann writes of the Nazi camps, "While some shortages were caused by growing pressures on resources during the war, the SS deliberately aggravated the situation." Wachsmann, *Kl*, 211.

47 See Margarete Buber-Neumann, *Under Two Dictators: Prisoner of Stalin and Hitler* (London: Pimlico, 2009). Her description of the rations document can be found on page 93 (quotations 162, 193).

48 As Viola argues, Stalinist planning often resembled what authorities wished to see in practice and did not always relate in any meaningful way to reality on the ground. Lynne Viola, "The Aesthetic of Stalinist Planning and the World of the Special Villages," *Kritika: Explorations and Russian and Eurasian History* 4, no. 1 (2004): 101–28.

49 There was not a difference in the main food norm for prisoners in ITKs compared with prisoners in ITLs.

50 See Bell, "Was the Gulag an Archipelago?" esp. 132–7.

51 For more discussion of this and for specific examples, see Applebaum, *Gulag*, 311; Barnes, *Death and Redemption*, 98–106; Wilson T. Bell, "Sex, Pregnancy, and Power in the Late Stalinist Gulag," *Journal of the History of Sexuality* 24, no. 2 (2015): 198–224; Buber-Neumann, *Under Two Dictators*, 69; Roy Robson, *Solovki: The Story of Russia Told through Its Most Remarkable Islands* (New Haven, CT: Yale University Press, 2004), 219; Olga Adamova-Sloizberg, "My Journey," in Simeon Vilensky, ed., *Till My Tale Is Told: Women's Memoirs of the Gulag* (Bloomington: Indiana University Press, 1999), 51. Sexual abuse was quite common in the 1930s, in the Soviet Union more generally and at the workplace particularly, as thousands upon thousands of women entered the workforce. For more, see Wendy Goldman, *Women at the Gates: Gender and Industry in Stalin's Russia* (Cambridge: Cambridge University Press, 2002), 227–30.

52 Krasil'nikov et al., eds., *Nasha malaia rodina*, 282–3. For another discussion of the release of invalids in the region during the war, see V.A. Isupov, *Glavnyi resurs Pobedy: Liudskoi potentsial Zapadnoi Sibiri v gody Vtoroi mirovoi voiny (1939-1945 gg.)* (Novosibirsk: Sova, 2008), 168–9.

53 See Golfo Alexopoulos, "Destructive-Labor Camps: Rethinking Solzhenitsyn's Play on Words," *Kritika: Explorations in Russian and Eurasian History* 16, no. 3 (2015): 499–526. Kondrashev's statement is reminiscent of Bauman's contention that the drive towards bureaucratic efficiency has no inherent moral boundaries. Zygmunt Bauman, *Modernity and the Holocaust* (New York: Columbia University Press, 1989).

54 GANO f. R-20, op. 4, d. 12 [Doklad o rabote prokuratury ITL ITK UNKVD [NSO] za 1943 god i 1-i kvartal 1944 god], ll. 14-15. The reluctance to release Article 58ers who were near death complicates Alexopoulos's

argument ("Destructive-Labor Camps"). Article 58ers tended to have the lengthiest sentences (particularly in the postwar period) and were treated worse than most other prisoners. Likely, a greater percentage of Article 58ers, compared to other prisoner contingents, would have found themselves at the point of near death. Yet if they were not being released early, one would expect to see an increase in the official Gulag mortality rate in the postwar years, rather than the reported decrease. Clearly, more investigation is needed on this crucial question.

55 See also Alexopoulos, "Destructive-Labor Camps."
56 See NKVD Order no. 067 from 2 March 1942, GARF f. 9401, op. 1a, d. 116, ll. 66–9.
57 GANO f. P-260, op. 1, d. 1, l. 21.
58 GANO f. P-260, op. 1, d. 1, l. 33.
59 On the average industrial wages, see Wendy Z. Goldman, "Not by Bread Alone: Food, Workers, and the State," in Wendy Z. Goldman and Donald Filtzer, eds., *Hunger and War: Food Provisions in the Soviet Union during World War II* (Bloomington: Indiana University Press, 2015), 44–97, esp. 80.
60 GANO f. P-260, op. 1, d. 1, l. 21.
61 Dan Healey, "Lives in the Balance: Weak and Disabled Prisoners and the Biopolitics of the Gulag," *Kritika: Explorations in Russian and Eurasian History* 16, no. 3 (2015): 527–56.
62 R.S. Bikmetov, "Siblag v gody Velikoi Otechestvennoi voiny," 113.
63 Alexopoulos, *Illness and Inhumanity*, 214.
64 For mortality rates during the war, see Applebaum, *Gulag*, 594, and Isupov, *Glavnyi resurs Pobedy*, 76, 113.
65 Ninel' Severiukhina, *Proshchanie s detstvom: Fragmenti semeinoi khroniki 1941–1944* (St. Petersburg: Izdatel'stvo imeni N.I. Novikova, 2004), 42. Here she notes that wartime rations were 400 grams of bread per day for *izhdiventsev*, 500 grams for *sluzhashchikh*, and for 800 grams for *rabochikh*. As noted earlier in this chapter, the 1939 Order on Gulag rations had called for 1,100 grams of bread per day.
66 Oleg Khlevniuk, "The Gulag and the Non-Gulag as One Interrelated Whole," trans. Simon Belokowsky, *Kritika: Explorations in Russian and Eurasian History* 16, no. 3 (2015): 479–98.
67 See Barnes, *Death and Redemption*, 116; and Alan Barenberg, *Gulag Town, Company Town: Forced Labor and Its Legacy in Vorkuta* (New Haven, CT: Yale University Press, 2014), 61–2. For the Norilsk figures, see Leonid Borodkin and Simon Ertz, "Nikel' v zapoliar'e: Trud zakliuchennykh Noril'laga," in L.I. Borodkin, P. Gregori [Gregory], and O.V. Khlevniuk, eds., *Gulag: Ekonomika prinuditel'nogo truda* (Moscow: Rosspen, 2005), 203–7.

68 For more on modern justification for punishment, see Philip L. Reichel, *Comparative Criminal Justice Systems: A Topical Approach*, 3rd ed. (Upper Saddle River, NJ: Prentice Hall, 2002), esp. 238–41. For more on the development of the modern prison, see Norval Morris and David J. Rothman, eds., *The Oxford History of the Prison: The Practice of Punishment in Western Society* (New York: Oxford University Press, 1995), and Michel Foucault, *Discipline and Punish: The Birth of the Prison*, 2nd ed., trans. Alan Sheridan (New York: Vintage Books, 1995). Foucault discusses justifications for punishment most clearly on pages 236–48.

69 For Foucault, forced labour was not economic at all but part of the disciplinary mechanism carried out on and through the prisoners' bodies. As he writes, "The prison is not a workshop; it is, it must be of itself, a machine whose convict-workers are both the cogs and the products." Foucault, *Discipline and Punish*, 242.

70 Patricia O'Brien, "The Prison on the Continent: Europe, 1865–1965," in Morris and Rothman, eds., *The Oxford History of the Prison*, 203–5.

71 Aidan Forth, "Britain's Archipelago of Camps: Labor and Detention in a Liberal Empire, 1871–1903," in Michael David-Fox, ed., *The Soviet Gulag: Evidence, Interpretation, Comparison* (Pittsburgh: Pittsburgh University Press, 2016), 199–223. Note that Forth discusses Britain's labour camps for the poor as part of "Britain's universe of camps" and also describes labour practices in the camps of the South African War, where white Boers were paid for their labour and involved in tasks in and around the camp itself. In some of the camps for black Africans, however, the prisoners were forced to conduct unremunerated agricultural work. See Forth, "Britain's Archipelago," 217–18.

72 Wachsmann, *Kl*, esp. 48–60.

73 See the report of the KVO UITLK NSO for the second half of 1943: GARF f. 9414 op. 1 d. 1463 l. 137.

74 N.P. Shuranov, "Razvitie promyshlennosti sibiri v period velikoi otechestvennoi voiny," *Izvestiia sibirskogo otdeleniia akademii nauk SSSR* 1 (1985): 15–20, info on 17.

75 I.M. Savitskii, "Oboronnaia promyshlennost' Novosibirskoi oblasti – frontu," *Nauka v Sibiri* 17–18 (2005): n.p., accessed 20 March 2017, http://www.nsc.ru/HBC/hbc.phtml?16+331+1.

76 Papkov, *Stalinksii terror v Sibiri*, 134–5. Siblag at the time consisted of twenty-seven subcamps housing 63,646 prisoners.

77 Kate Brown, "Out of Solitary Confinement: The History of the Gulag," *Kritika: Explorations in Russian and Eurasian History* 8, no. 1 (2007): 67–103,

esp. 77. See also Khlevniuk, "The Gulag and the Non-Gulag," and Barenberg, *Gulag Town, Company Town*.

78 Savitskii, "Oboronnaia promyshlennost' Novosibirskoi oblasti."

79 GANO f. P-4 op. 33 d. 238a l. 43.

80 See also Barenberg, *Gulag Town, Company Town*, esp. 9.

81 Two thousand were to come from Novosibirsk Province, 3,000 from Altai territory, 4,000 from Bashkir ASSR, and 2,000 from Kirov Province.

82 Rossiskii gosudarstvennyi arkhiv sotsial'no-politicheskoi istorii (RGASPI) f. 17 op. 162 d. 31 ll. 73–4.

83 See, for example, Protocol no. 216 point 4 of the Novosibirsk Obkom resolutions (25 September 1941): GANO f. P-4 op. 33 d. 503v ll. 70–8.

84 See also Khlevniuk, "The Gulag and the Non-Gulag," and Barenberg, *Gulag Town, Company Town*, for more on the grey areas between free and forced labour.

85 For the 10 September resolution, see GANO f. P-4 op. 33 d. 503v ll. 1–31, esp. l. 3. For the 14 October resolution, see ibid., ll. 83–96, esp. ll. 83–5.

86 GANO f. P-4, op. 33, d. 503d, ll. 112–14.

87 GARF f. 9414, op. 1, d. 45, l. 602.

88 GARF f. 9414, op. 1, d. 36, l. 23.

89 GARF f. 9414, op. 1, d. 35, l. 13.

90 Bell, "Was the Gulag an Archipelago?" 131–2.

91 GARF f. 9414, op. 1, d. 2513, l. 14.

92 Alin, *Malo slov, a goria rechen'ka…*, 130.

93 G.N. Gorchakov, *Vospominaniia* (Jerusalem: Ierusalim.izdat.tsentr, 1995), 113–14.

94 "Surrounded by Death," interview by Jehanne M. Gheith, in Geith and Catherine R. Jollock, *Gulag Voices: Oral Histories of Soviet Incarceration and Exile* (New York: Palgrave Macmillan, 2011), 87–97, esp. 92 and 95.

95 P. Kh. Ivanov, "Nezabytoe: Vospominaniia zhertv repressii," in I.V. Dobrovol'skii, *GULAG: Ego stroiteli, obitateli i geroi: raskulachivanie i gonenie na Pravoslavnuiu Tserkov' popolniali lageria GULAGa* (Frankfurt: Mezhdunarodnoe obshchestvo prav cheloveka, 1999), 371.

96 V.A. Isupov, "Na izlome: Smertnost' naseleniia Sibiri v nachale Velikoi Otechestvennoi voiny," in R.S. Vasil'evskii and N.Ia. Gushchin, eds., *Istoricheskaia demografiia Sibiri: sbornik nauchnykh trudov* (Novosibirsk: Nauka, 1992), 186, 193.

97 Donald Filtzer, "Starvation Mortality in Soviet Home-Front Industrial Regions during World War II," in Goldman and Filtzer, eds., *Hunger and War*, 265–338, esp. 266, 329.

98 For a good discussion of the effects of these laws, see Donald Filtzer, *Soviet Workers and Late Stalinism: Labour and the Restoration of the Stalinist System after World War II* (Cambridge: Cambridge University Press, 2002), esp. 27 and 162.

99 According to I.M. Savitskii, this turnover was directly related to poor living conditions. See See I.M. Savitskii, "Formirovanie kadrov oboronnoi promyshlennosti Novosibirskoi oblasti v gody Velikoi Otechestvennoi voiny," in V.A. Isupov, S.A. Papkov, and I.M. Savitskii, eds., *Zapadnaia Sibir' v Velikoi Otechestvennoi voine (1941–1945 gg.)* (Novosibirsk: Nauka-Tsentr, 2004), 17–19.

100 Martin Kragh, "Stalinist Labour Coercion during World War II: An Economic Approach," *Europe-Asia Studies* 63, no. 7 (2011): 1253–73.

101 See Nicholas Werth, "Vvedenie," in S.V. Mironenko and N. Werth, eds., *Istoriia stalinskogo Gulaga*, vol. 1, *Massovye represi v SSSR* (Moscow: Rosspen, 2004), 79.

102 V.V. Alekseev et al., *Rabochii klass Sibiri v period uprocheniia i razvitiia sotsialisma* (Novosibirsk: Nauka, 1984), 81.

103 V.A. Isupov, "Sotsial'no-demograficheskaia politika Stalinskogo pravitel'stva v gody Velikoi Otechestvennoi voiny (na materialakh Sibiri)," in V.A. Isupov, S.A. Papkov, and I.M. Savitskii, eds., *Zapadnaia Sibir' v Velikoi Otechestvennoi voine*, 115–43, esp. 120.

104 Tsentr Dokumentatsii noveishei istorii Tomskoi oblasti (TsDNI TO) f. 80 [Tomskii gorodskii komitet VKP(b)], op. 3, d. 91, ll. 200–1.

105 GANO f. P-4, op. 34, d. 171, l. 81

106 For more on lend-lease and the Gulag, see Applebaum, *Gulag*, 449; Barenberg, *Gulag Town, Company Town*, 44; and Martin Bollinger, *Stalin's Slave Ships: Kolyma, the Gulag Fleet, and the Role of the West* (Westport, CT: Praeger, 2003), 150.

107 V.N. Zemskov, *Spetsposelentsy v SSSR, 1930–1960* (Moscow: Nauka, 2005), 94.

108 For more on the Kalmyks, see documents 152–5 in S.N. Mironenko and N. Werth, eds., *Istoriia stalinskogo Gulaga*, vol. 1, *Massovye repressii v SSSR* (Moscow: Rosspen, 2004), 477–81.

109 "Telegrafnaia zapiska sekretaria Novosibirskogo obkoma VKP(b) v Narymskii okryzhkom partii o mobilizatsii trudposelentsev dlia raboty na voennykh zavodakh," in V.P. Danilov and S.A. Krasil'nikov, eds., *Spetspereselentsy v Zapadnoi Sibiri 1939–1945* (Novosibirsk: Ekor, 1996), 178–9.

110 Savitskii, "Formirovanie kadrov," 20–1.

111 Kuznetsov et al, eds., *Novonikolaevskaia guberniia – Novosibirskaia oblast'*, 157. For an interesting work on German POWs in the Soviet Union, see Andreas Hilger, *Deutsche Kriegsgefangene in der Sowjetunion, 1941–1956: Kriegsgefangenenpolitik, Lageralltag und Erinnerung* (Essen: Klartext-Verlag, 2000). Hilger argues that from central directives, the *intention* was to treat the German POWs humanely, but often inefficiencies on the ground undermined this effort.

112 See "Ykazaniia GULaga NKVD SSSR periferiinym organam o srochnom provedenii ucheta trudposelencheskoi molodezhi v sviazi s voennoi obstanovkoi," 14 November 1941, in Danilov and Krasil'nikov, eds., *Spetspereselentsy*, 109. For an example specific to Western Siberia, that included men from age eighteen to forty, see "Dokladnaia zapiska UNKVD po Novosibirskoi oblasti v GULag NKVD ob itogakh prizyva v RKKA trudposelentsev," in Danilov and Krasil'nikov, eds. *Spetspereselentsy*, 179–80.

113 "Spravka upravleniia NKVD po Novosibirskoi oblasti ob izmeneniiakh v sostave trudssylki za period 1930-1943 g.," in Danilov and Krasil'nikov, eds., *Spetspereselentsy*, 206–10.

114 See the November 1941 instruction in GARF f. 9479 op. 1 d. 71 ll. 202–3.

115 Quoted in Document 89 in T.V. Tsarevskaia-Diakina, ed., *Istoriia stalinskogo Gulaga*, vol. 5, *Spetspereselentsy v SSSR* (Moscow: Rosspen, 2004), 330.

116 J. Otto Pohl, Eric J. Schmaltz, and Ronald J. Vossler, "'In Our Hearts We Felt the Sentence of Death': Ethnic German Recollections of Mass Violence in the USSR, 1928–48," *Journal of Genocide Research* 11, no. 2/3 (2009): 323–54, esp. 335.

117 S.A. Papkov, "'Kontrrevoliutsionnaia prestupnost'' i osobennosti ee podavleniia v Sibiri v gody Velikoi Otechestvennoi voiny (1941–1945)," in Papkov and Teraiama, eds., *Ural i Sibir' v Stalinskoi politike*, 205–23, esp. 208–11.

118 Oleg Budnitskii, "The Great Patiotic War and Soviet Society: Defeatism, 1941–42," *Kritika: Explorations in Russian and Eurasian History* 15, no. 4 (2014): 767–97 (quotation 791).

119 *Gosudarstvennyi Komitet Oborony*, or GKO.

120 Zemskov, *Spetsposelentsy v SSSR*, 84–5.

121 J. Otto Pohl, "Persecution of Ethnic Germans in the USSR during World War II," *The Russian Review* 75 (2016): 284–303, esp. 289.

122 Siddiqi, "Scientists and Specialists in the Gulag," esp. 100–4.

123 Mark Harrison, *Accounting for War: Soviet Production, Employment, and the Defence Burden, 1940–1945* (Cambridge: Cambridge University Press,

1996), 98. Khlevniuk, in "The Gulag and the Non-Gulag," argues that there was a significant grey area of semi-forced labour, so we should be cautious about making clear-cut distinctions between free and forced labour in the Stalinist system.

124 Oleg Khlevniuk, *The History of the Gulag: From Collectivization to the Great Terror* (New Haven, CT: Yale University Press, 2004), 331–4.

125 K.M. Shchegolev, "Uchastie evakuirovannogo naseleniia v kolkhoznom proizvodstve Zapadnoi Sibiri v gody Velikoi Otechestvennoi voiny," *Istoriia SSSR* 2 (1959): 139–45.

126 Kristen Edwards, "Fleeing to Siberia: The Wartime Relocation of Evacuees to Novosibirsk, 1941–1943" (PhD diss., Stanford University, 1996), esp. 3–8. Note that I.M. Savitskii lists the 1939 population of Novosibirsk Province at just over 4 million. See Savitskii, "Formirovanie kadrov," 5. For more on wartime evacuations to the region, see Isupov, "Na izlome," 186–98. For more on the evacuations more generally, see Rebecca Manley, *To the Tashkent Station: Evacuation and Survival in the Soviet Union at War* (Ithaca, NY: Cornell University Press, 2009). Tashkent was one of the most famous evacuation destinations, as many prominent intellectuals spent the war there (including Anna Akhmatova), but Tashkent received fewer evacuees overall (100,000) than Novosibirsk (150,000). See Manley, *To the Tashkent Station*, 2, 6.

127 Kuznetsov et al., eds., *Novonikolaevskaia guberniia – Novosibirskaia oblast'*, 148. See also Edwards, "Fleeing to Siberia," 5–6. "Republican" status meant that Novosibirsk officials now answered directly to the Russian Soviet Republic, bypassing provincial authorities; this status was granted to cities deemed especially important for the war effort. For the quotation from the evacuee, see Severiukhina, *Proshchanie s detstvom*, 39.

128 Isupov, *Glavnyi resurs Pobedy*, 311.

129 GANO f. P-260 op. 1 d. 24 ll. 40–1ob.

130 GANO f. R-20, op. 4, d. 12, l. 10.

131 Edwin Bacon, *The Gulag at War: Stalin's Forced Labour System in the Light of the Archives* (New York: New York University Press, 1994), 132.

132 D.S. Krasil'nikov, "Lageria i kolonii na territorii Novosibirskoi oblasti," 62–3. For more on labour categories, see Alexopoulos, "Destructive Labor Camps," 506–12.

133 Alexopoulos, *Illness and Inhumanity*, 111.

134 Alexopoulos, "Destructive-Labor Camps."

135 See chapter 5 of the present study for more on this issue.

3 Patriotic Prisoners

1 As quoted in S.P. Zviagin, "K voprosu ob uchastii zakliuchennykh kuz-basskikh lagerei v pomoshchi frontu v gody Velikoi Otechestvennoi voiny," in A. T. Moskalenko et al., eds., *50 let velikoi pobedy pod Stalingradom* (Novosibirsk: UD SO RAN, 1993), 147.

2 For more on memory and the Gulag, see the epilogue of the present volume. The scholarly literature on memory and collective memory is voluminous, but see, for example, Maurice Halbwachs, *On Collective Memory*, trans. Lewis A Coser (Chicago: University of Chicago Press, 1992); and Sarah Gensburger, "Halbwachs' Sudies in Collective Memory: A Founding Text for Contemporary 'Memory Studies'?" *Journal of Classical Sociology* 16, no. 4 (2016): 396–413.

3 Oleg Budnitskii, "The Great Patriotic War and Soviet Society: Defeatism, 1941–42," trans. Jason Morton, *Kritika: Explorations in Russian and Eurasian History* 15, no. 4 (2014): 767–97, esp. 778–90.

4 On 1930s re-forging, see especially Steven A. Barnes, *Death and Redemption: The Gulag and the Shaping of Soviet Society* (Princeton, NJ: Princeton University Press, 2011), 57–68; Wilson T. Bell, "One Day in the Life of Educator Khrushchev: Labour and *Kul'turnost'* in the Gulag Newspapers," *Canadian Slavonic Papers* 46, no. 3/4 (2004): 289–313; and Julie S. Draskoczy, *Belomor: Criminality and Creativity in Stalin's Gulag* (Brighton, MA: Academic Studies Press, 2014).

5 For more on prisoners who retained loyalty to the regime, see Nanci Adler, *Keeping Faith with the Party: Communist Believers Return from the Gulag* (Bloomington: Indiana University Press, 2012).

6 As quoted in Barnes, *Death and Redemption*, 107–8.

7 P.I. Belykh, "Vospominaniia," in *Stalinsk v gody repressii: Vospominaniia. Pis'ma. Dokumenty*, 2nd ed., ed. L.I. Floigt (Novokuznetsk: Kuznetskaia krepost', 1995), 28.

8 Rossiskii gosudarstvennyi arkhiv sotsial'no-politicheskoi istorii (RGASPI) f. 560, op. 1, d. 22 [Vospominaniia Lazareva Vasiliia Nikiforovicha], l. 62.

9 See Applebaum, *Gulag: A History* (New York: Doubleday, 2003), 452–6.

10 N.A. Noskovich, "Vospominaniia 'pridurka,'" *Neva* 4 (2001): 170.

11 D.E. Alin, *Malo slov, a goria rechen'ka…: Nevydumannye rasskazy* (Tomsk: Volodei, 1997), 126.

12 V.V. Chernyshev had a long career in the Soviet security organs, having joined in 1920. He served as Gulag director from 1939–41, when he was promoted to vice-director of the NKVD and replaced as Gulag director

by Nasedkin (for more on Nasedkin, see the introduction of the present volume, note 21). He served in that position until 1952. For more, see N.V. Petrov and K.V. Skorkin, eds., *Kto rukovodil NKVD? Spravochnik* (Moscow: Zven'ia, 1999), accessed 7 May 2017, http://old.memo.ru/history/NKVD/kto/biogr/index.htm.

13 Gosudarstvennyi arkhiv Rossiskoi Federatsii (GARF) f. 9414, op. 1, d. 1167, especially ll. 2 (quotation) and 4 (figures for Novosibirsk Province).

14 Steve Barnes has discussed the Gulag's considerable emphasis on cultural activities during the war years, but few other scholars have studied this phenomenon. See Barnes, *Death and Redemption*, 128–34.

15 It is important to note that the term "home front" is used frequently in the cultural-educational department documents. For an example, see GARF f. 9414 op. 1 d. 1461 l. 196. In this way, then, prisoners were included as part of Soviet society.

16 GARF f. 9401 op. 1a d. 99 l. 157 [NKVD sekretnyi prikaz no. 0522/k "O reorganizatsii Kul'turno-Vospitatel'nykh otdelov (otdelenii) pri Politotdelakh v samostoiatel'nykh otdely (otdeleniia) ITL"].

17 Kate Brown describes the intricacies of Soviet reports from the periphery to the centre in *A Biography of No Place: From Ethnic Borderland to Soviet Heartland* (Cambridge, MA: Harvard University Press, 2004).

18 See GARF f. 9414 op. 1 d. 1432 ll. 36–8.

19 Memorial Society Archives f. 2, op. 2, d. 14 [Gebel' Ananii Semenovich, Kratkie epizody ternistigo puta s 1937 (iiun') do 1956 g.], l. 111.

20 Aleksandr Klein, *Kleimenye, ili, Odin sredi odinokikh: Zapiski katorzhnika* (Syktyvkar: n. pub., 1995), esp. 147, 168, 174. I thank Alan Barenberg for pointing me to this memoir.

21 G.N. Gorchakov, *Vospominaniia* (Jerusalem: Ierusalim.izdat.tsentr, 1995), 113.

22 See Noskovich, "Vospominaniia 'pridurka'," esp. 173–6. Noskovich was released at the end of her term in 1942 but was not allowed to leave Siberia; she continued to have various camp jobs until the end of the war, when she moved closer to her Leningrad home (she was still not allowed to live within 101 kilometres of major cities). She was rehabilitated in the 1960s and died in 1995.

23 Thomas Lahusen, *How Life Writes the Book: Real Socialism and Socialist Realism in Stalin's Russia* (Ithaca, NY: Cornell University Press, 1997).

24 GARF f. 9414 op. 1 d. 1432 ll. 6–7.

25 GARF f. 9414 op. 1 d. 1432 ll. 44–8. The four camp systems singled out were Siblag, OITK Kabardino-Balkarskoi ASSR, OITK Buriato-Mongol'skoi ASSR, and OITK Omskoi oblasti.

26 For the information about the Siblag KVO director, see GARF f. 9414 op. 1 d.
    1437 l. 39ob; on the use of cultural space for storing grain, see the same
    report, l. 45ob. For more on "red corners," see Stephen Kotkin, *Magnetic
    Mountain: Stalinism as a Civilization* (Berkeley: University of California
    Press, 1995), 180–2.
27 For this report, see GARF f. 9414, op. 1, d. 1437, l. 39ob.
28 For example, a typical fifteen-page report (GARF f. 9414 op. 1 d. 1463 ll.
    132–46) "On Cultural-Educational Work among the Prisoners of ITLK
    NKVD of Novosibirsk Province" for the second half of 1942 includes the
    following sections: cadres (half a page); mass-political work (three pages);
    mass-production work (four and a half pages); mass club work (one page);
    struggle against work-refusal (about three-quarters of a page); the press
    (one page); preparation for winter (one page); visual agitation (*nagliad-
    naia agitatsiia*) (one and a half pages); early release (half a page); and "our
    tasks" (half a page). Half of the section on mass-political work is devoted
    to stories of workers overfulfilling their norms following the department's
    political agitation. Statistical indices also include work-related data such
    as information about the numbers of prisoners in group "A" (healthy, able-
    bodied); the number of those involved in "labour competitions"; the num-
    ber not fulfilling their norms; the number of work refusals; and so on. See
    also, GARF f. 9414 op. 1 d. 1463 ll. 147–7ob.
29 For an example of prisoners supposedly gaining inspiration from Stalin's
    orders, see GARF f. 9414 op. 1 d. 1445 l. 15ob. The exploits of ex-prisoners
    at the front are a frequent theme in the reports. For an example of a so-
    called work-refuser (*otkazchik*) mending his ways following work by the
    KVCh, see GARF f. 9414 op. 1 d. 1463 l. 141.
30 GARF f. 9414 op. 1 d. 1437 l. 45.
31 Which is certainly not the case, as most film screenings likely would have
    been off limits to Article 58ers and especially dangerous offenders. The
    number of camps was constantly in flux, but S.A. Papkov reports that
    there were thirty-one at Siblag on the eve of the war, although the included
    chart lists only twenty-seven. See Papkov, *Stalinskii terror v Sibiri, 1928–
    1941* (Novosibirsk: Izdatel'stvo Sibirskogo Otdeleniia RAN, 1997),
    132–3.
32 In Kraslag prisoner Arsenii Formakov's letters to his family, mostly from
    the latter half of the war until 1947, he often mentions the films he was
    able to watch in the camps (including some American ones). These films
    are from the general repetoire of films screened in the Soviet Union at the
    time. See Arsenii Formakov, *Gulag Letters*, ed. and trans. Emily D. Johnson
    (New Haven, CT: Yale University Press, 2017), 62, 77, 131, 134, 163.

Johnson, in her introduction to the book, points to these films as evidence that "Soviet Labor camps were in many respects very closely integrated into the culture of the country as a whole" (16). Formakov generally, although not always, held privileged positions at Kraslag.

33 The statistical indices show 527 films screened in the second half of 1941 (interestingly, significantly less than the number in the report itself) and only 384 in the first half of 1942. See GARF f. 9414 op. 1 d. 1445 l. 18ob.

34 GARF f. 9414 op. 1 d. 1445 l. 17.

35 GARF f. 9414 op. 1 d. 1445 l. 32.

36 For the second half of 1942, UITLK NSO had 534 film screenings with an average of 370 persons attending, while Siblag had 186 screenings with an average attendance of "300–325." For the UITLK NSO figures, see GARF f. 9414 op. 1 d. 1445 l. 33ob; and for the Siblag statistics, see GARF f. 9414 op. 1 d. 1442 l. 213. In the first half of 1943, Siblag managed only 93 film screenings, but the figure for UITLK NSO jumps to 772. For the UITLK NSO statistics, see GARF f. 9414 op. 1 d. 1454 l. 106ob; the Siblag statistics can be found at GARF f. 9414 op. 1 d. 1452 l. 157ob.

37 Maddox suggests that soccer and other sports may not have been as prevalent during the war, due to harsh conditions, but also notes that cultural activities remained in place. See Steven Maddox, "Gulag Football: Competitive and Recreational Sport in Stalin's System of Forced Labor," *Kritika: Explorations in Russian and Eurasian History*, forthcoming.

38 See, for example, the "Spetsdonesenie" on the work of the KVO of Siblag for the second half of 1943. GARF f. 9414 op. 1 d. 1463 l. 192. This report mentions that the successes of the Red Army as well as the "freeing of tens of thousands of Soviet people from fascist katorga" had improved production levels at the camp.

39 One cultural report complains that the local cinefication office had not been sending proper equipment. See GARF f. 9414 op. 1 d. 1445 l. 32. For more on cinefication, see the documentary film Thomas Lahusen, Alexander Gershtein, Tracy McDonald, and Alexander Nikitin, dir., *The Province of Lost Film* (Chemodan Films, 2006).

40 Edwin Bacon, *The Gulag at War: Stalin's Forced Labour System in the Light of the Archives* (New York: New York University Press, 1994), 77.

41 GARF f. 9414 op. 1 d. 1437 l. 39.

42 This information comes from the signatures on the reports that have been cited throughout this section.

43 See Document no. 131, "Iz spravki Otdela kadrov GULAG o sostave kadrov po vsem periferiinym organam GULAG po sostoianiiu na 1 ianvaria 1945 g," in N.V. Petrov and N.I. Vladimirtsev, eds., *Istoriia stalinskogo*

Gulaga, vol. 2, *Karatel'naia sistema: struktura i kadry* (Moscow: Rosspen, 2004), 267. [Henceforth cited as *ISG*, 2]

44 Although we know, of course, from Galina Ivanova's research that, in general, the educational levels of guards and other officials was quite low. See Galina Ivanova, *Labor Camp Socialism: The Gulag in the Soviet Totalitarian System*, ed. Donald J. Raleigh, trans. Carol Flath (Armonk, NY: M.E. Sharpe, 2000), esp. 127–75. See also chapter 4 of the present study.

45 See GARF f. 9414 op. 1 d. 1445 l. 13.

46 For examples of party membership and gender composition, see the "Tsifrovye pokazateli" for UITLK NSO for the second half of 1943: GARF f. 9414 op. 1 d. 1463 l. 147.

47 See GARF f. 9414, op 1, d. 1463, l. 147; and GARF f. 9414 op. 1 d. 1461 l. 210. Political discussions and information sessions are the second-most frequent activity. At UITLK NSO, there were 1,125 of these in the second half of 1943; 72 reports and lectures; 280 theatrical performances, concerts, and amateur performances (*vecherov samodeiatel'nosti*); and 177 film screenings.

48 GARF f. 9414 op. 1 d. 1463 l. 147.

49 In the second half of 1943, UITLK NSO published 31 different wall newspapers and production bulletins with a total of 431 issues. I have not located wartime archival copies of these newspapers. For more on Gulag newspapers during the war, see A. Iu. Gorcheva, *Pressa Gulaga, 1918–1955* (Moscow: Izd-vo Moskovskogo Universiteta, 1996), 53–6.

50 GARF f. 9414, op. 1, d. 1463, l. 133.

51 GARF f. 9414, op. 1, d. 1463, l. 142. See also Bell, "One Day in the Life of Educator Khrushchev."

52 GARF f. 9414, op. 1, d. 1461, l. 196.

53 Bacon, *Gulag at War*, 106.

54 *ISG*, 2, Document no. 76: Reshenie Politburo VKP(b): "O lageriakh NKVD," 10 September 1939, p. 158. For more on workday credits and this decision, see Simon Ertz, "Trading Effort for Freedom: Workday Credits in the Stalinist Camp System," *Comparative Economic Studies* 47, no. 2 (2005): 476–91.

55 Barnes, *Death and Redemption*, 130.

56 See, for example, GARF f. 9414 op. 1 d. 1463 l. 145. The following discussion and quotations come from the same report.

57 GARF f. 9414, op. 1, d. 1463, l. 145.

58 R.S. Bikmetov, "Siblag v gody Velikoi otechestvennoi voiny," *Vestnik Kemerovskogo gosudarstvennogo universiteta* 61, no. 3 (2015): 110–15, esp. 113.

59 Lynne Viola, "Introduction," in Lynne Viola, ed., *Contending with Stalinism: Soviet Power and Popular Resistance in the 1930s* (Ithaca, NY:

Cornell University Press, 2002), 1–16 (quotation 14). See also her "Popular Resistance in the 1930s: Soliloquy of a Devil's Advocate," 17–43, in the same volume.

60 These forms of resistance are reminiscent of James Scott's description of peasant resistance in Southeast Asia. As Scott points out, open and organized resistance was "dangerous, if not suicidal." It is more important, then, that we understand *"everyday* forms of peasant resistance … the ordinary weapons of relatively powerless groups: foot dragging, dissimulation, desertion, false compliance, pilfering, feigned ignorance, slander, arson, sabotage, and so on." These types of activities are what Scott famously refers to as the "weapons of the weak," weapons that for the most part were readily available to – and widely used by – Gulag prisoners. See James C. Scott, *Weapons of the Weak: Everyday Forms of Peasant Resistance* (New Haven, CT: Yale University Press, 1985), esp. xv–xvi.

61 Wilson T. Bell, "Was the Gulag an Archipelago? De-Convoyed Prisoners and Porous Borders in the Camps of Western Siberia," *Russian Review* 72, no. 1 (2013): 116–41, esp. 117, 132.

62 TsDNITO f. 356, op. 1, d. 15, ll. 152–3.

63 Bell, "Was the Gulag an Archipelago?" 133.

64 See also, James Heinzen, "Corruption in the Gulag: Dilemmas of Officials and Prisoners," *Comparative Economic Studies* 47 (2005): 456–75.

65 Wilson T. Bell, "Sex, Pregnancy, and Power in the Late Stalinist Gulag," *Journal of the History of Sexuality* 24, no. 2 (2015): 198–224.

66 P. Kh. Ivanov, "Nezabytoe: Vospominaniia zhertv repressii," in I.V. Dobrovol'skii, ed., *GULAG: Ego stroiteli, obitateli i geroi: raskulachivanie i gonenie na Pravoslavnuiu Tserkov' popolniali lageria GULAGa* (Frankfurt: Mezhdunarodnoe obshchestvo prav cheloveka, 1999), 371.

67 TsDNITO f. 356, op. 1, d. 5, ll. 3*ob*, 6.

68 As I argue in Bell, "Sex, Pregnancy, and Power," this form of sexual barter in the Gulag is very similar to what Anna Hájková demonstrates took place in the Theresienstadt ghetto. See Hájková, "Sexual Barter in Times of Genocide: Negotiating the Sexual Economy of the Theresienstadt Ghetto," *Signs* 38, no. 3 (2013): 503–33.

69 See Bell, "Sex, Pregnancy, and Power," 206, and Margarete Buber-Neumann, *Under Two Dictators: Prisoner of Stalin and Hitler* (London: Pimlico, 2009), 95.

70 Anna Larina, *This I Cannot Forget: The Memoirs of Nikolai Bukharin's Widow*, trans. Gary Kern, intro. Stephen Cohen (New York: W.W. Norton, 1993).

71 Elena Glinka, "The Kolyma Tram," in Anne Applebaum, ed., *Gulag Voices: An Anthology* (New Haven, CT: Yale University Press, 2011), 39–48.

72 See Bell, "Sex, Pregnancy, and Power," and Adi Kuntsman, "'With a Shade of Disgust': Affective Politics of Sexuality and Class in Memoirs of the Stalinist Gulag," *Slavic Review* 68, no. 2 (2009): 308–28.

73 Dan Healey, *Homosexual Desire in Revolutionary Russia: The Regulation of Sexual and Gender Dissent* (Chicago: University of Chicago Press, 2001), 184–91.

74 Healey, *Homosexual Desire*, 230–4.

75 For more on homosexuality as resistance to Stalinism, see Dan Healey, "Sexual and Gender Dissent: Homosexuality as Resistance in Stalin's Russia," in Lynne Viola, ed., *Contending with Stalinism: Soviet Power and Resistance in the 1930s* (Ithaca, NY: Cornell University Press, 2002), 139–69.

76 Donald Filtzer, "Starvation Mortality in Soviet Home-Front Industrial Regions during World War II," in Wendy Z. Goldman and Donald Filtzer, eds., *Hunger and War: Food Provisions in the Soviet Union during World War II* (Bloomington: Indiana University Press, 2015), 265–338 (quotation 230). Note that Filtzer cites slightly lower mortality figures than those in table 3.1 for 1942 and 1943, stating that Gulag morality was "just over 20 percent in both 1942 and 1943." Filtzer, "Starvation Mortality," 330.

77 For a discussion of *tufta*, see Applebaum, *Gulag*, 350–60. Applebaum draws extensively on memoirs for this discussion. For another example, see N.M. Busarev's autobiography in RGASPI f. 560, op. 1, d. 4, ll. 104–5.

78 Evgeniia Borisovna Pol'skaia, *Eto my, Gospodi, pred Toboiu…* (Nevinnomyssk: n. pub, 1998), 203.

79 Memorial Society Archives f. 2, op. 1, d. 84, l. 46.

80 Kate Brown, *Plutopia: Nuclear Families, Atomic Cities, and the Great Soviet and American Plutonium Disasters* (Oxford: Oxford University Press, 2013), 96.

81 Oleg Khlevniuk, ed., *The History of the Gulag: From Collectivization to the Great Terror*, trans. Vadim A. Staklo (New Haven, CT: Yale University Press, 2004), 338.

82 Lynne Viola, "The Aesthetic of Stalinist Planning and the World of the Special Villages," *Kritika: Explorations in Russian and Eurasian History* 4, no. 1 (2004): 101–28, esp. 127–8.

83 Alin, *Malo slov, a goria rechen'ka…*, 147. Also quoted in Bell, "Was the Gulag an Archipelago?" 134.

84 Bell, "Was the Gulag an Archipelago?" 128.

85 Memorial Society Archives, f. 2, op. 2, d. 14 [Gebel' Ananii Semenovich, Kratkie epizody ternistigo puta s 1937 (iiun') do 1956 g. (ianvar')], ll. 136–42.

86 Dan Healey, "Lives in the Balance: Weak and Disabled Prisoners and the Biopolitics of the Gulag," *Kritika: Explorations in Russian and Eurasian History* 16, no. 3 (2015): 527–56, esp. 528–9.

87 Golfo Alexopoulos, "Destructive-Labor Camps: Rethinking Solzhenitsyn's Play on Words," *Kritika: Explorations in Russian and Eurasian History* 16, no. 3 (2015): 499–526.

88 Healey, "Lives in the Balance," 555.

89 As quoted in Golfo Alexopoulos, *Illness and Inhumanity in Stalin's Gulag* (New Haven, CT: Yale University Press, 2017), 130.

90 Alexander Etkind, "Bare Monuments to Bare Life: The Soon-to-be-Dead in Arts and Memory," *Gulag Studies* 1 (2008): 27–34.

91 Memorial Society Archives, f. 2, op. 2, d. 15, l. 143.

92 Eugenia Ginzburg, *Within the Whirlwind*, trans. Ian Boland (New York: Harvest/HBJ, 1982); Janusz Bardach and Kathleen Gleeson, *Man Is Wolf to Man: Surviving the Gulag* (Berkeley: University of California Press, 1999).

93 Healey, "Lives in the Balance," 529. For brief mention of the training of prisoner paramedics (*fel'dshera*) in Siblag, see also R.S. Bikmetov, "Siblag v gody Velikoi Otechestvennoi voiny," 112.

94 Zavgorodnii, who had been a member of the OGPU from 1921, was awarded the Order of the Red Banner of Labour (1942) and the Order of the Red Star (1944) for his successful direction of munitions production within the corrective-labour colony system. See A.I. Kokurin and N.V. Petrov, eds., *GULAG (Glavnoe upravlenie lagerei) 1918–1960* (Moscow: Materik, 2002), 816–17.

95 Document no. 84, "Iz dokladnoi zapiski zamestitelia nachal'nika GULAG G. S. Zavgorodnego v NKVD SSSR 'O rabote Glavnogo upravleniia lagerei i kolonii NKVD SSSR za vrenia s 15 iiulia po 15 noiabria 1941 goda,'" *ISG*, 4:199–204.

96 For information on order 0149 of April 1942, as well as on the censure of VOKhR commanders, see NKVD Operational Order 001478 from 13 July 1942 "O nalozhenii vzyskanii na rabotnikov Voenizirovannoi okhrany ispravitel'no-trudovykh lagerei i kolonii NKVD za dopusk pobegov gosudarstvennykh prestupnikov," GARF f. 9401, op. 1a, d. 113, l. 153 s ob.

97 See GARF f. 9401, op. 1a, d. 107, l. 80 [Tsirkuliar NKVD no. 87s/06/PR/29 ot 28 aprelia 1941 g. "Ob usilenii bor'by s pobegami z/k"].

98 The follow-up NKVD circular, from Chernyshev, dated 2 July 1941, clarifies that underage escapees should be sentenced only under article 82 of the RSFSR's criminal code, rather than 58-14, and that the death penalty should be carried out only against escapees who were especially dangerous (bandits, counter-revolutionaries, etc.) who had repeated an escape attempt. This follow-up circular also gave room to decide on the punishment based on individual circumstances. See GARF f. 9401, op. 1a, d. 113, l. 194.

99   Much of the story of Pavlik Morozov is likely untrue, although he was a
real person. See Catriona Kelly, *Comrade Pavlik: The Rise and Fall of a Soviet
Boy Hero* (London: Granta Publications, 2005).
100   Alin, *Malo slov, a goria rechen'ka...*, 147–54 (quotation 152). According to
Alin, camp officials simply noted that the third prisoner had died resist-
ing arrest during an escape attempt.
101   For more on the post-Stalin uprisings see, for example, Applebaum,
Gulag, 484–505; Barnes, *Death and Redemption*, 201–53; Alan Barenberg,
Gulag Town, Company Town: The Gulag and Its Legacy in Vorkuta (New
Haven, CT: Yale University Press, 2014), 130–49; and Marta Craveri, "The
Strikes in Norilsk and Vorkuta Camps, and their Role in the Breakdown
of the Stalinist Forced Labour System," in Marcel van der Linden and
Tom Brass, eds., *Free and Unfree Labour: The Debate Continues* (Bern: Peter
Lang, 1997), 363–78.
102   Barenberg, *Gulag Town, Company Town*, 45–52.
103   Document no. 15, "Iz ukazaniia Operativnogo otdela GULAG no. 45/4873
nachal'nikam operativno-chekistskikh otdelov (otdelenii) ispravitel'no-
trudovykh lagerei i kolonii o vyiavlenii v lageriakh povstancheskikh
nastroenii i formirovanii," in V.A. Kozlov and O.V. Lavinskaia, eds.,
Istoriia stalinskogo Gulaga, vol. 6, *Vosstaniia, bunty i zabastovki zakliuchennykh* (Moscow: Rosspen, 2004), 133–5. [Henceforth cited as *ISG*, 6]
104   Document no. 24, "Dokladnaia zapiska nachal'nika Operativnogo otdela
GULAG zamestitliu narkoma vnutrennikh del SSSR S.N.Kruglovu ob
usilenii "kontrrevoliutsionnykh proiavlenii" v ispravitel'no-trudovykh
lageriakh v sviazi s nastupleniiem germanskikh voisk," *ISG*, 6: 151–7,
Siblag information on 151–2.
105   GARF f. 9414, op. 1, d. 39, l. 145.
106   See Barnes, *Death and Redemption*, 108–13, for more on the prisoners from
the borderlands.
107   The phrasing in the documentation is inconsistent, as sometimes this
contingent is referred to as "refugees," sometimes as "special settlers,"
and sometimes as both ("special-settler refugees").
108   GARF f. 9401, op. 1a, d. 64, ll. 39–41.
109   V.N. Zemskov, *Spetsposelentsy v SSSR, 1930–1960* (Moscow: Nauka, 2005),
83–5. For more on these deportations, see Stanisław Ciesielski, Grzegorz
Hryciuk, and Aleksander Srebrakowski, *Masowe deportacje ludności
w Związku Radzieckim* (Toruń: Wydaw. Adam Marszałek, 2003); and
Stanisław Ciesielski, Wojciech Materski, and Andrzej Paczkowski, *Represje
sowieckie wobec Polaków i obywateli polskich* (Warsaw: Ośrodek Karta, 2002).
Special thanks to Daria Nałęcz for the Polish-language references.

110 Gosudarstvennyi arkhiv Novosibirskoi oblasti (GANO) f. P-4, op. 33, d. 238v, ll. 45–54: "Zamechaniia na biuro Obkoma VKP(b) po voprosu o Tomasinlage" from 14 Sept 1940. Information cited here on l. 45.

111 The commission's report can be found at GANO f. P-4, op. 33, d. 238v, ll. 32–6 (quotation l. 34).

112 The meeting protocol for this meeting can be found at GANO f. P-4, op. 33, d. 238v, ll. 37–44.

113 GANO f. P-4, op. 33, d. 238a, ll. 15–18: "Protokol No 55 p. 19. 6 Sept 1940. 'O besporiadkakh sredi bezhentsev-spetspereselentsev.'"

114 GANO f. P-4, op. 33, d. 238a, ll. 17–18. Note that the available documentation does not list the number of deaths amongst the "special-settler refugees."

115 Zemskov, *Spetsposelentsy v SSSR*, 89–90.

116 See, for example, the "European Memoirs of the Gulag: Sound Archives," accessed 9 May 2017, http://museum.gulagmemories.eu/en; V.N. Maksheev and A.I. Solzhenitsyn, eds., *Narymskaia khronika 1930–1945: Tragediia spetsperselentsev: Dokymenty i vospominaniia* (Moscow: Ruskii put', 1997); and U. Ruta, *Bozhe, kak eshche khotelos' zhit'*, trans. E. Ioffe (London: Overseas Publications Interchange, 1989). This source is in English and Russian, but I accessed it in Russian at the Sakharov Centre Gulag memoir database, 16 May 2017, http://www.sakharov-center.ru/asfcd/auth/?t=page&num=188.

117 Ruta, *Bozhe, kak eshche khotelos' zhit'*, esp. 16, 23–4, 28, 32–3, and 36.

118 The interviews of Rozentals have been partially translated into English, but can also be heard in the original Russian. They were conducted in Riga on 11 June 2008. See, in particular, "The Communists saved our lives," accessed 9 May 2017, http://museum.gulagmemories.eu/en/media/rozental-7-13; and "Reception in Siberia," accessed 9 May 2017, http://museum.gulagmemories.eu/en/media/rozental-4.

119 The interview with Peep Varju was conducted, in Russian, on 19 January 2009. See, in particular, "Peep Varju describes the death of his entire family and hunger in Siberia," accessed 9 May 2017, http://museum.gulagmemories.eu/en/media/clone-varju-2-1; and "Harsh life in the orphanage," accessed 9 May 2017, http://museum.gulagmemories.eu/en/media/varju-4.

120 See document 137 in Maksheev and Solzhenitsyn, eds., *Narymskaia khronika*, 178.

121 "Iz doklada upravleniia NKVD po Kemerovskoi oblasti v GULag NKVD o sostoianii trudssylki za pervoe polugodie 1943 g.," 29 August 1943, in V.P. Danilov and S.A. Krasil'nikov, eds., *Spetspereselentsy v Zapadnoi Sibiri 1939–1945* (Novosibirsk: Ekor, 1996), 216–24.

122 See discussion in Bell, "Was the Gulag an Archipelago?" 123n39.

123 Bardach and Gleeson, *Man Is Wolf to Man.*

124 Bacon, *The Gulag at War,* 24.

125 The exception to the trend of focusing on remote camps is O.V. Kornilova, who has published extensively over the last several years on Viazemlag, particularly focusing on the construction of the highway between Moscow and Minsk. Viazemlag had a very small percentage of prisoners sentenced under Article 58. See, for example, O.V. Kornilova, "Zakliuchennye GULAGa vtoroi poloviny 1930-kh gg.: lagkontingent Viazemlaga po stat'iam osuzhdeniia i srokom zakliucheniia," *Sotsial'naia istoriia* 23, no. 5 (2014): 569–83; and Kornilova, *Kak stroili pervuiu sovetskuiu avtomagistral' (1936–1941 gg.)* (Smolensk: Svitok, 2014).

126 Gosudarstvennyi arkhiv Tomskoi oblasti (GATO) has two collections that contain prisoner files, f. R-1151 and f. R-1152. In total there are around 350 files in these collections, from prisoners who ended their terms (either via release or death) in camps in the Tomsk area. It is unclear why these particular 350 files were transferred from the Tomsk MVD to the state archive, so there is no reason to think these files are representative (or not) of the population as a whole. Of these 350 files, moreover, I was able to examine around 50 over two separate trips, with the prisoner names redacted due to privacy concerns. Thus, I approach these files not as representative of the whole, but merely as examples that can provide insight into the variety of experiences and prisoners within the camps.

127 GATO f. 1151, op. 1, d. 205, esp. ll. 6, 11, 13.

128 GATO f. 1151, op. 1, d. 212, esp. ll. 7–7ob, 9, 18.

129 At only thirteen pages, this is also a short prisoner file. GATO f. R-1151, op. 1, d. 3, ll. 1–13.

130 Wendy Z. Goldman, "Not by Bread Alone: Food, Workers, and the State," in Wendy Goldman and Donald Filtzer, eds., *Hunger and War: Food Provisions in the Soviet Union during World War II* (Bloomington: Indiana University Press, 2015), 80.

131 Oddly, the copy of the sentence states that she has five children, while her arrest report, the *anketa arrestovannogo,* states the names of six children, three boys and three girls.

132 For more on children in the camps, as well as children of those arrested, see Cathy Frierson and Semyon Vilensky, eds., *Children of the Gulag* (New Haven, CT: Yale University Press, 2010), and Bell, "Sex, Pregnancy, and Power," esp. 216–19.

133 This 122-page file is GATO R-1151, op. 1, d. 195. See especially l. 2, l. 6 (these two documents reveal the 1936/37 discrepancy in his transfer to Tomsk); l. 40 for the diagnosis; ll. 33 and 56 for doctors' requests that he

be released to relatives; ll. 55 and 65 for two examples of letters from relatives; l. 107 for the document from the procurator revealing jurisdictional
issues; and ll. 111–120 for documents related to his release.

134 GATO R-1151, op. 1, d. 226.

135 GATO f. R-1151, op. 1, d. 222, esp. ll. 13, 41, 49, 51, 52, 53 (quotation 52).

136 GATO f. R-1151, op. 1, d. 83.

137 Etkind, "Bare Monuments to Bare Life."

138 Etkind points to the goner – the soon-to-be-dead – as exemplifying phi-
losopher Giorgio Agamben's idea of bare life. Agamben likens bare life to
the *homo sacer*, a figure banished completely outside of the law in ancient
Rome, who could neither be technically murdered nor sacrificed. His life,
in other words, had no meaning except for its biological functions. For
Agamben, the concentration camp (Agamben primarily considered the
Nazi camps) provides the modern framework for the reduction to bare
life, as the prisoners of the camp live within a state of exception, outside of any legal or social framework. They are beings whose lives have
become meaningless, aside, perhaps, from biological functions. Giorgio
Agamben, *Homo Sacer: Sovereign Power and Bare Life*, trans. Daniel Heller-
Roazen (Stanford: Stanford University Press, 1995), esp. 166–80.

139 Peter H. Solomon, Jr., *Soviet Criminal Justice under Stalin* (Cambridge:
Cambridge University Press, 1995).

4 Patriotic Personnel

1 Gosudarstvennyi arkhiv Novosibirskoi oblasti (GANO) fond P-260,
opis' 1, delo 54, listy 33–4.

2 V. Belousov [Sergei Vladimirov], *Zapiski dokhodiagi* (Ashkhabad,
Turkmenistan: n. pub., 1992), 127.

3 Although even for the Nazi camps, there have been few systematic studies of personnel. See Karin Orth, "The Concentration Camp Personnel,"
in Jane Caplan and Nikolaus Wachsmann, eds., *Concentration Camps in
Nazi Germany: The New Histories* (London: Routledge, 2010), 44–57. Still,
for the Nazi system more generally, the "question of the perpetrator"
has received widespread attention, from Arendt's famous discussion of
the banality of evil in *Eichmann in Jerusalem* to the widely read works
of Christopher Browning and Daniel Jonah Goldhagen.

4 Lynne Viola, "The Question of the Perpetrator in Soviet History,"
Slavic Review 72, no. 1 (2013): 1–23, esp. 10; also Wendy Z. Goldman,
"Comment: Twin Pyramids – Perpetrators and Victims," *Slavic Review* 72,
no. 1 (2013): 24–7.

5 Christopher Browning, *Ordinary Men: Reserve Police Battalion 101 and the Final Solution in Poland* (New York: HarperCollins, 1992). See also, Browning, *Nazi Policy, Jewish Workers, German Killers* (Cambridge: Cambridge University Press, 2000).

6 Galina Ivanova, *Labor Camp Socialism: The Gulag and the Soviet Totalitarian System*, ed. Donald J. Raleigh, trans. Carol A. Flath (Armonk, NY: M.E. Sharpe, 2000), 127.

7 Ivanova, *Labor Camp Socialism*, 139, 163, 165. Ivanova is somewhat contradictory on this point: on page 163 she states, "The Party organs did not seem to make any special efforts to improve the level of political awareness of the guards," while on page 165 she says, "The Gulag leadership made repeated attempts to raise the professional and educational level of their employees." These two statements are not necessarily contradictory, in part because "guards" and "employees" are not synonymous; but given that "political awareness" was a big part of education, further explanation is required.

8 Ivanova, *Labour Camp Socialism*, 149.

9 Anne Applebaum essentially follows Ivanova's analysis, arguing that "it seems that the Gulag administration openly functioned within the NKVD as a place of exile, a last resort for disgraced secret police." With some exceptions, officials took advantage of prisoners and dehumanized them. Anne Applebaum, *Gulag: A History* (New York: Doubleday, 2003) 261, 256–79; Steven A. Barnes, *Death and Redemption: The Gulag and the Shaping of Soviet Society* (Princeton, NJ: Princeton University Press, 2011), 49–50.

10 Oxana Ermolaeva, "Health Care, the Circulation of Medical Knowledge, and Research in the Soviet GULAG in the 1930s," *East Central Europe* 40 (2013): 341–65.

11 Alan Barenberg, *Gulag Town, Company Town: Forced Labor and Its Legacy in Vorkuta* (New Haven, CT: Yale University Press, 2014), esp. 66–78.

12 Barenberg, *Gulag Town, Company Town*, 72.

13 See Lynne Viola, *The Unknown Gulag: The Lost World of Stalin's Special Settlements* (New York: Oxford University Press, 2007), esp. 61–72.

14 Fyodor Mochulsky, *Gulag Boss: A Soviet Memoir*, trans. and ed. Deborah Kaple (New York: Oxford University Press, 2011), 33–7 and 41–2. Mochulsky generally comes across quite positively in his memoir. For a good discussion of this memoir as a historical source, see the October-November 2011 "Blog Conversation" on the memoir, accessed: 26 May 2015, http://russianhistoryblog.org/category/blog-conversations/gulagboss/.

15 Dietrich Beyrau, "Camp Worlds and Forced Labor: A Comparison of the National Socialist and Soviet Camp Systems," in Michael David-Fox, ed., *The Soviet Gulag: Evidence, Interpretation, Comparison* (Pittsburgh: University of Pittsburgh Press, 2016), 224–49 (quotation 248).

16 G.M. Ivanova, "Kadry GULAGa," in I.V. Dobrovol'skii and Ivanova, eds., *GULAG: ego stroiteli, obitateli i geroi: Rossiia po dorogam fanatizma i muchenichestva* (Moscow: Mezh.obshchestvo prav cheloveka, 1998), 40–59, esp. 53.

17 Donald Filtzer, *Soviet Workers and Late Stalinism: Labour and the Restoration of the Stalinist System after World War II* (Cambridge: Cambridge University Press, 2002), 26–7.

18 See N.V. Petrov, "Vvedenie," in Petrov and N.I. Vladimirtsev, eds., *Istoriia Stalinskogo Gulaga*, vol. 2, *Karatel'naia sistema: struktura i kadry* (Moscow: Rosspen, 2004), 44–5. [Henceforth cited as *ISG*, 2] In 1938 at Belbaltlag, for example, "more than half of the administrators and nearly half of the armed guards ... were former or actual prisoners" (Applebaum, *Gulag*, 257). Neftali Frenkel' is only the most famous prisoner who ended up as a Gulag administrator. He was a prisoner at Solovki in the 1920s and ended up working first in the Solovki administration, then as works chief on the White Sea–Baltic Canal, and then as head of construction at BAMLag in the Far East. Later he became the head of the Main Administration of Railway Construction Camps (GULZhDS). Petrov's introduction, as well as many of the documents contained within the volume itself, is particularly useful for questions of personnel shortages and general statistical information pertaining to Gulag cadres.

19 The "grey zone" in the Gulag was enormous. Holocaust survivor Primo Levi's various writings on his experience, notably *The Drowned and the Saved*, trans. Raymond Rosenthal (New York: Vintage, 1989), deal extensively with the idea that the perpetrator/victim dichotomy is an oversimplification of the Nazi camp structure. For Levi, for survival in the camps, a degree of moral ambiguity was necessary. In chapter 2 of *The Drowned and the Saved*, Levi termed this ambiguous area the "grey zone," an area that included the kapos and other inmates who helped the Nazis in one way or another in order to help themselves survive.

20 We do not have the equivalent, for the Gulag, of Rudolf Höss's memoir of his experience as commandant of Auschwitz. There have been memoirs from former NKVD officials, such as Anotoli Granovsky's *I Was an NKVD Agent* (New York: Devin-Adair, 1962), but even he cannot be considered representative, as he had been arrested before he became an agent and later defected to the west. Mochulsky, *Gulag Boss*, and Ivan

Chistyakov, *The Diary of a Gulag Prison Guard*, trans. Arch Tait, intro. Irina Shcherbakova (London: Granta, 2016) are more recent first-person examples that shed light on Gulag personnel.

21 Note that Oxana Ermolaeva, in an unpublished conference paper, makes excellent use of job application files for the positions of camp guard and camp Third Department worker, in order to answer pertinent questions about camp personnel. See Ermolaeva, "Making a Career in the GULAG Archipelago: The BBK-BBLag Personnel," paper for presentation at the 10th annual Young Researchers Conference, Miami University, Oxford, OH (2010). Ermolaeva was unfortunately unable to attend the conference but made her paper available. See also Ermolaeva, "Health Care," 351–3, for information on recruiting staff for Gulag medical positions.

22 Most of these documents are party meeting protocols for one camp party organization or another, which are either verbatim stenographic reports or close summaries of the meetings' proceedings It is ultimately impossible to know what has been omitted from these stenographic reports and meeting minutes. In some cases, they read as verbatim accounts, complete with notations for applause and questions from the floor. In other cases, particularly with the meeting minutes, some of the discussion has clearly been left out.

23 As Edwin Bacon notes, the camps' political departments, *politotdely* (singular, *politotdel*), focused their efforts on the staff. Edwin Bacon, *The Gulag at War: Stalin's Forced Labour System in the Light of the Archives* (New York: New York University Press, 1994), 79. See also Barnes, *Death and Redemption*, 49.

24 Exactly who the "civilians" were is not always clear. Many were ex-prisoners, hired on after the completion of their sentences (and frequently without a say in the matter). According to Jacques Rossi, the main guarding units, the VOKhR, were made up mostly of civilians on three-year contracts, usually demobilized soldiers who did not want to go back to the *kolkhoz*. See Zhak Rossi [Jacques Rossi], *Spravochnik po GULAGu* (Moscow: Prosvet, 1991), 62–3.

25 See the "STENOGRAMMA partiino-khoziaistvennogo aktiva Upravleniia ispravitel'no-trudovykh lagerei i kolonii po Novosibirskoi oblasti, 20–22 fev. 1941," GANO f. P-260, op. 1, d. 1, l. 2, for data on the civilian employees.

26 The 1 January 1941 population was 43,857 and the 1 January 1942 population was 77,919; most of the influx probably came after the outbreak of the war, but given the high turnover and rates of transfer of prisoners, the exact population throughout 1941 is difficult to know. For the population figures, see M.B. Smirnov, N.G. Okhotkin, and A.B. Roginskii, eds., *Sistema*

ispravitel'no-trudovykh lagerei v SSSR, 1923–1960: Spravochnik (Moscow: Zven'ia, 1998), 392. [Henceforth cited as *Sistema*]

27 For these figures, see Gosudarstvennyi arkhiv Rossiskoi Federatsii (GARF) f. 9414, op. 1 *dop*, d. 9, l. 5. The document is from October 1942 and has to do with a leadership change for the Novosibirsk Province Camp and Colony Administration.

28 GANO f. P-260, op. 1, d. 1, l. 33.

29 Mochulsky, *Gulag Boss*, 38.

30 This description is based mostly on private correspondence between Simon Ertz and myself (emails dated 8 and 9 February 2010, held on file). I am very grateful to Simon Ertz for his help in clarifying the varied terminology associated with guarding the camps.

31 GANO f. P-260, op. 1, d. 24, l. 28.

32 These, and many other examples, come from GANO f. P-260, op. 1, d. 24, l. 29.

33 The implications of this are considerable, and worth examining in further detail, as we must multiply the number of those who would have known a lot about Gulag conditions and operations.

34 V.P. Zinov'ev, "Poselok Chekist," in Zinov'ev, I.M. Rudaia, and V.O. El'blaus, eds., *Neizvestnyi Seversk: Sbornik statei* (Tomsk: Izd-vo TGU, 1996), 60–71, esp. 64.

35 Applebaum, *Gulag*, 261–2. Barenberg also discusses the conversion of barracks from prisoner to non-prisoner living quarters. See Barenberg, *Gulag Town, Company Town*, esp. 77, 186, 224–5, 229.

36 Wilson T. Bell, "Was the Gulag an Archipelago? De-Convoyed Prisoners and Porous Borders in the Camps of Western Siberia," *Russian Review* 72, no. 1 (2013): 116–41. See also Alan Barenberg, "Prisoners without Borders: *Zazonniki* and the Transformation of Vorkuta after Stalin," *Jahrbücher für Geschichte Osteuropas* 57, no. 4 (2009): 513–34.

37 Petrov, "Vvedenie," *ISG*, 2:34. This number was likely higher amongst the non-VOKhR guards. The VOKhR was the main guard unit, but there were also unarmed supervisors, or *nadzirateli*, within the camp compounds. Many prisoners, especially during the 1930s and then again in the late 1940s and early 1950s, were "self-guards," or *samookhraniki*.

38 Barenberg points out that at Vorkutlag, in 1948, 28 per cent (1,352) of all guards were prisoners, a number that had increased by 1950. See Barenberg, *Gulag Town, Company Town*, 116, for more on these "self-guards."

39 See Petrov, "Vvedenie," *ISG*, 2:48; Ivanova, *Labor Camp Socialism*, 141; and Applebaum, *Gulag*, 261.

40 Ivanova, *Labor Camp Socialism*, 146.

41 Chistyakov, *Diary of a Gulag Prison Guard.*

42 Petrov, "Vvedenie," *ISG*, 2:48.

43 Filtzer, *Soviet Workers*, 26–7. It is unclear from Filtzer's account whether this 9 per cent figure refers only to the VOKhR, or also to the *nadzirateli*. Likely, however, it is the VOKhR figure, as this was the formalized guard unit. This information is also discussed in Bell, "Was the Gulag an Archipelago?" 125.

44 D.S. Krasil'nikov, "Lageria i kolonii na territorii Novosibirskoi oblasti v gody Velikoi Otechestvennoi voiny 1941–1945" (diplomnaia rabota, Novosibirsk State University, 1999), 44.

45 GANO f. P-260, op. 1, d. 24, ll. 1–4.

46 GANO f. P-260, op. 1, d. 24, l. 29.

47 Tsentr dokumentatsii noveishei istorii Tomskoi oblasti (TsDNI TO) f. 356 op. 1 d. 15 ll. 152–3.

48 For more on black markets in the camps, see Bell, "Was the Gulag an Archipelago?" 132–7.

49 TsDNI TO f. 356 op. 1 d. 15 l. 153.

50 GARF f. 9401, op. 1a, d. 127, ll. 75–6.

51 Ermolaeva, "Health Care," 353.

52 *Strelki*, or riflemen, was another common term for members of the VOKhR.

53 GARF f. 9401, op. 1a, d. 128, ll. 9–10 *s ob* [Tsirkuliar no. 184s ot 4 maia 1942 g.].

54 GARF f. 9401, op. 1a, d. 128, l. 9*ob*.

55 GARF f. 9414 op. 1 d. 1994 l. 55. The letter is from Zavgorodnii, at the time the director of the Gulag's corrective-labour colonies (ITKs).

56 For this report, see GARF f. 9414, op. 1, d. 1437, l. 39ob.

57 GARF f. 9414 op. 1 d. 1437 l. 45ob.

58 Mochulsky, for example, was recruited right out of engineering school to work at Pechorlag in the far north of European Russia. Mochulsky, *Gulag Boss*, esp. 5–9.

59 Petrov, "Vvedenie," *ISG*, 2:46. Ermolaeva notes, however, that there was "an extensive network of medical schools" in the 1930s to train doctors for the camps. See Ermolaeva, "Health Care," 353.

60 Petrov, "Vvedenie," *ISG*, 2:46.

61 Document no. 122, "Spisok shkol GULAG, deistvovavshikh v 1944g." *ISG*, 2:244.

62 GARF f. 9401 op. 1a d. 118 l. 122.

63 The "general supply section" is the ChOS = *Chast'obshchego snabzheniia*.

64 The Kuibyshev school is likely the same as the 1930s Kharkov school. The Nazis occupied Kharkov until late summer 1943, and many administrative

offices from occupied or threatened areas (including Moscow) were relocated to Kuibyshev.

65 GARF f. 9401 op. 1a d. 165 ll. 88–90 *s ob.*

66 It is not clear what is meant by *inspektorskii sostav* in this 1944 document. Beria issued an order on 7 Februay 1940 (NKVD operational order number 00149), reorganizing several Gulag administrative departments. Order 00149 also created a fifteen-person *Kontrol'no-inspektorskaia gruppa* (Control-Inspection Group) within the central Gulag command to help monitor the work of the prison camps and colonies. It is likely that the *inspektorskii sostav* mentioned in the 1944 document refers to inspectors working under this group. However, it may also refer to inspectors of machinery. It is also worth noting that provincial and territorial procurators also had "camp procurators" on their staff, who inspected the camps on a semi-regular basis. For more on the Order 00149, see N. Petrov, "Istoriia imperii 'GULAG': Glava 8," accessed 28 May 2015, http://avkrasn.ru/article-2084.html.

67 In the Russian/Soviet education system, grades were assigned on a five-point scale, whereby five was the highest, roughly equivalent to an A.

68 See, for example, Yoram Gorlizki and Oleg Khlevniuk, *Cold Peace: Stalin and the Soviet Ruling Circle, 1945–1953* (Oxford: Oxford University Press, 2004), 128–9; Aleksei Tikhonov, "The End of the Gulag," in Paul R. Gregory and Valery Lazarev, eds., *The Economics of Forced Labor: The Soviet Gulag* (Stanford: Hoover Institution Press, 2003), 68, 72; Amy Knight, *Beria: Stalin's First Lieutenant* (Princeton, NJ: Princeton University Press, 1993), 105–6.

69 The Second Department was also called the URO (*Uchetno-raspredelitel'nyi otdel*), or Accounting and Distribution Department. See Rossi, *Spravochnik po GULAGu*, 428. For the circular and booklet, see GARF f. 9401, op. 1a, d. 81, ll. 12–37. The first two pages of this document are the text of the circular, no. 157 from 21 June 1940, while the remaining pages consist of a copy of a training booklet.

70 GANO f. P-260 op. 1 d. 24 ll. 1–4.

71 See also GARF f. 9414, op. 1 *dop*, d. 9, l. 5.

72 D.E. Alin, *Malo slov, a goria rechen'ka…: Nevydumannye rasskazy* (Tomsk: Volodei, 1997), 132.

73 Around 5 per cent of the incoming contingent were party or candidate party members (112 of 2,212), while only 3.3 per cent of the outgoing contingent had this status (83 of 2,533). 2.2 per cent (48 of 2,212) of the incoming contingent had completed some sort of higher education, while only 1.5 per cent (37 of 2,533) of the outgoing group had done so. In terms of

completed secondary education, the figures for the incoming contingent are 7.3 per cent compared to 6.7 per cent in the outgoing group.

74 Document no. 130, "Spravka Otdela kadrov NKVD SSSR o dvizhenii i sostave kadrov NKVD za 1944g.," *ISG*, 2:254–6.

75 The information on camp personnel shows a shortage of 15.3 per cent for the camp sector, 25.3 per cent for the production sector, 11.6 per cent for the Militarized Guard commanders; and 11.8 per cent for the leadership of the educational-political department (VPO – *Vospitatel'no-politicheskii otdel*). In absolute numbers, according the document (Document no. 131, "Iz spravki Otdela kadrov GULAG o sostave kadrov po vsem periferiinym organam GULAG po sostoia-niiu na 1 ianvaria 1945 g.," *ISG*, 2:266–71, esp. 266–7), the camp sector employed 23,703 persons (with a shortfall of 4,931); the production sector 23,479 persons (with a shortfall of 8,229); the VOKhR command-ers 5,185 (with a shortfall of 683); and the VPO leadership 848 (with a shortfall of 249).

76 OITK TO = The new administration for ITKs in Tomsk Province following the creation of Tomsk Province in 1944 out of Novosibirsk Province.

77 TsDNI TO f. 607, op. 1, d. 29, ll. 54–7.

78 Information in this paragraph comes from GARF f. 9414, op. 1, d. 2513 [Instruktsii i direktivy Gulaga NKVD SSSR po okhrane i rezhimu {Jan–Nov 1943}], ll. 83–4.

79 Ivanova, "Kadry GULAGa," 49.

80 See Document no. 49, "Prikaz NKVD SSSR no. 00690 «Ob organizatsii politotdela v sostave GULAGa NKVD i politotdelov v sostave Upravlenii lagerei». 22 oktiabria 1937," *ISG*, 2:134. See also Barnes, *Death and Redemption*, 49, and Beyrau, "Camp Worlds and Forced Labor," 247.

81 As of 10 March 1945, 99 per cent of the 756 *nomenklaturnykh rabotnikov* in the camp sector and the Militarized Guard (VOKhR) were party or candidate members. See Document no. 126, "Spravka GULAG o sostave rukovodiashchikh kadrov ispravitel'no-trudovykh lagerei i kolonii NKVD nomenklatury TsK VKP(b) ...," *ISG*, 2:250–1. For the 18 per cent figure as of 1 January 1945, see Petrov, "Vvedenie," in *ISG*, 2:47.

82 TsDNI TO f. 356, op. 1, d. 25 [Rukovodiashchikh direktiv politotdela UITLiK NKVD po NSO 1943 god], l. 148.

83 Barnes, *Death and Redemption*, 51.

84 See, for example. Protocol no. 11 of the operational-chekist primary party organization of Tomasinlag from 7 October 1940. Complaints at this meet-ing indicate that there was not enough study of the *Short Course*, and few communists had studied more than four chapters. TsDNI TO f. 242, op. 1,

d. 1 [Protokoly oper-chekistskoi pervichnoi partorganizatsii Tomasinlaga NKVD], ll. 43–5.

85 For more on the disciplining of party members outside of the camps, see Edward Cohn, *The High Title of a Communist: Postwar Party Discipline and the Values of the Soviet Regime* (DeKalb: Northern Illinois University Press, 2015).

86 The Control Commission was in charge of monitoring members for proper behaviour, and thus played a large role in issues of discipline and membership.

87 This information comes from the Party Commission report at the 3rd Party Conference of the Administration of Corrective Labour Camps and Colonies [Novosibirsk Province], held 22–3 January 1945. See GANO f. P-260, op. 1, d. 54, l. 33.

88 TsDNI TO f. 356, op. 1, d. 20, ll. 19–19ob.

89 See Cohn, *The High Title of a Communist.*

90 Bell, "Was the Gulag an Archipelago?" esp. 132–5.

91 Wilson T. Bell, "Sex, Pregnancy, and Power in the Late Stalinist Gulag," *Journal of the History of Sexuality* 24, no. 2 (2015): 198–224, esp. 213–15.

92 See Protocol no. 12, closed Party meeting of ITK 6, 4 June 1940. TsDNI TO f. 356, op. 1, d. 5, ll. 84–86.

93 See Protocol no. 1, closed Party meeting of ITK 6, 9 January 1940. TsDNI TO f. 356, op. 1, d. 5, l. 142.

94 This example comes from TsDNI TO f. 4151 [*Pervichnaia partorganizat- siia Tomsko-Asinskogo ispravitel'no-trudovogo lageria NKVD*], op. 1, d. 5, ll. 24–25 [1st party organization meeting protocol from 9 February 1940].

95 For the text of the letter, see TsDNI TO f. 356, op. 1, d. 15, l. 3. For more on intimate relations between personnel and prisoners, see Bell, "Sex, Pregnancy, and Power," 213–15.

96 *Sistema*, 392.

97 Closed letter from Gavrilin, a deputy director (*zam-nach*) of the Gulag's *Politotdel*, sent to all party and Komsomol organizations within GULAG and GLAVGIDROSTROI NKVD. The other camps listed are Karlag, Astrakhanlag, and Vladivostoklag. TsDNI TO f. 356, op. 1, d. 15, ll. 4–5.

98 See the unpublished memoir of Ananii Semenovich Gebel', "Kratkie epi- zody ternistigo puta s 1937 (iiun') do 1956 g. (ianvar')," held at Memorial, f. 2, op. 2, d. 14, l. 138.

99 Protocol no. 4 closed Party meeting of ITK no. 6, 1 February 1940. TsDNI TO f. 356, op. 1, d. 5, ll. 127–30.

100 See the Stenogramma partiino-khoziastvennogo aktiva Upravleniia ispravitel'no trudovykh lagerei i kolonii po Novosibirskoi oblasti, 20–22 February 1941: GANO f. P-260, op. 1, d. 1, ll. 235ob-236.

101 See TsDNI TO f. 4151, op. 1, d. 10 [Protokoly sobranii partorganizat-sii Siblaga], ll. 8–11 [Protokol no. 4 Obshchego zakrytogo sobranii pervichnoi partorganizatsii Asinovskogo otdeleniia Siblaga NKVD Novosibirskoi oblasti ot 25 iiunia 1941 goda].

102 Applebaum, *Gulag*, 418–19.

103 TsDNI TO f. 4151, op. 1, d. 10, l. 9.

104 TsDNI TO f. 4151, op. 1, d. 4, ll. 62–66, especially l. 64.

105 These statistics come from TsDNI TO f. 4151, op. 1, d. 12, l. 14*ob.*

106 TsDNI TO f. 4151, op. 1, d. 12, l. 16.

107 TsDNI TO f. 1492, op. 1, d. 1 [Dokumenta politotdela Siblaga NKVD SSSR ob usilenii partiino-propagandistskoi i kul'turno-vospitatel;noi raboty sredi sotrudnikov Siblaga i zakliuchennykh …], ll. 3–3ob. Unfortunately, the vast majority of Party Control Commission files are still classified at TsDNI TO; these could potentially yield a lot more information about party discipline. This particular document, a meeting protocol of the Party Commission of Siblag's *Politotdel* from 7 January 1942, probably has been declassified only because it was included within other *Politotdel* documents.

108 For more on issues facing Gulag prisoners after release, see Miriam Dobson, *Khrushchev's Cold Summer: Gulag Returnees, Crime, and the Fate of Reform after Stalin* (Ithaca, NY: Cornell University Press, 2009), and Nanci Adler, *The Gulag Survivor: Beyond the Soviet System* (New Brunswick, NJ: Transaction Publishers, 2002). For some of the issues in Novosibirsk Province, see Marc Elie, "Les politiques à l'égard des libérés du Goulag: amnistiés et réhabilités dans la région de Novossibirsk, 1953–1960," *Cahiers du monde russe* 47, no. 1–2 (2006): 327–48. Note that Barenberg, *Gulag Town, Company Town*, complicates the picture, as he shows that former prisoners in Vorkuta actually benefited from their connections to other former prisoners, who helped them secure new jobs and housing.

109 GANO f. P-260, op. 1, d. 1, l. 21. See also D.S. Krasil'nikov, "Lageria i kolonii," 37.

110 Indeed, it was a curious phenomenon in the Gulag that most prisoners would be overworked, underfed, underclothed, and forced to live in extremely harsh conditions, but that, once they were declared invalids by camp medical staff, considerable effort was usually made to nurse them back to health. Many extremely ill prisoners, of course, were never declared invalids and simply died. For more on the health and treatment of invalids, see Ermolaeva, "Health Care"; Golfo Alexopolous, "Destructive-Labor Camps: Rethinking Solzhenitsyn's Play on Words," *Kritika: Explorations in Russian and Eurasian History* 16, no. 3 (2015): 499–526; and Dan Healey, "Lives in the Balance: Weak and Disabled Prisoners

and the Biopolitics of the Gulag," *Kritika: Explorations in Russian and Eurasian History* 16, no. 3 (2015): 527–56.

111 Belousov, *Zapiski dokhodiagi*, 126–7.

112 Before moving to Orlovo-Rozovo, Kazachenko had been the director of the Antibes subdivision, an agricultural camp within Siblag that was in some ways a "model" camp. Antibes sent a delegation to the All-Union Agricultural Exhibition in 1940. See also "Netipichnyi geroi zhestokogo vremeni," *Vestnik UIS Kuzbassa* no. 4, 34–6; article can also be found at the Memorial f. 2, op. 1, d. 7.

113 See Memorial f. 2, op. 1, d. 84, ll. 34–5.

114 Memorial f. 2, op. 1, d. 7, l. 35.

115 I do not wish to give the impression that no personnel were motivated by ideology. J. Arch Getty and Oleg Naumov argue that Nikolai Ezhov, head of the NKVD during the Great Terror, was "not an amoral careerist, and he took ideology seriously." No doubt there were many within the NKVD like him. See J. Arch Getty and Oleg V. Naumov, eds., *Yezhov: The Rise of Stalin's "Iron Fist"* (New Haven, CT: Yale University Press, 2008), xxi.

116 Hannah Arendt, *Eichmann in Jerusalem: A Report on the Banality of Evil*, rev. ed. (New York: Penguin Books, 1994; original publication, 1963).

117 For an interesting discussion relating Arendt's theories to the Gulag, see Svetlana Boym, "'Banality of Evil,' Mimicry, and the Soviet Subject: Varlam Shalamov and Hannah Arendt," *Slavic Review* 67, no. 2 (2008): 342–63, esp. 349–52.

118 The presence of informal networks is an important theme of Barenberg's work. See *Gulag Town, Company Town*, esp. 66–72.

119 Christian Gerlach and Nicholas Werth, "State Violence – Violent Societies," in Michael Geyer and Sheila Fitzpatrick, eds., *Beyond Totalitarianism: Stalinism and Nazism Compared* (Cambridge: Cambridge University Press, 2009), 133–79.

5 The Gulag's Victory

1 David Dallin and Boris Nicolaevsky, *Forced Labor in Soviet Russia* (New Haven, CT: Yale University Press, 1947). See also Wilson T. Bell, "Gulag Historiography: An Introduction," *Gulag Studies* 2–3 (2009–10): esp. 4–5.

2 Albert Konrad Herling, *The Soviet Slave Empire* (New York: W. Funk, 1951); Charles Orr, *Stalin's Slave Camps: An Indictment of Modern Slavery* (Boston: Beacon Press, 1952); and Martha Chyz, *Woman and Child in the Modern System of Slavery – USSR*, trans. O. Pruchodko (New York: Dobrus, 1962).

3 S. Swianiewicz, *Forced Labour and Economic Development: An Enquiry into the Experience of Soviet Industrialization* (Oxford: Oxford University Press, 1965).

4 For example, see Václav Holešovský, "Review of S. Swianiewicz, *Forced Labour and Economic Development* and Paul Barton, *L'institution concentrationnaire en Russie (1930–1957)*," *Slavic Review* 26, no. 3 (1967): 505–7.

5 Marcel van der Linden, "Forced Labour and Non-Capitalist Industrialization: The Case of Stalinism (c. 1929–c. 1956)," in Tom Brass and van der Linden, eds., *Free and Unfree Labour: The Debate Continues* (Bern: Peter Lang, 1997), 351–62.

6 Paul R. Gregory, "An Introduction to the Economics of the Gulag," in Gregory and Valery Lazarev, eds., *The Economics of Forced Labor: The Soviet Gulag* (Stanford: Hoover Institution Press, 2003). See also Paul Gregory and Mark Harrison, "Allocation under Dictatorship: Research in Stalin's Archives," *Journal of Economic Literature* 43, no. 3 (2005): 721–61, esp. 737–8.

7 James Harris, "The Growth of the Gulag in the Urals Region, 1929–31," *The Russian Review* 56, no. 2 (1997): 265–80.

8 The most prominent example is Oleg Khlevniuk. See his "The Economy of the OGPU, NKVD, and MVD of the USSR, 1930–1953," in Gregory and Lazarev, eds., *Economics of Forced Labor*, 43–66.

9 Christian de Vito and Alex Lichtenstein, eds., *Global Convict Labour* (Leiden: Brill, 2015).

10 Jeffrey S. Hardy, *The Gulag after Stalin: Redefining Punishment in Khrushchev's Soviet Union* (Ithaca, NY: Cornell University Press, 2016), esp. 7, 71, and 86.

11 Tzvetan Todorov, *Facing the Extreme: Moral Life in the Concentration Camps* (New York: Henry Holt, 1996). He draws on the Gulag writings of Shalamov and Solzhenitsyn, among others. See, for example, 28, 32–5, 41.

12 Giorgio Agamben, *Homo Sacer: Sovereign Power and Bare Life*, trans. Daniel Heller-Roazen (Stanford: Stanford University Press, 1995), 42, 52, 148.

13 Hannah Arendt, *The Origins of Totalitarianism* (New York: Harcourt, 1968), 437–59, esp. 437 and 445.

14 Dietrich Beyrau, "Camp Worlds and Forced Labor: A Comparison of the National Socialist and Soviet Camp Systems," trans. Nicole Eaton, in Michael David-Fox, ed., *The Soviet Gulag: Evidence, Interpretation, Comparison* (Pittsburgh: Pittsburgh University Press, 2016), 224–49; Alan Barenberg, "Forced Labor in Nazi Germany and the Stalinist Soviet Union," in David Eltis, Stanley Engerman, Seymour Drescher, and David Richardson, eds., *AD 1804–AD 2016*, vol. 4 of *The Cambridge World History of Slavery* (Cambridge: Cambridge University Press, 2017), 633–54.

15 Beyrau, "Camp Worlds and Forced Labor," 248.

16 Barenberg, "Forced Labor," 653.

17 Steven A. Barnes, *Death and Redemption: The Gulag and the Shaping of Soviet Society* (Princeton, NJ: Princeton University Press, 2011), 53.

18 Zygmunt Bauman, *Modernity and the Holocaust* (New York: Columbia University Press, 1989).

19 See David L. Hoffman, *Stalinist Values: The Cultural Norms of Soviet Modernity, 1917–1941* (Ithaca, NY: Cornell University Press, 2003); Peter Holquist, "State Violence as Technique: The Logic of Violence in Soviet Totalitarianism," in Amir Weiner, ed., *Landscaping the Human Garden: Twentieth-Century Population Management in a Comparative Framework* (Stanford: Stanford University Press, 2003), 19–45; Weiner, "Introduction: Landscaping the Human Garden," in Weiner, ed., *Landscaping the Human Garden*, 1–18.

20 Stephen Kotkin, "Modern Times: The Soviet Union and the Interwar Conjuncture," *Kritika: Explorations in Russian and Eurasian History* 2, no. 1 (2001): 110–63, especially 111–12.

21 A.I. Kokurin and N.V. Petrov, eds., *GULAG (Glavnoe upravlenie lagerei) 1918–1960* (Moscow: Materik, 2002), 30. See also chapter 1, on the evolution of prisoner labour in the Soviet Union.

22 The full text of this document can be found in Gosudarstvennyi arkhiv Rossiskoi Federatsii (GARF) f. 9401, op. 1a, d. 35, ll. 16–29 *c ob.*; and as Document 112, "Prikaz no. 00889 […]," in Kokurin and Petrov, eds., *GULAG*, 456–76.

23 See Document 36, "Prikaz NKVD SSSR no. 0161 …" in Kokurin and Petrov, eds., *GULAG*, 117–28, esp. 119.

24 GARF f. 9401, op. 1a, d. 37, ll. 93–101 *s ob.*

25 The censor would look out for hidden items and evidence of anti-Soviet statements, as well as for information about the camp, such as its location, the number of prisoners, statements pertaining to regimen, conditions, the guards, escapes, type of production, problems with living conditions, illnesses and epidemics in the camps, camp rules, and complaints to judicial organs.

26 NKVD Operational Order no. 00555 from 5 May 1940, "O vvedenii v podrazdeleniiakh lagerei NKVD i koloniiakh UITK, OITK NKVD, UNKVD dolzhnosti tsenzora," GARF f. 9401 op. 1a d. 56 l. 187.

27 Arsenii Formakov, *Gulag Letters*, ed., trans., and intro. Emily D. Johnson (New Haven, CT: Yale University Press, 2017).

28 Richard W. Ireland, *"A Want of Order and Good Discipline": Rules, Discretion and the Victorian Prison* (Cardiff: University of Wales Press, 2007), 192.

29 See chapter 4 in this book for more on personnel shortages in the Gulag.

30 Terry Martin, "Modernization or Neo-Traditionalism: Ascribed Nationality and Soviet Primordialism," in Sheila Fitzpatrick, ed., *Stalinism: New Directions* (New York: Vintage Books, 2000), 348–67; and Ken Jowitt, "Soviet Neotraditionalism: The Political Corruption of a Leninist Regime," *Soviet Studies* 35, no. 3 (1983): 275–97.

31 Michael David-Fox argues that we should think about multiple modernities when considering the Soviet Union, thus allowing scholars to highlight similarities with other states as well as elements particular to the Soviet Union. He takes issue with the neo-traditional approach, as this approach downplays the many similarities the Soviet Union shared with other states of the twentieth century. See Michael David-Fox, *Crossing Borders: Modernity, Ideology, and Culture in Russia and the Soviet Union* (Pittsburgh: University of Pittsburgh Press, 2015), esp. 21–47.

32 GARF f. 9401, op. 1a, d. 234, l. 29ob.

33 J. Otto Pohl, *The Stalinist Penal System: A Statistical History of Soviet Repression and Terror, 1930–1953* (London: McFarland, 1997), 28. The main differences in terms of prisoners' sentences were not surprisingly at the extremes. In ITLs, only 0.2 per cent of prisoners were serving sentences of less than one year, while that figure was 7 per cent in ITKs, while 6.8 per cent of ITL prisoners had sentences of over twenty years, compared with only 1.8 per cent of ITK prisoners. Still, overall, there are surprisingly few differences.

34 GARF f. 9401, op. 1a, d. 234, l. 29.

35 See Richard Ek, "Giorgio Agamben and the Spatialities of the Camp: An Introduction," *Geografiska Annaler. Series B, Human Geography* 88, no. 4 (2006): 363–86; Agamben, *Homo Sacer*; and Agamben, *State of Exception*, trans. Kevin Artell (Chicago: University of Chicago Press, 2005).

36 Carl Schmitt, *Political Theology: Four Chapters on the Concept of Sovereignty*, trans. Charles Schwab (Chicago: University of Chicago Press, 2005), 5. Schmitt was writing in an interwar context that was fearful of the rise of communism, and no doubt would have been perplexed to see his own theories on sovereignty applied, however indirectly, to the Soviet Union.

37 Agamben, *Homo Sacer*, 20.

38 Derek Gregory, "The Black Flag: Guantanamo Bay and the Space of Exception," *Geografiska Annaler* 88, no. 4 (2006): 405–27.

39 The Enabling Act of 1933 essentially declared a state of exception, allowing Hitler and the Nazis to rule by emergency decree.

40 Amir Weiner, *Making Sense of War: The Second World War and the Fate of the Bolshevik Revolution* (Princeton, NJ: Princeton University Press, 2001), 87.

41 Weiner, *Making Sense of War*, 190.
42 Anne Applebaum, *Gulag: A History* (New York: Doubleday, 2003), 591.
43 Mark Harrison, *Accounting for War: Soviet Production, Employment, and the Defence Burden, 1940–1945* (Cambridge: Cambridge University Press, 1996), 98.
44 Document 69, T.V. Tsarevskaia-Diakina, ed., *Istoriia stalinskogo Gulaga*, vol. 5, *Spetspereselentsy v SSSR* (Moscow: Rosspen, 2004), 270.
45 V.N. Zemskov, *Spetsposelentsy v SSSR, 1930–1960* (Moscow: Nauka, 2005), 122.
46 Lynne Viola, *The Unknown Gulag: The Lost World of Stalin's Special Settlements* (New York: Oxford University Press, 2007), 178–9.
47 For a file on the mobilization of special settlers for the Red Army, see GARF f. 9479, op. 1, d. 113. Novosibirsk Province is discussed in numerous documents in this file, including ll. 13, 78–80, 99–100, 202–3. As of 12 May 1942, Novosibirsk Province had mobilized 9,500 special settlers, more than every region except Central Asia.
48 Michael H. Westren, "Nations in Exile: 'The Punished Peoples' in Soviet Kazakhstan, 1941–1961" (PhD diss., University of Chicago, 2012).
49 Norman Naimark, *Stalin's Genocides* (Princeton, NJ: Princeton University Press, 2011).
50 For some of the trouble the regime had enforcing its harsh labour laws, see Martin Kragh, "Stalinist Labour Coercion during World War II: An Economic Approach," *Europe-Asia Studies* 63, no. 7 (2011): 1253–73. For more on the partial relaxation of measures affecting religion and the cultural elite, see Bernd Bonwetsch, "War as a 'Breathing Space': Soviet Intellectuals and the 'Great Patriotic War,'" in Robert W. Thurston and Bonwetsch, eds., *The People's War: Responses to World War II in the Soviet Union* (Urbana: University of Illinois Press, 2000), 146.
51 Nikolaus Wachsmann, *Kl: A History of the Nazi Concentration Camps* (New York: Farrar, Straus and Giroux, 2015), 61.
52 Jonathan Hyslop, "The Invention of the Concentration Camp: Cuba, Southern Africa and the Philippines, 1896–1907," *South African Historical Journal* 63, no. 2 (2011): 251–76.
53 Wolfgang Sofsky, *The Order of Terror: The Concentration Camp*, trans. W. Templer (Princeton, NJ: Princeton University Press, 1997), 159–61.
54 For scholarship on the Gulag as an integrated part of Soviet society, see Alan Barenberg, *Gulag Town, Company Town: Forced Labor and Its Legacy in Vorkuta* (New Haven, CT: Yale University Press, 2014); Wilson T. Bell, "Was the Gulag an Archipelago? De-Convoyed Prisoners and Porous Borders in the Camps of Western Siberia," *Russian Review* 72, no. 1 (2013): 116–41;

Kate Brown, "Out of Solitary Confinement: The History of the Gulag," *Kritika: Explorations in Russian and Eurasian Studies* 8, no. 2 (2007): 67–103; and Oleg Khlevniuk, "The Gulag and the Non-Gulag as One Interrelated Whole," trans. Simon Belokowsky, *Kritika: Explorations in Russian and Eurasian History* 16, no. 3 (2015): 479–98.

55 For a discussion of "high modernism," see James C. Scott, *Seeing like a State: How Certain Schemes to Improve the Human Condition Have Failed* (New Haven, CT: Yale University Press, 1998). See also Kate Brown, *A Biography of No Place: From Ethnic Borderland to Soviet Heartland* (Cambridge, MA: Harvard University Press, 2004).

56 Beyrau, "Camp Worlds and Forced Labor," 235–8.

57 Barenberg, *Gulag Town, Company Town*.

58 For more on the postwar issues facing home front cities, see Robert Dale, "Divided We Stand: Cities, Social Unity and Post-War Reconstruction in Soviet Russia, 1945–1953," *Contemporary European History* 24, no. 4 (2015): 493–516. The literature on reconstruction of cities directly affected by front-line fighting is more developed. See, for example, Karl D. Qualls, *From Ruins to Reconstruction: Urban Identity in Soviet Sevastopol after World War II* (Ithaca, NY: Cornell University Press, 2009); and Steven Maddox, *Saving Stalin's Imperial City: Historic Preservation in Leningrad, 1930–1950* (Bloomington: Indiana University Press, 2015).

59 V.V. Alekseev et al., eds., *Rabochii klass Sibiri v period uprocheniia i razvitiia sotsializma* (Novosibirsk: Nauka, 1984), 149.

60 Timothy Snyder, *Bloodlands: Europe between Hitler and Stalin* (New York: Basic Books, 2010).

61 Barnes, *Death and Redemption*, 155–200, esp. 166–74.

62 Golfo Alexopoulos, *Illness and Inhumanity in Stalin's Gulag* (New Haven, CT: Yale University Press, 2017), esp. 221–31.

63 Dale, "Divided We Stand," 494.

64 For a discussion of the spike in escapes in early 1946 (Siblag was one of the camps singled out), see Order no. 10/ss of the Administration for Guarding and Regimen of the Gulag, "O nakazanii vinovnikov neobespecheniia izoliatsii i okhrany zakliuchennykh v ispravitel'no-trudovykh lageriakh i koloniiakh NKVD i priniatii mer k prekrashcheniiu pobegov," from 15 February 1946. GARF f. 9414, op. 1, d. 2527, ll. 36–7. In *Cold Peace*, Gorlizki and Khlevniuk argue that escapes remained common in the postwar years, but certainly relative to the 1930s there was a major improvement. See Yoram Gorlizki and Oleg Khelvniuk, *Cold Peace: Stalin and the Soviet Ruling Circle, 1945–1953* (Oxford: Oxford University Press, 2004), 126.

65 Golfo Alexopolous, "Amnesty 1945: The Revolving Door of Stalin's Gulag," *Slavic Review* 64, no. 2 (2005): 290.

66 Applebaum, *Gulag*, 590–3.

67 In March of 1946 the NKVD split into two ministries, the MGB (Ministry of State Security) and the MVD (Ministry of Internal Affairs), with the MGB (the precursor to the KGB) in charge of counter-intelligence and the MVD in charge internal security, including the regular police and fire-fighting services but also, of course, the Gulag. See Applebaum, *Gulag*, 468.

68 These arguments come from Gorlizki and Khlevniuk, who note that Beria (head of the MVD) in particular sought incentives to improve the efficiency of Gulag labour. By 1950, 27 per cent of prisoners were in camps that were again using workday credits, while from 1949 to Stalin's death, various measures were passed to give certain prisoners wages for their labour. See Gorllizki and Khlevniuk, *Cold Peace*, 128–9.

69 Alexopolous, "Amnesty 1945," 299.

70 See Document no. 100, "Spravki 1 spetsotdela MVD SSSR o kolichestve arestovannykh i osuzhdennykh v period 1921-1953 gg.," in Kokurin and Petrov, eds., *GULAG*, 431.

71 Peter H. Solomon, Jr., *Soviet Criminal Justice under Stalin* (Cambridge: Cambridge University Press, 1996), 404. See also, Donald Filtzer, *Soviet Workers and Late Stalinism: Labour and the Restoration of the Stalinist System after World War II* (Cambridge: Cambridge University Press, 2002), 27. The increasing arbitrariness of the system runs counter to one of Foucault's keys to modern punishment, namely that the punishment appear just. See Michel Foucault, *Discipline & Punish: The Birth of the Prison*, 2nd ed., trans. Alan Sheridan (New York: Vintage Books, 1995), 94–9.

72 Siblag figures come from *Sistema ispravitel'no-trudovykh lagerei v SSSR, 1923–1960: Spravochnik*, comp. M.B. Smirnov, ed. N.G. Okhotin and A.B. Roginskii, (Moscow: Zven'ia, 1998), 392 [henceforth cited as *Sistema*], while the Gulag figures are from Applebaum, *Gulag*, 579. For the Western Siberian estimates, see Wilson T. Bell, "The Gulag and Soviet Society in Western Siberia, 1929–1953" (PhD diss., University of Toronto, 2011), 257.

73 Applebaum, *Gulag*, 298.

74 Oleg Khlevniuk, "Vvedenie," in Khlevniuk, ed., *Istoriia Stalinskogo Gulaga*, vol. 3, *Ekonomika Gulaga* (Moscow: Rosspen, 2004), 47. For a good discussion of the "Special Camps" and their effects on political prisoners, see Barnes, *Death and Redemption*, 164–85. See also Aleksandr Solzhenitsyn, *The GULAG Archipelago 1918–1956: An Experiment in Literary Investigation*, vol. 3, trans. Harry Willitts (New York: Harper & Row, 1978), 37; and Applebaum, *Gulag*, 477.

75 Zemskov, *Spetsposelentsy v SSSR*, 122.

76 John Goldlust, "A Different Silence: The Survival of More Than 200,000 Polish Jews in the Soviet Union during World War II as a Case Study in Cultural Amnesia," *Australian Jewish Historical Society Journal* 21 (2012): 13–60, esp. 40–6.

77 Alexopolous, "Amnesty 1945," 301. See also "Appendix (b): USSR Custodial Populations, 1943–1953," in J. Arch Getty, Gabor T. Rittersporn, and Viktor N. Zemskov, "Victims of the Soviet Penal System in the Pre-War Years: A First Approach on the Basis of Archival Evidence," *The American Historical Review* 98, no. 4 (1993): 1049.

78 Applebaum, *Gulag*, 295.

79 Bell, "Gulag and Soviet Society," 255–7.

80 G.N. Gorchakov, *Vospominaniia* (Jerusalem: Ierusalim.izdat.tsentr, 1995), 116.

81 These figures come from Filtzer, *Soviet Workers and Late Stalinism*, 23.

82 Information about the postwar Gulag economic activity in Western Siberia can be found in *Sistema*, 194, 281, 290, 305, 386, 392, 439, 482, 483, 520. See also L.I. Gvozdkova, A. A. Mit', eds., *Prinuditel'nyi trud: Ispravitel'no-trudovye lageria v Kuzbasse (30-50-e gg.)*, 2 vols. (Kemerovo: Kuzbassvuzizdat, 1994), for information on UITLK KO, and Gosudarstvennyi arkhiv Novosibirskoi oblasti (GANO) f. R-20, op. 1, dd. 378, 404, for information on UITLK NSO.

83 Alexopoulos, *Illness and Inhumanity*, 183–207.

84 Gosudarstvennyi arkhiv Novosibirskoi oblasti (GANO) f. R-20, op. 1, d. 378, l. 9. I have also come across this *Ukaz* in a prisoner file: one prisoner at the OITK TO was "released" early (after serving about one year of a two-year term) because of this *Ukaz*, but was to serve out the remainder of his term as a civilian ("*v/n*") worker. The *Ukaz* of the Supreme Soviet of the USSR is listed as no. 108/59 for 1947. See Gosudarstvennyi arkhiv Tomskoi oblasti (GATO) f. R-1151, op. 1, d. 51, l. 20. This *Ukaz* does not appear in M.I. Iumashev and B.A. Zhaleiko, eds., *Sbornik zakonov SSSR i Ukazov Prezidiuma Verkhovnogo Soveta SSSR (1938-iul' 1956)* (Moscow: Gos. Izd. Iuridicheskoi literatury, 1956).

85 See Donald Filtzer, "The Standard of Living of Soviet Industrial Workers in the Immediate Postwar Period, 1945–1948," *Europe-Asia Studies* 51, no. 6 (1999): 1013–38, esp. 1018–24.

86 These numbers are higher than what Moscow wanted and, indeed, what it called for in its directives on health categories. See Golfo Alexopoulos, "Destructive-Labor Camps: Rethinking Solzhenitsyn's Play on Words," *Kritika: Explorations in Russian and Eurasian History* 16, no. 3 (2015): 499–526.

87 GANO f. R-20, op. 1, d. 404 [*Doklady o rabote prokuatury UITLiK UMVD po Novosibirskoi oblasti za 1948 god*] l. 8.

88 GANO f. R-20, op. 1, d. 404, l. 8ob.

89 See Document 43, "Spravka 2-go Upravleniia GULAG o napravlenii osuzhdennykh k katorzhnym rabotam v spetsial'nye lagernye podrazdelenie," in A.B. Bezborodov, I.V. Bezborodova, and V.M. Khrustalev, eds., *Istoriia Staliniskogo Gulaga*, vol. 4, *Naselenie Gulaga: chislennost' i usloviia soderzhaniia* (Moscow: Rosspen, 2004), 122.

90 James Heinzen, "Corruption in the Gulag: Dilemmas of Officials and Prisoners," *Comparative Economic Studies* 47 (2005): 456–75.

91 I describe this instance in Bell, "Was the Gulag an Archipelago?" 131–2.

92 See Hava Volovich, "My Past," in Simeon Vilensky, ed., *Till My Tale Is Told: Women's Memoirs of the Gulag*, trans. John Crowfoot et al. (Bloomington: Indiana University Press, 1999), 241–78.

93 Wilson T. Bell, "Sex, Pregnancy, and Power in the Late Stalinist Gulag," *Journal of the History of Sexuality* 24, no. 2 (2015), esp. 210.

94 For more on the post-Stalin amnesties and how they affected Western Siberia, see Marc Elie, "Les politiques à l'égard des libérés du Goulag: amnistiés et réhabilités dans la région de Novossibirsk, 1953–1960," *Cahiers du monde russe* 47, no. 1–2 (2006): 327–48.

95 For the shift in labour use of prisoners, see Hardy, *The Gulag after Stalin*, esp. 77–80. Official mortality rates fell below 1 percent in 1950 and then continued to fall, although we should question the reliability of these statistics. See Applebaum, *Gulag*, 583.

Epilogue

1 For some of the ambiguities of post-Stalin Gulag reforms, see the work of Jeffrey S. Hardy, especially "The Camp Is Not a Resort: The (re)Imposition of Order in the Soviet Gulag, 1957–1961," *Kritika: Explorations in Russian and Eurasian History* 13, no. 1 (2012): 89–212; and Hardy, *The Gulag after Stalin: Redefining Punishment in Khrushchev's Soviet Union* (Ithaca, NY: Cornell University Press, 2016).

2 Aleksandr Solzhenitsyn, *One Day in the Life of Ivan Denisovich*, trans. Harry T. Willetts (New York: Farrar, Straus and Giroux, 1991); and Miriam Dobson, *Khrushchev's Cold Summer: Gulag Returnees, Crime, and the Fate of Reform after Stalin* (Ithaca, NY: Cornell University Press, 2009).

3 See, for example, "'My breathing mom was among the corpses': Putin recalls his parents' World War II ordeal," *RT* [*Russia Today*], 30 April 2015, accessed 21 January 2016, https://www.rt.com/

news/254445-putin-family-details-wwii/. See also Masha Gessen, *The Man without a Face: The Unlikely Rise of Vladimir Putin* (New York: Penguin, 2012); and Elizabeth Wood, "Performing Memory: Vladimir Putin and the Celebration of World War II in Russia," *Soviet and Post-Soviet Review* 38, no. 2 (2011): 172–200.

4 Wood, "Performing Memory," 174.

5 Kathleen E. Smith, *Remembering Stalin's Victims: Popular Memory and the End of the USSR* (Ithaca, NY: Cornell University Press, 1996).

6 The volume of Russian scholarship on the Gulag is enormous and includes many document collections and an increasing number of monographs and journal articles. The most prominent published example is the seven-volume document collection, *Istoriia stalinskogo Gulaga*, which has been used extensively in the present study. For more, see Wilson T. Bell and Marc Elie, comps., "Selected Bibliography of Historical Works on the Gulag," *Gulag Studies* 1 (2008): 143–60, and updates in volumes 4 and 5/6 of the same journal.

7 Gleb Panfilov, dir., *V kruge pervom* (Kinokompaniia "Vera," 2006) (based on Solzhenitsyn's novel of the same name); and Nikolai Dostal', dir., *Zaveshchanie Lenina* (Rossiia, 2007) (based on Varlam Shalamov's *Kolymskie rasskazy*). Both television series had relatively high production values and appeared on the television station Rossiia, one of the main state-sponsored television stations.

8 Given the general tendency of the Western media to highlight the partial rehabilitation of Stalin under Putin's rule, the reaction to the opening of the new Gulag museum in Moscow was decidedly muted. For an example, see the BBC News story, "New Russian Gulag Museum Recreates Soviet Terror," 30 October 2015, accessed 22 January 2016, http://www.bbc.com/news/world-europe-34675413. For more on the new Gulag monument in Moscow, see, for example, the BBC's coverage: "Wall of Grief: Putin Opens Russia's First [sic] Soviet Victims Memorial," BBC News, 30 October 2017, accessed 30 November 2017, http://www.bbc.com/news/world-europe-41809659.

9 Thomas Sherlock, "Russian Politics and the Soviet Past: Reassessing Stalin and Stalinism under Vladimir Putin," *Communist and Post-Communist Studies* 49, no. 1 (2016): 45–59 (quotation 54).

10 On Perm' 36, see Mikhail Danilovich and Robert Coalson, "Revamped Perm-36 Museum Emphasises Gulag's 'Contribution to Victory," Radio Free Europe, 25 July 2015, accessed 22 January 2016, https://www.rferl.org/content/russia-perm-gulag-museum-takeover-contribution-to-victory/27152188.html. For coverage of the crackdowns against the Memorial

Society and the Sakharov Centre, see Priyanka Boghani, "Putin's Legal Crackdown on Civil Society," PBS, 13 January 2015, accessed 22 January 2016, https://www.pbs.org/wgbh/frontline/article/putins-legal-crackdown-on-civil-society/; and "Court Fines Sakharov Center NGO for Violating 'Foreign Agents' Law," *The Moscow Times*, 30 September 2015, accessed 22 January 2016, http://www.themoscowtimes.com/news/article/court-fines-sakharov-center-ngo-for-violating-foreign-agents-law/536321.html.

11 Eva-Clarita Onken, "The Baltic States and Moscow's 9 May Commemoration: Analysing Memory Politics in Europe," *Europe-Asia Studies* 59, no. 1 (2007): 23–46 (quotation 23).

12 Zuzanna Bogumił, Dominique Moran, and Elly Harrowell, "Sacred or Secular? 'Memorial,' the Russian Orthodox Church, and the Contested Commemoration of Soviet Repression," *Europe-Asia Studies* 67, no. 9 (2015): 1416–44. Note that Sherlock sees Putin's acceptance of some official memory of Stalinist repression as part of a rapprochement with the "rule of law" coalition that loosely backs Medvedev. See Sherlock, "Russian Politics and the Soviet Past," esp. 57. My thanks to my research assistant Elena Plotnikoff for research on the memory of Stalinism in today's Russia.

13 Maria M. Tumarkin, "The Long Life of Stalinism: Reflections on the Aftermath of Totalitarianism and Social Memory," *Journal of Social History* 44, no. 4 (2011): 1047–61, esp. 1052.

14 Alexander Etkind, *Warped Mourning: Stories of the Undead in the Land of the Unburied* (Stanford: Stanford University Press, 2013), 18 and 245.

15 Etkind, "Hard and Soft in Cultural Memory: Political Mourning in Russia and Germany," *Grey Room* 16 (2004): 36–59.

16 Xenia Cherkaev, "On Warped Mourning and Omissions in Post-Soviet Historiography," *Ab Imperio* 4 (2014): 365–85 (quotation 367).

17 Wilson T. Bell, "Tomsk Regional Identity and the Legacy of the Gulag and Stalinist Repression," in Edith Clowes, Ani Kokobobo, and Gisela Erbsloh, eds., *Russia's Regional Identities* (London: Routledge, 2018), 206–25.

Bibliography

Archives

GANO (*Gosudarstvennyi arkhiv Novosibirskoi oblasti* / State Archive of Novosibirsk Province)
    fond P-4 (Novosibirsk Province Party Committee)
    fond P-260 (Political Department of the Novosibirsk Province Corrective Labour Camp and Colony Administration)
    fond R-20 (Novosibirsk Province Procuracy)
GARF (*Gosudarstvennyi arkhiv Rossiskoi Federatsii* / State Archive of the Russian Federation)
    fond 9401, opis' 1a (NKVD operational orders)
    fond 9414 (Gulag)
    fond 9479 (Special Settlements)
GATO (*Gosudarstvennyi arkhiv Tomskoi oblasti* / State Archive of Tomsk Province)
    fond R-1151 (Corrective-Labour Colonies of Tomsk Province)
    fond R-1152 (Tomasinlag)
Memorial Society Archives
    fond 2 (Personal memoirs)
RGASPI (*Rossiskii gosudarstvennyi arkhiv sotsial'no-politicheskoi istorii* / Russian State Archive of Socio-Political History)
    fond 17 (Central Committee of the Communist Party)
    fond 560 (Memoirs relating to the "period of the cult of personality")
RGAE (*Rossiskii gosudarstvennyi arkhiv ekonomiki* / Russian State Archive of the Economy)
    fond 7486 (Ministry of Agriculture)
    fond 7733 (Ministry of Finance)

Tomsk Memorial Society Archives
TsDNI TO (*Tsentr dokumentatsii noveishei istorii Tomskoi oblasti* / The Centre for
   the Documentation of the Contemporary History of Tomsk Province)
   fond 80 (Tomsk City Party Committee)
   fond 242 (Political Department of Tomasinlag)
   fond 356 (Party Organization of the Third Camp Station of Siblag)
   fond 607 (Tomsk Province Party Committee)
   fond 1492 (Party Organization of the Tomsk region ITK no. 7)
   fond 4151 (Primary Party Organization of Tomasinlag)

Published Document Collections

Bezborodov, A.B., I.V. Bezborodova and V.M. Khrustalev, eds. *Istoriia
   Stalinskogo Gulaga*. Vol. 4, *Naselenie Gulaga: chislennost' i usloviia soderzhaniia*.
   Moscow: Rosspen, 2004.
Bol'shakova, V.A., S.A. Krasil'nikov, and B.P. Trenin, eds. *Nazinskaia tragediia:
   Iz istorii zemli Tomskoi: Dokumental'noe nauchnoe izdanie*. Tomsk: Nauka, 2002.
Danilov, V.P., R.T. Manning, and L. Viola, eds. *Tragediia sovoteskoi derevni: kolle-
   ktivizatsiia i raskulachivanie: dokumenty i materialy v piat' tomakh, 1927–1939*.
   5 vols. Moscow: Rosspen, 1999.
Danilov, V.P., and S.A. Krasil'nikov, eds. *Spetspereselentsy v Zapadnoi Sibiri,
   1939–1945*. Novosibirsk: Ekor, 1996.
– eds. *Spetspereselentsy v Zapadnoi Sibiri 1931–1933*. Novosibirsk: Nauka, 1992.
Frierson, Cathy, and Semyon Vilensky, eds. *Children of the Gulag*. New Haven,
   CT: Yale University Press, 2010.
Getty, J. Arch, and Oleg V. Naumov, eds. *Yezhov: The Rise of Stalin's "Iron Fist."*
   New Haven, CT: Yale University Press, 2008.
– eds. *The Road to Terror: Stalin and the Self-Destruction of the Bolsheviks,
   1932–1939*. New Haven, CT: Yale University Press, 1999.
The GULAG Press 1920–1937. Leiden, The Netherlands: IDC Publishers, 1999.
   Microfiche.
Gvozdkova, L.I., and A.A. Mit', eds. *Prinuditel'nyi trud: Ispravitel'no-trudovye
   lageria v Kuzbasse (30–50-e gg.)*. 2 vols. Kemerovo: Kuzbassvuzizdat, 1994.
Khlevniuk, Oleg, ed. *The History of the Gulag: From Collectivization to the Great
   Terror*. Translated by Vadim A. Staklo. New Haven, CT: Yale University
   Press, 2004.
– ed. *Istoriia Stalinskogo Gulaga*. Vol. 3, *Ekonomika Gulaga*. Moscow: Rosspen,
   2004.
Kokurin, A.I., and N.V. Petrov, eds. *GULAG (Glavnoe upravlenie lagerei)
   1918–1960*. Moscow: Materik, 2002.

Kozlov, V.A., and O.V. Lavinskaia, eds. *Istoriia Stalinskogo Gulaga*. Vol. 6, *Vosstaniia, bunty i zabastovki zakliuchennykh*. Moscow: Rosspen, 2004.

Krasil'nikov, S.A., V.A. Il'inykh, G.A. Spitsyna, and O.K. Kavtsevich, eds. *Nasha malaia rodina: Khrestomatiia po istorii Novosibirskoi oblasti, 1921–1991*. Novosibirsk: Ekor, 1997.

Kuznetsov, I.S. et al., eds. *Novonikolaevskaia guberniia – Novosibirskaia oblast': 1921–2000: Khronika. Dokumenty*. Novosibirsk: Sibirskoe otdelenie RAN, 2001.

Maksheev, V., and A. Solzhenitsyn, eds. *Narymskaia khronika, 1930–1945: Tragediia spetspereselentsev: Dokumenty i vospominaniia*. Moscow: Russkii put', 1997.

Mironenko, S.V. and N. Werth, eds. *Istoriia Stalinskogo Gulaga*. Vol. 1, *Massovye repressii v SSSR*. Moscow: Rosspen, 2004.

Petrov, N.V., and N.I. Vladimirtsev, eds. *Istoriia Stalinskogo Gulaga*. Vol. 2, *Karatel'naia sistema: struktura i kadry*. Moscow: Rosspen, 2004.

Pipes, Richard, ed. *The Unknown Lenin: From the Secret Archives*. New Haven, CT: Yale University Press, 1996.

Tsarevskaia-Diakina, T.V., ed. *Istoriia Stalinskogo Gulaga*. Vol. 5, *Spetspereselentsy v SSSR*. Moscow: Rosspen, 2004.

Viola, Lynne, V.P. Danilov, N.A. Ivnitskii, and Denis Kozlov, eds. *The War against the Peasantry, 1927–30*. Translated by Steven Shabad. New Haven, CT: Yale University Press, 2005.

Published Literary and First-Person Accounts

Adamova-Sloizberg, Olga. "My Journey." In Simeon Vilensky, ed., *Till My Tale Is Told: Women's Memoirs of the Gulag*. Translated by John Crowfoot et al., 1–86. Bloomington: Indiana University Press, 1999.

Alin, D.E. *Malo slov, a goria rechen'ka…: Nevydumannye rasskazy*. Tomsk: Volodei, 1997.

Bardach, Janusz, and Kathleen Gleeson. *Man Is Wolf to Man: Surviving the Gulag*. Berkeley: University of California Press, 1999.

Belousov, V. [Sergei Vladimirov.] *Zapiski dokhodiagi*. Ashkhabad, Turkmenistan: n. pub., 1992.

Belykh, P.I. "Vospominaniia." In L.I. Floigt, ed., *Stalinsk v gody repressii: Vospominaniia. Pis'ma. Dokumenty*. 2nd ed., 14–34. Novokuznetsk: Kuznetskaia krepost', 1995.

Berger, Iosif. *Krushenie pokoleniia. Vospominania*. Translated by Ia. Berger. Florence: Aurora, 1973.

Boldyrev, N.N. "Zigzagi sud'by." In Aleksandr Solzhenitsyn, comp. *Pozhivshi v GULAGe: Sbornik vospominanii*, 73–140. Moscow: Rus. put', 2001.

Buber-Neumann, Margarete. *Under Two Dictators: Prisoner of Stalin and Hitler.* London: Pimlico, 2009.

Chistyakov, Ivan. *The Diary of a Gulag Prison Guard.* Translated by Arch Tait, with an introduction by Irina Shcherbakova. London: Granta: 2016.

"European Memoirs of the Gulag: Sound Archives." http://museum. gulagmemories.eu/en.

Fel'tgeim", O. "Konets ssylki." *Annales contemporaines/Sovermennyia zapiski* 68 (1939).

Formakov, Arsenii. *Gulag Letters.* Edited, translated, and with an introduction by Emily D. Johnson. New Haven, CT: Yale University Press, 2017.

Ginzburg, Eugenia. *Within the Whirlwind.* Translated by Ian Boland. New York: Harvest/HBJ, 1982.

Glinka, Elena. "The Kolyma Tram." In Anne Applebaum, ed., *Gulag Voices: An Anthology*, 39–48. New Haven, CT: Yale University Press, 2011.

Gorchakov, G.N. *Vospominaniia.* Jerusalem: Ierusalim.izdat.tsentr, 1995.

Granovsky, Anotoli. *I Was An NKVD Agent.* New York: Devin-Adair, 1962.

Ivanov, P.Kh. "Nezabytoe: Vospominaniia zhertv repressii." In I.V. Dobrovol'skii, ed., *GULAG: Ego stroiteli, obitateli i geroi: raskulachivanie i gonenie na Pravoslavnuiu Tserkov' popolniali lageria GULAGa*, 370–1. Frankfurt: Mezhdunarodnoe obshchestvo prav cheloveka, 1999.

Klein, Aleksandr. *Kleimenye, ili, Odin' sredi odinokikh: Zapiski katorzhnika.* Syktyvkar: n. pub., 1995.

Larina, Anna. *This I Cannot Forget: The Memoirs of Nikolai Bukharin's Widow.* Translated by Gary Kern, with an introduction by Stephen Cohen. New York: W.W. Norton, 1993.

Levi, Primo. *The Drowned and the Saved.* Translated by Raymond Rosenthal. New York: Vintage, 1989.

Mochulsky, Fyodor Vasilevich. *Gulag Boss: A Soviet Memoir.* Translated and edited by Deborah Kaple. New York: Oxford University Press, 2011.

Noskovich, N.A. "Vospominaniia 'pridurka.'" *Neva* 4 (2001): 165–83.

Pol'skaia, Evgeniia Borisovna. *Eto my, Gospodi, pred Toboiu...* Nevinnomyssk: n. pub, 1998.

Ruta, U. *Bozhe, kak eshche khotelos' zhit'.* Translated by E. Ioffe. London: Overseas Publications Interchange, 1989.

Sats, Nataliia Il'inichna. *Zhizn' – iavlenie polosatoe.* Moscow: Novosti, 1991.

Severiukhina, Ninel'. *Proshchanie s detstvom: Fragmenti semeinoi khroniki 1941–1944.* St. Petersburg: Izdatel'stvo imeni N.I. Novikova, 2004.

Shalamov, Varlam. *Kolyma Tales.* Translated by John Glad. New York: W.W. Norton & Company, 1980.

Shapovalov, Veronica, ed. *Remembering the Darkness: Women in Soviet Prisons.* Lanham, MD: Rowman & Littlefield, 2001.

Sidorov, Sergei Alekseevich. *Zapiskia sviashchennika Sergiia Sidorova: S pril. ego zhizneopisaniia, sost. docher'iu, V. S. Bobrinskoi*. Moscow: Pravoslav. Sviato-Tikhonov. Bogoslov In-t., 1999.

Solzhenitsyn, Aleksandr. *One Day in the Life of Ivan Denisovich*. Translated by Harry T. Willetts. New York: Farrar, Straus and Giroux, 1991.

Vilensky, Simeon, ed. *Till My Tale Is Told: Women's Memoirs of the Gulag*. Bloomington: Indiana University Press, 1999.

Volovich, Hava. "My Past." In Simeon Vilensky, ed., *Till My Tale Is Told: Women's Memoirs of the Gulag*. Translated by John Crowfoot et al., 241–76. Bloomington: Indiana University Press, 1999.

Secondary Sources

Adler, Nanci. *Keeping Faith with the Party: Communist Believers Return from the Gulag*. Bloomington: Indiana University Press, 2012.

– *The Gulag Survivor: Beyond the Soviet System*. New Brunswick, NJ: Transaction Publishers, 2002.

Agamben, Giorgio. *State of Exception*. Translated by Kevin Artell. Chicago: University of Chicago Press, 2005.

– *Homo Sacer: Sovereign Power and Bare Life*. Translated by Daniel Heller-Roazen. Stanford: Stanford University Press, 1995.

Alekseev, V.V., and Z.G. Karpenko. "Razvitie narodnogo khoziastvo." In V.V. Alekseev et al., eds., *Rabochii klass Sibiri v period uprocheniia i razvitiia sotsializma*, 148–71. Novosibirsk: Nauka, 1984.

Alexopoulos, Golfo. *Illness and Inhumanity in Stalin's Gulag*. New Haven, CT: Yale University Press, 2017.

– "Destructive-Labor Camps: Rethinking Solzhenitsyn's Play on Words." *Kritika: Explorations in Russian and Eurasian History* 16, no. 3 (2015): 499–526.

– "Amnesty 1945: The Revolving Door of Stalin's Gulag." *Slavic Review* 64, no. 2 (2005): 274–306.

Applebaum, Anne. *Gulag: A History*. New York: Doubleday, 2003.

Arendt, Hannah. *Eichmann in Jerusalem: A Report on the Banality of Evil*. Revised and enlarged edition. New York: Penguin Books, 1994.

– *The Origins of Totalitarianism*. New York: Harcourt, 1968.

Bacon, Edwin. *The Gulag at War: Stalin's Forced Labour System in the Light of the Archives*. New York: New York University Press, 1994.

Badcock, Sarah. *A Prison without Walls? Eastern Siberian Exile in the Last Years of Tsarism*. Oxford: Oxford University Press, 2016.

Barenberg, Alan. "Forced Labor in Nazi Germany and the Stalinist Soviet Union." In David Eltis, Stanley Engerman, Seymour Drescher, and David

Richardson, eds., *AD 1804–AD 2016*. Vol. 4 of *The Cambridge World History of Slavery*, 633–54. Cambridge: Cambridge University Press, 2017.

– *Gulag Town, Company Town: Forced Labor and Its Legacy in Vorkuta*. New Haven, CT: Yale University Press, 2014.

– "Prisoners without Borders: *Zazonniki* and the Transformation of Vorkuta after Stalin." *Jahrbücher für Geschichte Osteuropas* 57, no. 4 (2009): 513–34.

Barnes, Steven A. *Death and Redemption: The Gulag and the Shaping of Soviet Society*. Princeton, NJ: Princeton University Press, 2011.

– "All for the Front, All for Victory! The Mobilization of Forced Labor in the Soviet Union during World War Two." *International Labor and Working-Class History* 58 (2000): 239–60.

Baron, Nick. "Production and Terror: The Operation of the Karelian Gulag, 1933–1939." *Cahiers du Monde russe* 43, no. 1 (2002): 139–79.

– "Conflict and Complicity: The Expansion of the Karelian Gulag, 1923–1933." *Cahiers du Monde russe* 42, no. 2–4 (2001): 615–48.

Bauman, Zygmunt. *Modernity and the Holocaust*. New York: Columbia University Press, 1989.

Beer, Daniel. *The House of the Dead: Siberian Exile under the Tsars*. New York: Alfred A. Knopf, 2017.

– "Penal Deportation to Siberia and the Limits of State Power, 1801–1881." In Michael David-Fox, ed., *The Soviet Gulag: Evidence, Interpretation, Comparison*, 173–98. Pittsburgh: Pittsburgh University Press, 2016.

Bell, Wilson T. "Tomsk Regional Identity and the Legacy of the Gulag and Stalinist Repression." In Edith Clowes, Ani Kokobobo, and Gisela Erbsloh, eds., *Russia's Regional Identities*, 206–25. London: Routledge, 2018.

– "Sex, Pregnancy, and Power in the Late Stalinist Gulag." *Journal of the History of Sexuality* 24, no. 2 (2015): 198–224.

– "Was the Gulag an Archipelago? De-Convoyed Prisoners and Porous Borders in the Camps of Western Siberia." *The Russian Review* 72, no. 1 (2013): 116–41.

– "The Gulag and Soviet Society in Western Siberia, 1929–1953." PhD diss., University of Toronto, 2011.

– "One Day in the Life of Educator Khrushchev: Labour and *Kul'turnost'* in the Gulag Newspapers." *Canadian Slavonic Papers* 46, no. 3/4 (2004): 289–314.

Bell, Wilson T., and Marc Elie, comps. "Selected Bibliography of Historical Works on the Gulag." *Gulag Studies* 1 (2008): 143–60.

Bellamy, Chris. *Absolute War: Soviet Russia in the Second World War*. New York: Alfred A. Knopf, 2007.

Beyrau, Dietrich. "Camp Worlds and Forced Labor: A Comparison of the National Socialist and Soviet Camp Systems." Translated by Nicole

Eaton. In Michael David-Fox, ed., *The Soviet Gulag: Evidence, Interpretation, Comparison*, 224–49. Pittsburgh: Pittsburgh University Press, 2016.

Bikmetov, R.S. "Siblag v gody Velikoi Otechestvennoi voiny." *Vestnik Kemerovskogo gosudarstvennogo universiteta* 61, no. 3 (2015): 110–15.

– "Uchastie spetskontingenta v formirovanii infrastruktury gorodov Kuzbassa v 1930-e–1950-e gg." In Iu. V. Kupert and K.V. Fadeev, eds., *Problemy urbanizatsii vostochnykh regionov Rossii v XIV–XX vv*, 132–42. Tomsk: Izd-vo TGASU, 2007.

Blackwell, William. *The Beginnings of Russian Industrialization, 1800–1860.* Princeton, NJ: Princeton University Press, 1968.

Bogumił, Zuzanna, Dominique Moran, and Elly Harrowell. "Sacred or Secular? 'Memorial', the Russian Orthodox Church, and the Contested Commemoration of Soviet Repression." *Europe-Asia Studies* 67, no. 9 (2015): 1416–44.

Bollinger, Martin. *Stalin's Slave Ships: Kolyma, the Gulag Fleet, and the Role of the West.* Westport, CT: Praeger, 2003.

Bonwetsch, Bernd. "War as a 'Breathing Space': Soviet Intellectuals and the 'Great Patriotic War.'" In Robert W. Thurston and Bonwetsch, eds., *The People's War: Responses to World War II in the Soviet Union.* Urbana: University of Illinois Press, 2000.

Borodkin, Leonid, and Simon Ertz. "Coercion vs. Motivation: Forced Labor in Norilsk." In Paul Gregory and Valery Lazarev, eds., *The Economics of Forced Labor: The Soviet Gulag*, 75–104. Stanford: Hoover Institution Press, 2003.

– "Nikel' v zapoliar'e: Trud zakliuchennykh Noril'laga." In L.I. Borodkin, P. Gregori (Gregory), and O.V. Khlevniuk, eds., *Gulag: Ekonomika prinuditel'nogo truda*, 197–238. Moscow: Rosspen, 2005.

Bosworth, Mary, ed. *The Encyclopedia of Prisons & Correctional Facilities.* 2 vols. London: Sage Publications, 2005.

Boym, Svetlana. "'Banality of Evil,' Mimicry, and the Soviet Subject: Varlam Shalamov and Hannah Arendt." *Slavic Review* 67, no. 2 (2008): 342–63.

Brown, Kate. *Plutopia: Nuclear Families, Atomic Cities, and the Great Soviet and American Plutonium Disasters.* Oxford: Oxford University Press, 2013.

– "Out of Solitary Confinement: The History of the Gulag." *Kritika: Explorations in Russian and Eurasian History* 8, no. 1 (2007): 67–103.

– *A Biography of No Place: From Ethnic Borderland to Soviet Heartland.* Cambridge, MA: Harvard University Press, 2004.

Browning, Christopher. *Nazi Policy, Jewish Workers, German Killers.* Cambridge: Cambridge University Press, 2000.

– *Ordinary Men: Reserve Police Battalion 101 and the Final Solution in Poland.* New York: HarperCollins, 1992.

Budnitskii, Oleg. "The Great Patriotic War and Soviet Society: Defeatism, 1941–42." Translated by Jason Morton. *Kritika: Explorations in Russian and Eurasian History* 15, no. 4 (2014): 767–97.

Channon, John. "Siberia in Revolution and Civil War, 1917–1921." In Alan Wood, ed., *The History of Siberia: From Russian Conquest to Revolution*, 158–80. London: Routledge, 1991.

Cherkaev, Xenia. "On Warped Mourning and Omissions in Post-Soviet Historiography." *Ab Imperio* 4 (2014): 365–85.

Chickering, Roger. "Total War: The Use and Abuse of a Concept." In Manfred Boerneke, Roger Chickering, and Stig Forster, eds., *Anticipating Total War: The German and American Experiences*, 13–28. Cambridge: Cambridge University Press, 1999.

Chyz, Martha. *Woman and Child in the Modern System of Slavery – USSR*. Translated by O. Pruchodko. New York: Dobrus, 1962.

Ciesielski, Stanisław, Grzegorz Hryciuk, and Aleksander Srebrakowski. *Masowe deportacje ludności w Związku Radzieckim*. Toruń: Wydaw. Adam Marszałek, 2003.

Ciesielski, Stanisław, Wojciech Materski, and Andrzej Paczkowski. *Represje sowieckie wobec Polaków i obywateli polskich*. Warsaw: Ośrodek Karta, 2002.

Cohn, Edward. *The High Title of a Communist: Postwar Party Discipline and the Values of the Soviet Regime*. DeKalb: Northern Illinois University Press, 2015.

Conquest, Robert. *Kolyma: The Arctic Death Camps*. London: MacMillan, 1978.

Craveri, Marta. "The Strikes in Norilsk and Vorkuta Camps, and their Role in the Breakdown of the Stalinist Forced Labour System." In Tom Brass and Marcel van der Linden, eds., *Free and Unfree Labour: The Debate Continues*, 363–78. Bern: Peter Lang, 1997.

Dale, Robert. "Divided We Stand: Cities, Unity and Post-War Reconstruction in Soviet Russia, 1945–1953." *Contemporary European History* 24, no. 4 (2015): 493–516.

Dallin, David J., and Boris I. Nicolaevsky. *Forced Labor in Soviet Russia*. New Haven, CT: Yale University Press, 1947.

David-Fox, Michael, ed. *The Soviet Gulag: Evidence, Interpretation, Comparison*. Pittsburgh: Pittsburgh University Press, 2016.

– *Crossing Borders: Modernity, Ideology, and Culture in Russia and the Soviet Union*. Pittsburgh: University of Pittsburgh Press, 2015.

Davies, R.W. "Stalin as Economic Policy-Maker: Soviet Agriculture, 1931–36." In Sarah Davies and James Harris, eds. *Stalin: A New History*, 121–39. Cambridge: Cambridge University Press, 2005.

de Vito, Christian, and Alex Lichtenstein, eds. *Global Convict Labour*. Leiden, The Netherlands: Brill, 2015.

Dobson, Miriam. *Khrushchev's Cold Summer: Gulag Returnees, Crime, and the Fate of Reform after Stalin.* Ithaca, NY: Cornell University Press, 2009.

Draskoczy, Julie S. *Belomor: Criminality and Creativity in Stalin's Gulag.* Brighton, MA: Academic Studies Press, 2014.

Edwards, Kristen. "Fleeing to Siberia: The Wartime Relocation of Evacuees to Novosibirsk, 1941–1943." PhD diss., Stanford University, 1996.

Ek, Richard. "Giorgio Agamben and the Spatialities of the Camp: An Introduction." *Geografiska Annaler. Series B, Human Geography* 88, no. 4 (2006): 363–86.

Elie, Marc. "Les politiques à l'égard des libérés du Goulag: amnistiés et réhabilités dans la région de Novossibirsk, 1953–1960." *Cahiers du monde russe* 47, no. 1–2 (2006): 327–48.

Epstein, Mikhail. "The Dialectics of *Hyper*: From Modernism to Postmodernism." In Epstein, A.A. Genis, and S.M Vladiv-Glover, eds., *Russian Postmodernism: New Perspectives on Post-Soviet Culture*, 2nd ed., 23–50. Providence: Berghan Books, 2015.

Ermolaeva, Oxana. "Health Care, the Circulation of Medical Knowledge, and Research in the Soviet GULAG in the 1930s." *East Central Europe* 40 (2013): 341–65.

– "Making a Career in the GULAG Archipelago: The BBK-BBLag Personnel." Paper for presentation at the 10th annual Young Researchers Conference, Miami University, Oxford, OH, 2010.

Ertz, Simon. "Trading Effort for Freedom: Workday Credits in the Stalinist Camp System." *Comparative Economic Studies* 47, no. 2 (2005): 476–91.

– "Building Norilsk." In Paul Gregory and Valery Lazarev, eds., *The Economics of Forced Labor: The Soviet Gulag*, 127–150. Stanford: Hoover Institution Press, 2003.

Esper, Thomas. "The Condition of the Serf Workers in Russia's Metallurgical Industry, 1800–1861." *The Journal of Modern History* 50, no. 4 (1978): 660–79.

Etkind, Alexander. *Warped Mourning: Stories of the Undead in the Land of the Unburied.* Stanford: Stanford University Press, 2013.

– "Bare Monuments to Bare Life: The Soon-to-be-Dead in Arts and Memory." *Gulag Studies* 1 (2008): 27–34.

– "Hard and Soft in Cultural Memory: Political Mourning in Russia and Germany." *Grey Room* 16 (2004): 36–59.

Figes, Orlando. *Just Send Me Word: A True Story of Love and Survival in the Gulag.* London: Allen Lane, 2012.

Filtzer, Donald. "Starvation Mortality in Soviet Home-Front Industrial Regions during World War II." In Wendy Z. Goldman and Donald Filtzer, eds., *Hunger and War: Food Provisions in the Soviet Union during World War II*, 265–338. Bloomington: Indiana University Press, 2015.

– *Soviet Workers and Late Stalinism: Labour and the Restoration of the Stalinist System after World War II.* Cambridge: Cambridge University Press, 2002.

– "The Standard of Living of Soviet Industrial Workers in the Immediate Postwar Period, 1945–1948." *Europe-Asia Studies* 51, no. 6 (1999): 1013–38.

Fitzpatrick, Sheila. "Ascribing Class: The Construction of Social Identity in Soviet Russia." In Sheila Fitzpatrick, ed., *Stalinism: New Directions*, 20–46. London: Routledge, 2000.

– *Everyday Stalinism: Ordinary Life in Extraordinary Times: Soviet Russia in the 1930s.* New York: Oxford University Press, 1999.

– *The Russian Revolution.* 2nd ed. Oxford: Oxford University Press, 1994.

Forth, Aidan. "Britain's Archipelago of Camps: Labor and Detention in a Liberal Empire, 1871–1903." In Michael David-Fox, ed., *The Soviet Gulag: Evidence, Interpretation, Comparison*, 199–223. Pittsburgh: Pittsburgh University Press, 2016.

Foucault, Michel. *Discipline and Punish: The Birth of the Prison.* 2nd ed. Translated by Alan Sheridan. New York: Vintage Books, 1995.

Gensburger, Sarah. "Halbwachs' Studies in Collective Memory: A Founding Text for Contemporary 'Memory Studies'?" *Journal of Classical Sociology* 16, no. 4 (2016): 396–413.

Gentes, Andrew W. "Katorga: Penal Labor and Tsarist Siberia." In Eva-Maria Stolberg, ed., *The Siberian Saga: A History of Russia's Wild East*, 75–85. Frankfurt am Main: Peter Lang, 2005.

Gerlach, Christian, and Nicholas Werth. "State Violence – Violent Societies." In Michael Geyer and Sheila Fitzpatrick, eds., *Beyond Totalitarianism: Stalinism and Nazism Compared*, 133–79. Cambridge: Cambridge University Press, 2009.

Gessen, Masha. *The Man without a Face: The Unlikely Rise of Vladimir Putin.* New York: Penguin, 2012.

Getty, J. Arch, Gabor T. Rittersporn, and Viktor N. Zemskov. "Victims of the Soviet Penal System in the Pre-War Years: A First Approach on the Basis of Archival Evidence." *The American Historical Review* 98, no. 4 (1993): 1017–49.

Geyer, Michael, and Sheila Fitzpatrick, eds. *Beyond Totalitarianism: Stalinism and Nazism Compared.* Cambridge: Cambridge University Press, 2009.

Gheith, Jehanne M., and Katherine R. Jolluck. *Gulag Voices: Oral Histories of Soviet Incarceration and Exile.* New York: Palgrave Macmillan, 2011.

Goldlust, John. "A Different Silence: The Survival of More Than 200,000 Polish Jews in the Soviet Union during World War II as a Case Study in Cultural Amnesia." *Australian Jewish Historical Society Journal* 21 (2012): 13–60.

Goldman, Wendy Z. "Not by Bread Alone: Food, Workers, and the State." In Wendy Z. Goldman and Donald Filtzer, eds., *Hunger and War: Food Provisions in the Soviet Union during World War II*, 44–97. Bloomington: Indiana University Press, 2015.

– "Comment: Twin Pyramids – Perpetrators and Victims." *Slavic Review* 72, no. 1 (2013): 24–7.

– *Women at the Gates: Gender and Industry in Stalin's Russia*. Cambridge: Cambridge University Press, 2002.

Gorcheva, A.Iu. *Pressa Gulaga, 1918–1955*. Moscow: Izd-vo Moskovskogo Universiteta, 1996.

Gorlizki, Yoram, and Oleg Khlevniuk. *Cold Peace: Stalin and the Soviet Ruling Circle, 1945–1953*. Oxford: Oxford University Press, 2004.

Gregory, Derek. "The Black Flag: Guantanamo Bay and the Space of Exception." *Geografiska Annaler* 88, no. 4 (2006): 405–27.

Gregory, Paul. *Politics, Murder, and Love in Stalin's Kremlin: The Story of Nikolai Bukharin and Anna Larina*. Stanford: Hoover Institution Press, 2010.

Gregory, Paul, and Mark Harrison. "Allocation under Dictatorship: Research in Stalin's Archives." *Journal of Economic Literature* 43, no. 3 (2005): 721–61.

Gregory, Paul, and Valery Lazarev, eds. *The Economics of Forced Labor: The Soviet Gulag*. Stanford: Hoover Institution Press, 2003.

Gushchin, N.Ia. "Demograficheskoe razvitie sovetskoi Sibiri." In R.S. Vasil'evskii and N.Ia. Gushchin, eds., *Istoricheskaia demografiia Sibiri: sbornik nauchnykh trudov*, 124–85. Novosibirsk: Nauka, 1992.

Hagen, Mark von. "New Directions in Military History, 1900–1950: Questions of Total War and Colonial War." *Kritika: Explorations in Russian and Eurasian History* 12, no. 4 (2011): 867–84.

Hagenloh, Paul. *Stalin's Police: Public Order and Mass Repression in the USSR, 1926–1941*. Baltimore: Johns Hopkins University Press, 2009.

Hájková, Anna. "Sexual Barter in Times of Genocide: Negotiating the Sexual Economy of the Theresienstadt Ghetto." *Signs* 38, no. 3 (2013): 503–33.

Halbwachs, Maurice. *On Collective Memory*. Translated by Lewis A. Coser. Chicago: University of Chicago Press, 1992.

Hardy, Jeffrey S. *The Gulag after Stalin: Redefining Punishment in Khrushchev's Soviet Union*. Ithaca, NY: Cornell University Press, 2016.

– "The Camp Is Not a Resort: The (re)Imposition of Order in the Soviet Gulag, 1957–1961." *Kritika: Explorations in Russian and Eurasian History* 13, no. 1 (2012): 89–212.

Harris, James R. "The Growth of the Gulag: Forced Labor in the Urals Region, 1929–31." *The Russian Review* 56, no. 2 (1997): 265–80.

Harrison, Mark. *Accounting for War: Soviet Production, Employment, and the Defence Burden, 1940–1945.* Cambridge: Cambridge University Press, 1996.

Healey, Dan. "Lives in the Balance: Weak and Disabled Prisoners and the Biopolitics of the Gulag." *Kritika: Explorations in Russian and Eurasian History* 16, no. 3 (2015): 527–56.

– "Sexual and Gender Dissent: Homosexuality as Resistance in Stalin's Russia." In Lynne Viola, ed., *Contending with Stalinism: Soviet Power and Resistance in the 1930s*, 139–69. Ithaca, NY: Cornell University Press, 2002.

– *Homosexual Desire in Revolutionary Russia: The Regulation of Sexual and Gender Dissent.* Chicago: University of Chicago Press, 2001.

Heinzen, James. "Corruption in the Gulag: Dilemmas of Officials and Prisoners." *Comparative Economic Studies* 47 (2005): 456–75.

Hellie, Richard. "The Economy, Trade and Serfdom." In Maureen Perrie, ed., *The Cambridge History of Russia.* Volume 1: *From Early Rus' to 1689*, 539–58. Cambridge: Cambridge University Press, 2006.

Herling, Albert Konrad. *The Soviet Slave Empire.* New York: W. Funk, 1951.

Hilger, Andreas. *Deutsche Kriegsgefangene in der Sowjetunion, 1941–1956. Kriegsgefangenenpolitik, Lageralltag und Erinnerung.* Essen: Klartext-Verlag, 2000.

Hoffman, David L. *Stalinist Values: The Cultural Norms of Soviet Modernity, 1917–1941.* Ithaca, NY: Cornell University Press, 2003.

Holquist, Peter. "State Violence as Technique: The Logic of Violence in Soviet Totalitarianism." In Amir Weiner, ed., *Landscaping the Human Garden: Twentieth-Century Population Management in a Comparative Framework*, 19–45. Stanford: Stanford University Press, 2003.

– *Making War, Forging Revolution: Russia's Continuum of Crisis, 1914–1921.* Cambridge, MA: Harvard University Press, 2002.

Holzman, Franklyn D. "The Soviet Ural-Kuznetsk Combine: A Study in Investment Criteria and Industrialization Policies." *The Quarterly Journal of Economics* 71, no. 3 (1957): 368–405.

Hyslop, Jonathan. "The Invention of the Concentration Camp: Cuba, Southern Africa and the Philippines, 1896–1907." *South African Historical Journal* 63, no. 2 (2011): 251–76.

Ireland, Richard W. *"A Want of Order and Good Discipline': Rules, Discretion and the Victorian Prison.* Cardiff: University of Wales Press, 2007.

Isupov, V.A. *Glavnyi resurs Pobedy: Liudskoi potentsial Zapadnoi Sibiri v gody Vtoroi mirovoi voiny (1939–1945 gg.).* Novosibirsk: Sova, 2008.

– "Sotsial'no-demograficheskaia politika Stalinskogo pravitel'stva v gody Velikoi Otechestvennoi voiny (na materialakh Sibiri)." In V.A. Isupov, S.A.

Papkov, and I.M. Savitskii, eds., *Zapadnaia Sibir' v Velikoi Otechestvennoi voine (1941–1945 gg.)*, 115–43. Novosibirsk: Nauka-Tsentr, 2004.

– "Na izlome: Smertnost' naseleniia Sibiri v nachale Velikoi Otechestvennoi voiny." In R.S. Vasil'evskii and N.I. Gushchin, eds., *Istoricheskaia demografiia Sibiri: sbornik nauchnykh trudov*, 186–98. Novosibirsk: Nauka, 1992.

Iumashev, M.I., and B.A. Zhaleiko, eds. *Sbornik zakonov SSSR i Ukazov Prezidiuma Verkhovnogo Soveta SSSR (1938-iul' 1956)*. Moscow: Gos. Izd. Iuridicheskoi literatury, 1956.

Ivanova, Galina. *Labour Camp Socialism: The Gulag in the Soviet Totalitarian System*. Edited by Donald J. Raleigh. Translated by Carol Flath. Armonk, NY: M.E. Sharpe, 2000.

– "Kadry GULAGa." In I.V. Dobrovol'skii and G.M. Ivanova, eds., *GULAG: ego stroiteli, obitateli i geroi: Rossiia po dorogam fanatizma i muchenichestva*, 40–59. Moscow: Mezh.obshchestvo prav cheloveka, 1998.

Jakobson, Michael. *Origins of the GULAG: The Soviet Prison-Camp System, 1917–1934*. Lexington: University Press of Kentucky, 1993.

Johnson, Robert E. "Family Life-Cycles and Economic Stratification: A Case-Study in Rural Russia." *Journal of Social History* 30, no. 3 (1997): 705–31.

Jowitt, Ken. "Soviet Neotraditionalism: The Political Corruption of a Leninist Regime." *Soviet Studies* 35, no. 3 (1983): 275–97.

Kelly, Catriona. *Comrade Pavlik: The Rise and Fall of a Soviet Boy Hero*. London: Granta Publications, 2005.

Kennan, George. *Siberia and the Exile System*. New York: The Century Co., 1891.

Khlevniuk, Oleg. "The Gulag and the Non-Gulag as One Interrelated Whole." Translated by Simon Belokowsky. *Kritika: Explorations in Russian and Eurasian History* 16, no. 3 (2015): 479–98.

– "The Economy of the OGPU, NKVD, and MVD of the USSR, 1930–1953: The Scale, Structure, and Trends of Development." In Paul Gregory and Valery Lazarev, eds., *The Economics of Forced Labor: The Soviet Gulag*, 43–66. Stanford: Hoover Institution Press, 2003.

Knight, Amy. *Beria: Stalin's First Lieutenant*. Princeton, NJ: Princeton University Press, 1993.

Kondrashin, V.V. *Golod 1932–1933 godov: tragediia rossiskoi derevni*. Moscow: Rosspen, 2008.

Kornilova, O.V. *Kak stroili pervuiu sovetskuiu avtomagistral' (1936–1941 gg.)*. Smolensk: Svitok, 2014.

– "Zakliuchennye GULAGa vtoroi poloviny 1930-kh gg.: lagkontingent Viazemlaga po stat'iam osuzhdeniia i srokom zakliucheniia." *Sotsial'naia istoriia* 23, no. 5 (2014): 569–83.

Kotkin, Stephen. "Modern Times: The Soviet Union and the Interwar Conjuncture." *Kritika: Explorations in Russian and Eurasian History* 2, no. 1 (2001): 110–63.

– *Magnetic Mountain: Stalinism as a Civilization.* Berkeley: University of California Press, 1995.

Kotsonis, Yanni. "The Problem of the Individual in the Stolypin Reforms." *Kritika: Explorations in Russian and Eurasian History* 12, no. 1 (2011): 25–52.

Kragh, Martin. "Stalinist Labour Coercion during World War II: An Economic Approach." *Europe-Asia Studies* 63, no. 7 (2011): 1253–73.

Krasil'nikov, Danila S. "Lageria i kolonii na territorii Novosibirskoi Oblasti v gody Velikoi Otechestvennoi voiny (1941–1945)." Diplomnaia rabota, Novosibirsk State University, 1999.

Krasil'nikov, S.A. "Spetspereselentsy, spetsarteli i spetsorgany: mekhanizmy i rezul'taty spetskolonizatsii severa Zapadnoi Sibiri v 1930-e gg." In. L.D Borodkin, P. Gregori [Paul Gregory], and O.V. Khlevniuk, eds., *GULAG: Ekonomika prinuditel'nogo truda,* 279–316. Moscow: Rosspen, 2005.

– *Serp i Molokh: Krest'ianskaia ssylka v Zapadnoi Sibiri v 1930-e gody.* Moscow: Rosspen, 2003.

Lahusen, Thomas. *How Life Writes the Book: Real Socialism and Socialist Realism in Stalin's Russia.* Ithaca, NY: Cornell University Press, 1997.

Ledeneva, Alena. *Russia's Economy of Favours: Blat, Networking and Informal Exchange.* Cambridge: Cambridge University Press, 1998.

Lenin, Vladimir. *The Development of Capitalism in Russia.* Moscow: Foreign Languages Publishing House, 1956.

Lewin, Moshe. *The Making of the Soviet System: Essays in the Social History of Interwar Russia.* New York: The New Press, 1994.

Lichtenstein, Alex. *Twice the Work of Free Labor: The Political Economy of Convict Labor in the New South.* London: Verso, 1996.

Lincoln, W. Bruce. *The Conquest of a Continent: Siberia and the Russians.* Ithaca, NY: Cornell University Press, 2007.

Lonsdale, Richard E. "Siberian Industry before 1917: The Example of Tomsk Guberniya." *Annals of the Association of American Geographers* 53, no. 4 (1963): 479–93.

Maddox, Steven. "Gulag Football: Competitive and Recreational Sport in Stalin's System of Forced Labor." *Kritika: Explorations in Russian and Eurasian History,* forthcoming.

– *Saving Stalin's Imperial City: Historic Preservation in Leningrad, 1930–1950.* Bloomington: Indiana University Press, 2015.

Malia, Martin. *The Soviet Tragedy: A History of Socialism in Russia, 1917–1991.* New York: The Free Press, 1994.

Mancini, Michael. *One Dies, Get Another: Convict Leasing in the American South, 1866–1928*. Columbia: University of South Carolina Press, 1996.

Manley, Rebecca. *To the Tashkent Station: Evacuation and Survival in the Soviet Union at War*. Ithaca, NY: Cornell University Press, 2009.

Martin, Terry. "Modernization or Neo-Traditionalism: Ascribed Nationality and Soviet Primordialism." In Sheila Fitzpatrick, ed., *Stalinism: New Directions*, 348–67. New York: Vintage Books, 2000.

Marks, Steven G. *Road to Power: The Trans-Siberian Railroad and the Colonization of Asian Russia 1850–1917*. Ithaca, NY: Cornell University Press, 1991.

Moon, David. *The Russian Peasantry, 1600–1930: The World the Peasants Made*. London: Longman, 1999.

Morris, Norval, and David J. Rothman, eds. *The Oxford History of the Prison: The Practice of Punishment in Western Society*. New York: Oxford University Press, 1995.

Naimark, Norman. *Stalin's Genocides*. Princeton, NJ: Princeton University Press, 2011.

Nordlander, David. "Magadan and the Economic History of Dalstroi in the 1930s." In Paul Gregory and Valery Lazarev, eds., *The Economics of Forced Labor: The Soviet Gulag*, 105–26. Stanford: Hoover Institution Press, 2003.

Onken, Eva-Clarita. "The Baltic States and Moscow's 9 May Commemoration: Analysing Memory Politics in Europe." *Europe-Asia Studies* 59, no. 1 (2007): 23–46.

Orr, Charles. *Stalin's Slave Camps: An Indictment of Modern Slavery*. Boston: Beacon Press, 1952.

Orth, Karin. "The Concentration Camp Personnel." In Jane Caplan and Nikolaus Wachsmann, eds., *Concentration Camps in Nazi Germany: The New Histories*, 44–57. London: Routledge, 2010.

Papkov, S.A. "Kontrrevoliutsionnaia prestupnost' i osobennosti ee podavleniia v Sibiri v gody Velikoi Otechestvennoi voiny (1941–1945)." In S.A. Papkov and K. Teraiama, eds., *Ural i Sibir' v Stalinskoi politike*, 205–23. Novosirbisk: Sibirskii khronograf, 2002.

– *Stalinskii terror v Sibiri, 1928–1941*. Novosibirsk: Izdatel'stvo Sibirskogo Otdeleniia Rossiiskoi Akademii Nauk, 1997.

Pereira, N.G.O. *White Siberia: The Politics of Civil War*. Montreal: McGill-Queen's University Press, 1995.

Petrov, N.V. "Istoriia imperii 'GULAG': Glava 8." Accessed 28 May 2015. http://avkrasn.ru/article-2084.html.

Petrov, N.V., and K.V. Skorkin, eds. *Kto rukovodil NKVD? Spravochnik*. Moscow: Zven'ia, 1999.

Plamper, Jan. "Foucault's Gulag." *Kritika: Explorations in Russian and Eurasian History* 3.2 (2002): 255–280.

Pohl, J. Otto. "Persecution of Ethnic Germans in the USSR during World War II." *The Russian Review* 75 (2016): 284–303.

– *The Stalinist Penal System: A Statistical History of Soviet Repression and Terror, 1930–1953*. London: McFarland, 1997.

Pohl, J. Otto, Eric J. Schmaltz, and Ronald J. Vossler. "'In Our Hearts We Felt the Sentence of Death': Ethnic German Recollections of Mass Violence in the USSR, 1928–48." *Journal of Genocide Research* 11, no. 2/3 (2009): 323–54.

Qualls, Karl D. *From Ruins to Reconstruction: Urban Identity in Soviet Sevastopol after World War II*. Ithaca, NY: Cornell University Press, 2009.

Raleigh, Donald J. *Experiencing Russia's Civil War: Politics, Society, and Revolutionary Culture in Saratov, 1917–1922*. Princeton, NJ: Princeton University Press, 2002.

Reichel, Philip L. *Comparative Criminal Justice Systems: A Topical Approach*. 3rd ed. Upper Saddle River, NJ: Prentice Hall, 2002.

Robson, Roy. *Solovki: The Story of Russia Told through Its Most Remarkable Islands*. New Haven, CT: Yale University Press, 2004.

Rossi, Zhak [Jacques Rossi]. *Spravochnik po GULAGu*. Moscow: Prosvet, 1991.

Roth, Mitchel P. *Prisons and Prison Systems: A Global Encyclopedia*. London: Greenwood Press, 2006.

Savitskii, I.M. "Formirovanie kadrov oboronnoi promyshlennosti Novosibirskoi oblasti v gody Velikoi Otechestvennoi voiny." In V.A. Isupov, S.A. Papkov, and I.M. Savitskii, eds., *Zapadnaia Sibir' v Velikoi Otechestvennoi voine (1941–1945 gg.)*, 3–35. Novosibirsk: Nauka-Tsentr, 2004.

– "Sozdanie v Novosibirske krupneishego v Sibiri tsentra oboronnoi pro-myshlennosti v gody Velikoi Otechestvennoi voiny." In S.A. Papkov and K. Teraiama, eds., *Ural i Sibir' v Stalinskoi politike*, 192–204. Novosibirsk: Sibirskii khronograf, 2002.

Samuelson, Lennart. *Plans for Stalin's War Machine: Tukhachevskii and Military-Economic Planning, 1925–1941*. New York: St. Martin's Press, 2000.

Scherer, John L., and Michael Jakobson. "The Collectivisation of Agriculture and the Soviet Prison Camp System." *Europe-Asia Studies* 45, no. 3 (1993): 533–46.

Schmitt, Carl. *Political Theology: Four Chapters on the Concept of Sovereignty*. Translated by Charles Schwab. Chicago: University of Chicago Press, 2005.

Schrader, Abby M. "Unruly Felons and Civilizing Wives: Cultivating Marriage in the Siberian Exile System, 1822–1860." *Slavic Review* 66, no. 2 (2007): 230–56.

Scott, James C. *Seeing Like a State: How Certain Schemes to Improve the Human Condition Have Failed*. New Haven, CT: Yale University Press, 1998.

– *Weapons of the Weak: Everyday Forms of Peasant Resistance.* New Haven, CT: Yale University Press, 1985.

Shanin, Teodor. *The Awkward Class: Political Sociology of Peasantry in a Developing Society: Russia 1910–1925.* Oxford: Clarendon Press, 1972.

Shchegolev, K.M. "Uchastie evakuirovannogo naseleniia v kolkhoznom proizvodstve Zapadnoi Sibiri v gody Velikoi Otechestvennoi voiny." *Istoriia SSSR* 2 (1959): 139–45.

Shearer, David. "Mastering the Soviet Frontier: Western Siberia in the 1930s." In Eva-Maria Stolberg, ed., *The Siberian Saga: A History of Russia's Wild East*, 159–72. Frankfurt am Main: Peter Lang, 2005.

Sherlock, Thomas. "Russian Politics and the Soviet Past: Reassessing Stalin and Stalinism under Vladimir Putin." *Communist and Post-Communist Studies* 49, no. 1 (2016): 45–59.

Shuranov, N.P. "Razvitie promyshlennosti sibiri v period velikoi otechestvennoi voiny." *Izvestiia sibirskogo otdeleniia akademii nauk SSSR* 1 (1985): 15–20.

Siddiqi, Asif. "Scientists and Specialists in the Gulag: Life and Death in Stalin's *Sharashka*." In Michael David-Fox, ed., *The Soviet Gulag: Evidence, Interpretation, and Comparison*, 87–113. Pittsburgh: University of Pittsburgh Press, 2016.

Slezkine, Yuri. *Arctic Mirrors: Russia and the Small Peoples of the North.* Ithaca, NY: Cornell University Press, 1994.

Smirnov, M.B., comp. N.G. Okhotin, and A.B. Roginskii, eds. *Sistema ispravitel'no-trudovykh lagerei v SSSR, 1923–1960: Spravochnik.* Moscow: Zven'ia, 1998.

Smith, Kathleen E. *Remembering Stalin's Victims: Popular Memory and the End of the USSR.* Ithaca, NY: Cornell University Press, 1996.

Snyder, Timothy. *Bloodlands: Europe between Hitler and Stalin.* New York: Basic Books, 2010.

Sofsky, Wolfgang. *The Order of Terror: The Concentration Camp.* Translated by W. Templer. Princeton, NJ: Princeton University Press, 1997.

Solomon, Peter H., Jr. *Soviet Criminal Justice under Stalin.* Cambridge: Cambridge University Press, 1996.

Solzhenitsyn, Aleksandr I. *The Gulag Archipelago, 1918–1956: An Experiment in Literary Investigation*, 3 vols. Volumes 1 and 2 translated by Thomas P. Whitney. Volume 3 translated by Harry Willetts. New York: Harper & Row, 1974–8.

Stolberg, Eva-Maria. "The Genre of Frontiers and Borderlands: Siberia as a Case Study." In Eva-Maria Stolberg, ed., *The Siberian Saga: A History of Russia's Wild East*, 13–27. Frankfurt am Main: Peter Lang, 2005.

Sunderland, Willard. "Imperial Space: Territorial Thought and Practice in the Eighteenth Century." In Jane Burbank, Mark von Hagen, and Anatolyi

Remnev, eds., *Russian Empire: Space, People, Power, 1700–1930*, 33–66.
Bloomington: Indiana University Press, 2007.

Suverov, V.M., and E.V. Suverov. "Povstancheskoe dvizhenie v Sibiri
1920–1923 gg." In S.V. Makarchuk, ed., *Sibir': XX vek*, 53–60. Kemerovo:
Kuzbassvuzizdat, 1997.

Swianiewicz, S. *Forced Labour and Economic Development: An Enquiry into the
Experience of Soviet Industrialization*. Oxford: Oxford University Press, 1965.

Tikhonov, Aleksei. "The End of the Gulag." In Paul R. Gregory and Valery
Lazarev, eds., *The Economics of Forced Labor: The Soviet Gulag*, 67–74.
Stanford: Hoover Institution Press, 2003.

Todorov, Tzvetan. *Facing the Extreme: Moral Life in the Concentration Camps*.
New York: Henry Holt, 1996.

Tumarkin, Maria M. "The Long Life of Stalinism: Reflections on the Aftermath
of Totalitarianism and Social Memory." *Journal of Social History* 44, no. 4
(2011): 1047–61.

Uimanov, V.N. *Likvidatsiia i reabilitatsiia: politicheskie repressii v Zapadnoi Sibiri
v sisteme bol'sevitskoi vlasti (konets 1919–1941 g.)*. Tomsk: Izd-vo Tomskogo
Universiteta, 2012.

– *Penitentsiarnaia Sistema Zapadnoi Sibiri (1920–1941 gg.)*. Tomsk: Izd-vo
Tomskogo Universiteta, 2011.

van der Linden, Marcel. "Forced Labour and Non-Capitalist Industrialization:
The Case of Stalinism (c. 1929–c. 1956)." In Tom Brass and Marcel van der
Linden, eds., *Free and Unfree Labour: The Debate Continues*, 501–23. Bern:
Peter Lang, 1997.

Viola, Lynne. "The Question of the Perpetrator in Soviet History." *Slavic
Review* 72, no. 1 (2013): 1–23.

– *Peasant Rebels under Stalin: Collectivization and the Culture of Peasant
Resistance*. New York: Oxford University Press, 2007.

– *The Unknown Gulag: The Lost World of Stalin's Special Settlements*. New York:
Oxford University Press, 2007.

– "The Aesthetic of Stalinist Planning and the World of the Special Villages."
Kritika: Explorations in Russian and Eurasian History 4, no. 1 (2004): 101–28.

– ed. *Contending with Stalinism: Soviet Power and Popular Resistance in the 1930s*.
Ithaca, NY: Cornell University Press, 2002.

– "'Tear the Evil from the Root': The Children of the *Spetspereselentsy* of the
North." *Studia Slavica Finlandensia* 17 (2000): 34–72.

Wachsmann, Nikolaus. *Kl: A History of the Nazi Concentration Camps*. New
York: Farrar, Straus and Giroux, 2015.

Weiner, Amir, ed. *Landscaping the Human Garden: Twentieth-Century Population
Management in a Comparative Framework*. Stanford: Stanford University
Press, 2003.

– *Making Sense of War: The Second World War and the Fate of the Bolshevik Revolution.* Princeton, NJ: Princeton University Press, 2001.

Werth, Nicholas. *Cannibal Island: Death in a Siberian Gulag.* Translated by Steven Rendall. Princeton, NJ: Princeton University Press, 2007.

Westren, Michael H. "Nations in Exile: 'The Punished Peoples' in Soviet Kazakhstan, 1941–1961." PhD diss., University of Chicago, 2012.

Wheatcroft, Stephen G. "Crises and the Condition of the Peasantry in Late Imperial Russia." In Esther Kingston-Mann and Timothy Mixter, eds., *Peasant Economy, Culture, and Politics of European Russia, 1800–1921*, 128–74. Princeton, NJ: Princeton University Press, 1991.

Wood, Elizabeth. "Performing Memory: Vladimir Putin and the Celebration of World War II in Russia." *Soviet and Post-Soviet Review* 38, no. 2 (2011): 172–200.

Young, Sarah J. "Selected Bibliography of Gulag Narratives and Secondary Sources." *Gulag Studies* 7–8 (2014–2015): 110–40.

Zemskov, V.N. *Spetsposelentsy v SSSR, 1930–1960.* Moscow: Nauka, 2005.

Zinov'ev, V.P. "Poselok Chekist." In V.P. Zinov'ev, I.M. Rudaia, and V.O. El'blaus, eds., *Neizvestnyi Seversk: Sbornik statei*, 60–71. Tomsk: Izd-vo TGU, 1996.

Zviagin, S.P. "K voprosu ob uchastii zakliuchennykh kuzbasskikh lagerei v pomoshchi frontu v gody Velikoi Otechestvennoi voiny." In A.T. Moskalenko et al., eds., *50 let velikoi pobedy pod Stalingradom*, 147–51. Novosibirsk: UD SO RAN, 1993.

Films

Dostal', Nikolai, director. *Zaveshchanie Lenina.* Rossiia, 2007.

Lahusen, Thomas, Alexander Gershtein, Tracy McDonald, and Alexander Nikitin, directors. *The Province of Lost Film.* Chemodan Films, 2006.

Panfilov, Gleb director. *V kruge pervom.* Kinokompaniia "Vera," 2006.

Recent News Articles

Boghani, Priyanka. "Putin's Legal Crackdown on Civil Society." PBS. 13 January 2015. Accessed 22 January 2016. https://www.pbs.org/wgbh/frontline/article/putins-legal-crackdown-on-civil-society/.

"Court Fines Sakharov Center NGO for Violating 'Foreign Agents' Law." *The Moscow Times*, 30 September 2015. Accessed 22 January 2016. http://www.themoscowtimes.com/news/article/court-fines-sakharov-center-ngo-for-violating-foreign-agents-law/536321.html.

Danilovich, Mikhail, and Robert Coalson. "Revamped Perm-36 Museum Emphasises Gulag's 'Contribution to Victory." Radio Free Europe.

25 July 2015. Accessed 22 January 2016. https://www.rferl.org/content/russia-perm-gulag-museum-takeover-contribution-to-victory/27152188.html.

"'My Breathing Mom Was among the Corpses': Putin Recalls His Parents' World War II Ordeal." *RT* [*Russia Today*], 30 April 2015. Accessed 21 January 2016. https://www.rt.com/news/254445-putin-family-details-wwii/.

"New Russian Gulag Museum Recreates Soviet Terror." BBC News, 30 October 2015. Accessed 22 January 2016. http://www.bbc.com/news/world-europe-34675413.

"Wall of Grief: Putin Opens Russia's First Soviet Victims Memorial." BBC News, 30 October 2017. Accessed 30 November 2017. http://www.bbcvvv.com/news/world-europe-41809659.

Index